GERMAN POLITICAL SYSTEMS

Theory and Practice in the Two Germanies

Editors
Klaus von Beyme
Max Kaase
Ekkehart Krippendorff
Volker Rittberger
Kurt L. Shell

German Political Studies Volume 2
sponsored by the German Political Science Association

For information address:

SAGE Publications Ltd.
44 Hatton Garden
London E.C.1

SAGE Publications Inc.
275 South Beverly Drive
Beverly Hills, California 90212

First Printing
Printed and Bound in Great Britain by
Biddles Ltd., Guildford, Surrey
International Standard Book Number: 8039-9963-1
Library of Congress Catalog Card Number: 74–82535
ISSN 0307-7233

GERMAN POLITICAL SYSTEMS

Theory and Practice in the Two Germanies

Contents

Editors' Preface

IN THE FIRST VOLUME of *German Political Studies* the editors intended to give the reader a general idea as to the breadth of theoretical and empirical research interests in contemporary West German political science. Inevitably, the choices made could not claim to be fully representative in terms of research areas nor could they do justice to all major theoretical and methodological approaches. In this volume, then, the editors attempt to shift the emphasis in their selections in two directions: studies on political behavior and in political sociology, as well as research in international politics, are more strongly represented than they were in the first volume. Moreover, the editors succeeded in raising the ratio of original contributions.

The first three pieces selected for the second volume of *German Political Studies* analyse such major behavioural and structural changes in West German politics as have taken place since the late 1960s. At the same time, two of them demonstrate the degree to which empirical methods, in particular interview and survey research, are being utilized by researchers with different theoretical persuasions.

The phenomenon of protest and unconventional political behaviour in general — little noticed by political scientists in the 1950s and early 1960s — is dealt with in the paper by Max Kaase. Signs of a new militancy among industrial workers form the background of the research on union consciousness in the paper by Christel Eckardt et al. The raising of the level of manifest social conflict in West Germany has resulted in efforts to develop political-administrative strategies and mechanisms of conflict management and societal guidance. The study of Heribert Schatz, written from the vantage point of a participant observer, gives an authoritative account of how political planning developed at the level of the federal government.

The next two articles, written specifically at the request of the editors, are both surveys and reviews of the literature in two major fields of work of West German political science. Heide Gerstenberger's paper should be seen as a sequel to the articles of Luhmann and Offe published in the first volume of *German Political Studies*. From a Marxist point of view she discusses critically recent contributions to the theory of the state and indicates some problems which, in her view, Marxist theories of the state have yet to solve. The article by Clemens Burrichter and Eckart Förtsch is less focussed and serves the purpose of giving the reader who may be unfamiliar with research on the German Democratic Republic a general introduction to this field. The editors plan to have more topical studies on different aspects of East German politics included in subsequent volumes of *German Political Studies*.

The last three contributions selected for this volume contain analyses of crucial changes both in the setting and in the focus of public policy-making, particularly in Western Europe. Gerd Junne describes the internationalisation of banking and investigates the impact of this process on the effectiveness of the state in capitalist society as the paramount public policy-making institution. Gerda Zellentin's article asks whether supranational institutions are necessary, or are capable of taking over some of the public policy-making functions fulfilled by the national state thus far. Since these contributions deal exclusively with changes in the international politics of the developed capitalist countries it was felt appropriate, in the aftermath of Helsinki, to include the study of Ulricht Albrecht and Udo Rehfeldt on the structural conditions of East-West cooperation.

The editors hope that this second volume of *German Political Studies* will convince an increasing number of our colleagues abroad that the work of West German political scientists is relevant to their own scientific interests.

Heidelberg
December 1975

POLITICAL IDEOLOGY, DISSATISFACTION AND PROTEST

A Micro Theory of Unconventional Political Behavior

Max Kaase

INTRODUCTORY REMARKS

IN 1971, A GROUP OF SOCIAL SCIENTISTS from different countries met for the first time to discuss the possibility of co-operating in a research project dealing with problems of social and political change. This research project has grown into an eight-nation study which is now collecting and beginning to analyse data.*

Although the project had to accomodate a variety of individual research interests, it was clear that it had to be held together by some sort of agreement on common theoretical concerns. Some of the key concepts that were developed and discussed in the research group are rooted in theories of unconventional political behavior which reflect my particular interest in the broader context of the project.

In the first part of this paper I will elaborate on those concepts in greater detail. In the second part I will briefly discuss the operationalization of the key concepts. In the final part of the paper some results of a first empirical analysis are reported. This analysis is extremely limited in scope and empirical basis and should be understood accordingly; it is solely based on the second German pretest for the study with 67 respondents.

The focus of the following discussion will be on unconventional political behavior, undoubtedly a very ambiguous term if one were to try to define it as a specific, concrete set of activities. What may be unconventional today will very frequently be part of the standard repertoire of political activities tomorrow. This problem is linked to communication and diffusion patterns,[1] the symbolic meaning

---

* My German collaborators in this study are Klaus Allerbeck from Cologne and Hans D. Klingemann from Mannheim. The article was completed in the Fall of 1974.

of political acts[2] and, above all, to social and political change. Consideration of these aspects is extremely important within the theoretical frame of reference of this article. They will, however, not be dealt with explicitly or extensively.

Unconventional political behavior can be defined as behavior that does not correspond to the norms of law and custom which regulate political participation under a particular regime. In this sense, Lester Milbrath could correctly write in 1965 that political demonstrations are a type of participation that 'does not fit into the hierarchy of political involvement in the United States'.[3] In many post-industrial democratic societies, peaceful demonstrations have by now become part of the 'normal' way of expressing political sentiments, and other actions have taken their place as unconventional and, therefore, frequently very effective expressions of political dissatisfaction.

The relative newness of these phenomena in many of the highly developed countries provided social scientists with considerable puzzlement. Seymour Martin Lipset probably summed up the feelings of many political scientists in the late fifties when he wrote that 'the democratic class struggle will continue, but it will be a fight without ideologies, without red flags, without May Day parades'.[4] This conclusion sounded plausible enough against the background of economic well-being and undisturbed growth in the post-war industrialized societies and the impact that the economic crises of the twenties and thirties had had on many democracies. The return of the ideologies, flags and parades in the movements for civil rights, for peace in Vietnam and for more participation constituted a definite challenge to the understanding and explanatory capabilities of social scientists. In particular: why were these movements overwhelmingly supported by the well-to-do classes?

The first explanations offered bore a definitely ad hoc character and were accordingly unsatisfactory. One major reason for this was clearly the lack of systematic empirical information about forms of and conditions for unconventional political behavior.[5] This comparative study is intended to fill at least part of this information gap.

A SYSTEMS PERSPECTIVE OF UNCONVENTIONAL POLITICAL BEHAVIOR

Collective political violence, defined as the collective use of physical force against objects or persons for political reasons, seems to be a permanent aspect of human existence through time.[6] Still, it appeared for a while that increasing wealth in the industrialized, democratically organized nations would lead to the 'end of ideology' and would consequently insulate these countries against internal political violence as a means of political and social conflict. Furthermore, public attitudes towards violence — at least as an abstract concept — are extremely negative.[7] The shock of an experience for which nobody was really prepared may in part account for the intensely hostile public reaction against the social and political movements of the late sixties which, after an initial period of uncertainty and adjustment, accepted the use of violence as a very efficient and therefore legitimate means in their fight against perceived injustice and deprivation.

The fact that the same mass publics which are so strongly opposed to the use of political violence overwhelmingly support types of legalized violence like capital punishment,[8] points firstly to an imbalance in the means of political influence and control that are available for political authorities on the one hand and mass publics on the other. Secondly, it becomes apparent that violence is a highly ambiguous concept when it is treated abstractly and not analyzed in a specific context.[9]

The imbalance in political means is not only constituted by the coercive control potential of the state.[10] It is also considerably aided by the overall legitimacy beliefs of the public, which are based among other things, on assumptions of system responsiveness. Let me elaborate on this a little further.

Following good traditions, one can regard politics as a process that produces decisions about the production and distribution of scarce resources. This frame of reference naturally points to the high conflict potential of the process. Unquestionably, the successful management of this conflict potential bears directly on the chances that any society has to survive. In this sense then, the institutionalization of potent patterns of conflict management enables a society to achieve its goals without permanent danger of self destruction.

Positions of influence in a political and social system at a given point in time reflect more or less the economic, technological, organizational and ideological resources that the actors in the system command. Therefore, the participants in conflicts which are regarded as legitimate — such as between employers and labor unions or government and opposition — and which are usually highly ritualized, reflect more or less the societal status quo. Since — which may seem trivial enough — societies and also resources change, there will necessarily always be groups which have not as yet gained access to channels of influence. Consequently non-institutionalized, non-coopted conflicts represent a system state in which newly-defined interests are denied what they regard as their proper rights.

According to fundamental democratic principles, however, democratic societies guarantee individual citizens or social groupings at least *the chance to influence the political situation.* To the extent that this principle is realized (or rather believed to be realized), any recourse to collective political violence or the threat thereof would be unnecessary and illegitimate. On the other hand, lack of system responsiveness would legitimately (although not legally) allow for the use of violence as the final point of a continuum of unconventional types of political behavior.

Relating mass publics and political authorities in a dynamic cross-level model, collective political protest in any of its concrete forms can then be conceptualized as an exchange process of expectations and interaction between political authorities and non-élites. Its central variables are the trust of the non-élites in the political authorities, their accordingly chosen means of influence, the perceived success of their influence attempts, the ability of authorities to change outcome decisions and their definition of the situation in terms of their social control chances and the accordingly chosen means of influence.[11]

A perspective or policy formation that does not postulate specific origins and directions of political influence on a priori normative grounds is extremely desirable. This kind of perspective does not assume that 'the people' originate demands which are then processed by the political system and transferred into policy content. It does at least account for the possibility that political authorities themselves define political goals and create the public support that is necessary to carry them out.[12] It is in this sense that the frequent complaint about the manipulation of the masses gains its justification and shows, at the same time, its ideological bias, having to assume an independent, engaged citizen reflecting freedom and dignity which, as Skinner has shown, is rather more myth than reality.[13]

It hardly seems necessary to stress the importance of organizational prerequisites of *successful* political inputs, although it might be justifiably argued that the development of the electronic mass communication systems has at least somewhat reduced the importance of demand *organization,* though at the same time favored the chances of rapid establishment of such organizational structures. The particular pitfalls of perspective[14] and the technical and financial problems that are tied to empirical, longitudinal analyses of political processes have as yet revealed little systematic information about conditions favoring the development of political beliefs which are hostile to the ruling authorities, or the conditions under which either new organizational structures are developed to back up these beliefs, or existing organizational structures redefine their organizational goals and co-opt these beliefs.[15]

Even without such information, however, it is apparent that the analytic approach to collective unconventional behavior is a rationalistic one. It assumes that such types of behavior are rationally considered as the ultimate means by which non-élites achieve certain goals that do not seem to be achievable otherwise because of the unresponsiveness of the political authorities and the corresponding political structures. It does not assume, however, that this calculation (which is 'zweck-rational' in Max Weber's sense) is done independently of all external social stimuli and influence structures. Therefore it is not identical with or similar to the concept of the rational individual 'political man' who actively collects all available and necessary information and then makes up his mind accordingly – an ideal type that has been successfully done away with by modern empirical political sociology. Neither is it identical with the traditional 'ruling élite'-model since it no longer assumes that the organizational structures necessary to pose a realistic threat to the governing elites must be based on traditional, well-established influence positions.

ELEMENTS OF AN INDIVIDUALISTIC MODEL
OF UNCONVENTIONAL POLITICAL BEHAVIOR

The Concept of Relative Deprivation

Whether a high degree of public participation is a necessary condition for a successful revolution may, in the light of some of the most influential revolutions of the past, at least be an open question. Still, public participation has usually been explained by the 'nothing to loose' hypothesis, implying that the average situation for the participating citizens was so bad that the high risk factor involved in participating in the revolution appeared not so high, considering the available alternatives for action. The logic of this type of explanation also invariably assumed that the distribution of wealth and income is the prime determinant of public dissatisfaction. Doubtful as this assumption may have been to start with, it was the civil rights movement in the United States and the student movement in many countries which attracted participants who could not, by any stretch of the imagination, be regarded as economically deprived. Lately Ron Inglehart[16] has now proposed an explanation for the puzzling use of the psychological theory of a need hierarchy proposed by Abraham Maslow.[17] In short, this theory postulates that individual needs are hierarchically organized, and that satisfaction of one stage of the hierarchy leads to the actualization of needs located one step lower in the hierarchy.

Without discussing this theory in any greater detail,[18] at least one general hypothesis related to the appearance on the scene of unconventional political behavior can be formulated: Contrary to many expectations, satisfaction of the physical and safety needs (now at least in sight in many of the post-industrial societies) will not eliminate political conflict. Rather, the conflicts in these societies will now shift to values related to the sphere of lower priority needs like self-actualization and the feeling of belonging.

However far the satisfaction of needs has gone, the central variable that would have to be causally linked to participation in unconventional political behavior would be the concept of relative deprivation, defined for example, as the 'perceived discrepancy between men's value expectations and their value capabilities'[19] or the 'discrepancy between present social aspirations and expectations, on the one hand, and social achievements, on the other'.[20]

The concept of relative deprivation is, of course, all but new.[21] Nevertheless, it has as yet hardly been systematically applied to empirical *survey* research.[22] Therefore, it is not at all surprising that a recent examination of empirical analyses of unconventional political behavior applying the concept of relative deprivation concludes that 'there is considerable reason for rejecting the sociological and popular cliche that absolute or relative deprivation and the ensuing frustration of discontent or despair is the root cause of rebellion'.[23] Still, a careful analysis of the operationalization of such a complex concept as relative deprivation in the re-analysed studies reveals that such a far-reaching conclusion is not at all warranted. Rather, it appears that it should be regarded as bad research policy that the unavailability of adequate data encourages operationalizations that are not founded in the corresponding theory they are supposed to test.[24]

Empirical research on the relationship between frustration and aggression (which can be regarded as the psychological expression of the relative deprivation concept), leaves little doubt that there is indeed such a relationship.[25] It is, however, not as simple and direct as was initially assumed. Notwithstanding the discussion whether aggression is a basic drive or a learned type of behavior, Berkowitz names at least two major factors which intervene between frustration (i.e. blocking of goal-directed behavior) and aggression: the appropriate cues in a given situation that must be present to 'pull out' the aggressive behavior, and the intensity of inhibitions against the use of violence.[26]

The Collective Character of Unconventional Political Behavior

With the emphasis on *collective* forms of unconventional political behavior, some important qualifications must be made. First, the emphasis on the collective character of such types of behavior implies that the protest is supported by a sufficiently large number of individuals or groups to constitute a realistic threat to the existence of a given society. Secondly, although much of the available data on distrust and dissatisfaction suggests that these sentiments are much more widely shared than shows up when it comes to actual protest behavior, it has to be kept in mind that decades of psychological research into the relationship between attitudes and behavior have demonstrated that there is no direct transition from attitudes to behaviors.[27] While correspondingly, it will not be argued that a predisposition to unconventional political behavior will in fact lead to such behavior, it will be hypothesized that such a predisposition is a necessary condition for an engagement in unconventional political behavior.

Problems with the dependent variable: What is unconventional political behavior?

The particular activities which at a given point may be termed unconventional political behavior may not remain so over a longer period of time. This is, of course, a major problem when it comes to the operationalization and quanitification of a potential for political protest. Not only may a particular protest activity be unacceptable for selection because of its specific symbolic connotations with which an individual cannot identify (e.g. draft card burning),[28] but it is also conceivable that, at a certain time a sufficient repertoire of such symbolic activities is simply not available to allow for satisfactory identification and differentiation of potential protest. Therefore, instead of inquiring about behavioral *intentions* in terms of socially well-defined and well-diffused activities that are available for imitative identification, it may be sufficient to measure the extent of politically oriented dissatisfaction. This could then serve as a starting point for a multi-level analysis of the conditions that may lead to political protest.

As long as the main objective of analysis is the ex-post explanation of certain events, the operationalization and measurement problems may not be regarded as too serious. So, to give one example, the strategy of Edward N. Muller in his Waterloo study[29] to measure his dependent variable of potential for political violence as a set of questions about approval of a set of obvious protest activities of different intensity following a Guttman scale pattern, and the probability of own participation in such activities is perfectly acceptable. As soon, however, as the objective changes to the development of predictive theories, this strategy becomes more problematic simply because it cannot sufficiently cope with the dynamics of social processes on different system levels that redefine social and political contexts.

Problems with the main independent variable: Who is relatively deprived of what?

This problem shows up even more clearly when the analysis turns to the concept of relative deprivation. Not unexpectedly, objective aggregate measures of relative deprivation have hardly shown any noticeable relationship with proneness to participate in unconventional political behavior.[30] But also, an individual, static measure of discrepancy between the individual's best possible achievement in certain areas (in this case, so-called welfare values) and his personal standing in these areas at the time of the interview (using a Cantril Self-Anchoring Scale), did not reveal any systematic relationship to the potential for political violence.[31] That same analysis, however, shows very interesting relationships to the potential for political violence when the concept of relative deprivation is operationalized in more dynamic terms (i.e. a positive or negative change in value expectations), although the available data cover only one single point in time and connect past experiences and future expectations exclusively via the perception of the individual at the time of the interview. It need hardly be stressed that changes in the extent of perceived relative deprivation can be produced by changes in the subjective definition of the value optimum, the perceived achievement or both, all falling under the J-curve hypothesis,[32] and definitely demanding independent measures over time in order to assess adequately the individual changes on these dimensions.[33]

The emphasis on independent measurements over time is not only intended to deal with problems of reliability and validity. Much more interesting is the analysis of the conditions that produce shifts of established value dimensions over time, and of the conditions that make for the appearance of new value dimensions. The latter aspect refers to the notion that certain deprivations may be unconsciously — if at all — present but require the action of social groupings to move over the threshold of political relevance. At this point, then, the analysis of individual deprivations has to be paralleled by the analysis of social and political actors — individuals or groups — who try to gain a following by producing collective feelings of deprivation, and the analysis of the conditions under which they are successful.

Only three such conditions will be briefly discussed here. First, the idea of a need hierarchy will be taken up again. According to Maslow, individuals who have been deprived of certain needs at a time will have a tendency to continue to evaluate satisfaction of these needs very highly, even if they are satisfied consistently over a longer time. They may periodically switch over to needs lower in the hierarchy for satisfaction, but will always be extremely unstable in that respect as soon as the satisfaction of the more basic needs seems to be threatened. In contrast to these individuals, those who have continuously experienced satisfaction of the more basic needs will attach much more importance to the satisfaction of less basic needs, and the threat of interrupted satisfaction of more basic needs will not influence the relatively higher importance of the less basic needs.[34]

These assumptions are most likely to be met by younger and more well-to-do people. In correspondence with these hypotheses, Ronald Inglehart has been able to suggest at least empirically that the expected differences in value preferences do indeed seem to be present.[35] This would, at the same time, also qualify any assumption about the unlimited manipulability of individual policy preferences and provide a more balanced picture of the influence opportunities of authorities and other social actors.

A second major factor is the condition that collective deprivations, once they have crossed the individual's threshold of awareness, have to be tied to actors or institutions who are clearly held responsible for the deprivation. In this respect, it may be conceivable to maintain the differentiation between collective unconventional behavior including violence, and collective *political* unconventional behavior including violence,[36] and therefore distinguish between aggressive acts directed towards social actors and aggressive acts directed towards political actors. In complex post-industrial societies, however, this distinction appears somewhat artificial, since it is difficult to imagine a social conflict of some magnitude that will not sooner or later also involve the political system. Therefore, it seems sufficient to require that in order to be added to the potential for political protests, an individual who has experienced some deprivation, must place the reasons and responsibilities for his deprivation in the public and not the private sphere.

Finally, it should be kept in mind that the high degree of social stratification and the corresponding differences in wealth and income in the post-industrial societies make it very unlikely that all population groups will be frustrated on equal value dimensions at the same time. Let us assume for a moment that the discussed age differences in value preferences do not turn out to be a passing fancy. Then it is probable that the corresponding value differences will increase the chance for social conflicts if the output of the political and social system does not permanently guarantee the satisfaction of all basic needs, so that demands by some groups for the satisfaction of less basic needs can be fulfilled at not too high costs for the overall system.[37]

Some intervening variables: Legitimacy beliefs and attitudes towards violence

Political dissatisfaction as a result of deprivation and potential for unconventional political behavior are obviously not identical. For an operative theory it is therefore essential to define the variables that intervene between the independent and the dependent variable. In order to identify such variables, one has to consider some of the problems that I have already discussed in previous parts of the article. The most difficult problem is the processual perspective of political unrest, which must be seen as a dynamic, multi-level phenomenon.

A few remarks may help to clarify this point. If the assumption of a systematic relationship between dissatisfaction and unrest is correct, then the first problem that has to be considered is that there cannot be time identity between dissatisfaction and unrest. There may be social actors who anticipate and define deprivation and push it over the threshold of individual awareness, or it may happen that certain actors take up existing individual deprivations and organize as well as articulate them: there has to be an interaction between actors on different system levels over time to start off the process of unrest. The process itself — and this leads to the second problem — is strongly incluenced by factors based on the value system as well as on organizational and structural properties of the participants in the conflict, notwithstanding the dynamics of the confrontation situation itself.

The interactional and transactional qualities of this process have been stressed many times, although with different emphases and unequal sophistication.[38] Still, the theoretical work has not as yet been sufficiently paralleled by corresponding mathematical models and empirical work. Here, it can surely be argued that the present developmental stage of the empirical social sciences simply does not allow for the complexity of approach that is so badly wanted and needed. On the other hand, the researcher facing the dilemma of wanting to explain complex phenomena with relatively simple means should at least be aware of the shortcomings of his research, which can usually cover only limited aspects of the problem at hand.

Macro-level theories have used concepts like coercive and respecting regime coercive control (Gurr) or social control (Smelser, Gamson) to refer to factors which externally influence the probability of dissatisfaction leading to overt protest behavior. Variables of this class would intervene in the process of transformation of a protest potential into protest behavior. A micro-level theory aiming at an explanation of individual protest behavior has to consider the same variables, although they would have to be mediated through the perception of the individual actor. In addition to these and other structural factors,[39] a micro-theory of unconventional political behavior has to search also for attitudinal variables which might influence the availability for such behavior.[40]

As I have argued in previous sections of the article, the propensity to participate in unconventional political activities should be systematically related to the perception of the responsiveness of the political system and its actors. Such perception can be understood as a generalized belief about this property of the system which may be widely divorced from any realistic assessment of the objective degree of system responsiveness. Whether this belief is called legitimacy (Max Weber) or trust (Gamson) is not really important. What is important, however, is an understanding of the functions that such a generalized attitude serves on the system level. Following Gamson, it is maintained that it allows political authorities a 'blank cheque' for their actions and allows citizens to regard politics as an aspect of life to which they do not have to commit too many resources.[41]

If this state of affairs is regarded as equilibrium, the question to consider is under what conditions this equilibrium could be destroyed. Even restricting consideration to variables operating on the individual level, the question is very difficult to answer because of the multiplicity of functions that the legitimacy beliefs may fulfill, depending on the stage of the process that the political system is in. Restricting the analysis to one point in time, a very plausible hypothesis is that a high level of relative deprivation will lead to a high potential for unconventional political behavior under conditions of low legitimacy beliefs, and to a low potential for unconventional political behavior under conditions of high legitimacy beliefs.[42] It must however be assumed that, according to psychological balance or consonance theories, legitimacy beliefs will – in the long run – not be independent of feelings of deprivation, especially if such feelings are clearly directed towards parts of the political system. Whether the balance of the internal belief system can be restored without changing the overall legitimacy beliefs may depend to a larger extent on the centrality of the value dimension in which the individual feels deprived.

However, the decisive point is that any static conceptualization as one-way causation without feed-back of the role that legitimacy beliefs play in the process of building up a potential for political protest may be highly misleading.

Two more considerations further complicate the picture. First, empirical evidence about legitimacy beliefs indicates that they are multidimensional in a way that requires explicit distinction.[43] In particular, the overall sense of system responsiveness (which seems to be very close to the old ISR-Political Efficacy Scale[44]) has to be distinguished from the personal confidence in one's own political potency. Moreover, these different dimensions also have an unequal chance of being confronted with social and political reality, leading to unequal probabilities of attitude change and the chance of conflict between legitimacy dimensions.[45] Secondly, the concept of legitimacy beliefs cannot be treated so easily in a causal framework of the Simon-Blalock type because, besides the problem of reciprocal causation already mentioned, the necessary assumption of uncorrelated error terms would be very questionable in the case of deprivation and legitimacy, if both of these concepts were contained in a recursive causal model with unconventional political behavior as the dependent variable.[46]

At first sight the second intervening variable, attitudes towards violence, seems to pose less severe theoretical and methodological problems. The argument is straightforward: the more negative the attitude towards violence, the lesser the probability of participation in unconventional political behavior, since such behavior – because of its very nature and its situational properties – always contains at least the possibility of violent confrontation with control agencies. Unfortunately, the results of an extensive study about attitudes towards violence show that the situation is more complicated.[47] According to this study, there is a consistent perceptual bias in the way that certain social groupings think of specific actions as violent or non-violent. In order to achieve cognitive consonance, they simply define acts that are ideologically close to them and supposedly help their cause as non-violent. With this, they are then able to maintain their notion of the fundamental evil of violence.

While these remarks point to the ambiguity of an abstract understanding of violence, they nevertheless also point to the fact that because of the negative associations with violence, the psychological 'trick' of subjective definitions of specific actions as violent or non-violent can be overridden if sufficient social influence or social control is exerted. The initial hypothesis would then still hold, provided that certain kinds of behavior were clearly and unanimously labeled as violent. Of course, there may also be groups who consciously and, usually on the basis of comprehensive ideology, regard violence as a desirable means of achieving what they think is a desirable state of the world.[48]

Another aspect of political violence that may well become part of an individual's frame of reference is his assessment of the success of previous violence.[49] The use of this concept at the micro-level stresses the rationalistic character of the explanation for unconventional political behavior. At the macro-level it points to questions of political strategy and conflict management.

Some Concluding remarks on the theory of unconventional political behavior

Let me now briefly summarize the main concepts and relationships that are hypothesized to explain the appearance on the scene of unconventional political behavior in post-industrial societies.

The basic relationship that is postulated between the degree of relative deprivation and the potential for unconventional political behavior: the higher the subjectively perceived deprivation, the more central the value dimensions on which deprivations are experienced and the clearer the perceived responsibility of political authorities for these deprivations, the higher the potential for unconventional political behavior.

In addition, two intervening variables have been introduced: legitimacy beliefs and attitudes towards violence. High legitimacy beliefs and negative attitudes towards violence suppress the potential for unconventional political behavior, whereas low legitimacy beliefs and positive attitudes towards violence enhance it.[50]

Under conditions of high deprivation and high legitimacy beliefs, however, it is possible that this conflict can be resolved through increased participation within the system. This outcome is particularly likely when the *personal efficacy dimension* of the legitimacy beliefs is well developed, and this expectation is in line with the theoretical conceptualization on the system level that Gamson has proposed and which has been previously discussed. Sketchy empirical evidence from West Germany seems to indicate that, indeed, part of the student protest movement went out of the universities and into political parties. Of course, this hypothesis has consequences for the empirical research strategy: it requires also the measurement of conventional political behavior over a period of time.

Under conditions of high deprivation, low legitimacy beliefs and negative attitudes towards violence or sceptical evaluation of the success of past violence, the expected outcome would be alienation and apathy.[51]

Very little empirical evidence is as yet available which could be regarded as an adequate test of the outlined theoretical approach to the explanation of unconventional political behavior. The analysis of Edward N. Muller's Waterloo study certainly comes closest to what could be regarded as a serious test. The amount of variation that he is able to explain in his dependent variable – potential for political violence – is not overwhelming: about 30 per cent, corresponding to a multiple correlation coefficient of less than 0.6.[52] On the other hand, considering the various limitations of his study these results are far more impressive than most of the other relationships that have been reported.[53]

It should be clear from the discussion of the theoretical propositions developed in the first part of the article that the survey data which will be collected in this new study will all most probably come from one point in time – though from eight nations – and have substantial shortcomings. In this respect, the decision to apply only the survey approach is an uneasy compromise between what would have been desirable and what was financially and technically feasible.

THE OPERATIONALIZATION OF THE CORE VARIABLES

Relative Social Deprivation

Insofar as empirical research has employed the concept of relative deprivation, it seems safe to summarize one result of that research by saying that the explanatory power of the concept depends on the extent to which the *subjective and collective* property of relative deprivation has been taken into account. In other words: relative deprivation must be consciously and individually experienced as a deprivation in comparison with something or somebody.[54] In addition however I would argue that relative deprivation must be perceived collectively, that is as a *shared* deprivation, and that its cause must be related to concrete social or political structures in a given society.

It is of course difficult to translate these considerations into a concrete research strategy. Two major difficulties, and their solutions chosen by our research group, will be briefly discussed here. First, the processual, dynamic aspect of relative deprivation requires an anticipation of the distinctive areas of life satisfaction which may, under certain circumstances, be actualized as collective deprivations. In this respect we have drawn heavily on the work of Ron Inglehart on value change in post-industrial societies.[55] The specific selection of satisfaction domains reflects the notion of a spectrum of different values in the need hierarchy (e.g. economic welfare, safety, a feeling of belonging) which may be of unequal importance to population groups of widely differing affluence. The concrete description of the domains, on the other hand, has been designed to correspond to the assumption that most of the relevant deprivations which people can experience are extremely close to the center of their daily life. The seven domains were:

a. housing
b. safety in the neighborhood
c. standard of living
d. daily work
e. way of spending leisure time
f. family income
g. degree of friendliness and consideration of friends and neighbors

The second problem is how the necessary dynamization of the concept of the relative deprivation should be achieved from the multiplicity of available and theoretically meaningful alternatives. Unfortunately, lack of interview space prevented the inclusion of all the measures that had come into consideration on theoretical grounds. The compromise to concentrate on present and future domain satisfaction and to leave out past satisfaction and satisfaction entitlement reflected the emphasis on the analysis of transition from acquisitive to post-acquisitive values in the study. These *future-oriented* change indicators of domain satisfaction, however, did not perform as expected in the pretest analysis. In this respect, we were lucky to have at least included a measure for overall life satisfaction which was taken at three different points in time (five years ago, today, five years from now), as well as for the theoretically significant assessment of subjective satisfaction entitlement.[56] On the basis of these measures, indicators of change in overall life satisfaction were also constructed.[57]

Political Deprivation

Particularly in societies like the US, where personal success or failure is attributed much more to individual than to system characteristics, it becomes very important to develop a measure for specific political dissatisfaction that is not operationally related to general life dissatisfaction. Such a measure has to be comparatively complex in order to reflect the different theoretical dimensions of the concept. On a concrete level it has to get at the processes by which citizens themselves relate to the output and problem-solving capacity of the political system, in other words: its handling of the political issues.

In order to be able to hypothesize a relationship between political dissatisfaction and potential for unconventional political behavior, the following three conditions should hold in particular:

a. the issue should be politicized and be of high personal relevance to the respondent;

b. a clear responsibility for action in the specific issue area should be assigned to the political authorities;

c. the respondent should evaluate the performance of the political authorities in the specific area negatively.

Following a design proposed by Milbrath,[58] we had our respondents evaluate the following 13 issues according to the three dimensions of personal relevance, responsibility for action and performance of political authorities:

a. care for the aged

b. protecting personal freedom in sexual matters

c. stabilizing prices

d. guaranteeing equal rights for women and men

e. leveling differences between the rich and the poor

f. guaranteeing everybody's right to work

g. guaranteeing good educational opportunities

h. guaranteeing good health services for everybody

i. offering more adequate housing

j. making sure that police do not abuse their rights

k. fighting pollution

l. making sure that people in this neighborhood are safe at night

m. guaranteeing equal rights for foreign workers

Whether the three dimensions of personal relevance, responsibility and performance of political authorities were sufficiently independent to warrant separate treatment was first ascertained in a series of factor analyses and regression analyses. The results of these analyses clearly supported the assumption of independence. In a next step, the three assessments were summed across each individual issue to produce a measure of individual issue dissatisfaction.[59] Then, a global measure of political dissatisfaction was calculated by averaging the 13 individual issue dissatisfaction scores.

An inspection of the issues selected for presentation to the respondents shows that the issue areas have been chosen with the intention of covering a broad range of political problems whose personal relevance should be widely influenced by the general value preferences of acquisitiveness versus post-acquisitiveness which are also reflected in the operationalizations in the life domain satisfaction part of the study. Even more than in the case of life domain satisfaction, however, the selection of concrete political issues for measuring political dissatisfaction runs the danger of not covering the issues that are really relevant to some people and thereby failing to achieve a valid measure of political dissatisfaction.

In addition to such validity considerations, I would like to stress again the importance of the fact that political and social deprivations are not purely individualistic phenomena which, to everybody's surprise, materialize out of the blue. Collective deprivation — and only collective deprivation is theoretically relevant in a model for the explanation of unconventional political behavior — is a threshold phenomenon which requires interactions between élites and mass publics.

Intervening Variables

Empirical research has demonstrated time and again that politics is an aspect of life which the majority of people perceive only very broadly and which, under normal circumstances, is not a central part of their daily pleasures and worries. It is, therefore, extremely functional for the average citizen to orient himself in a very generalized way towards the political system. Gamson speaks of two general ways by which a citizen relates to politics and can be consequently alienated from politics: on the output dimension the feeling of *necessity* to influence political outcomes, (political trust), on the input dimension the feeling of *ability* to influence political outcomes (political efficacy).[60]

The first analysis of the Waterloo study clearly shows that political trust warrants an inclusion into an *additive* model of potential for political protest.[61] Unfortunately, we had not included in the pretest a measure that covers the dimension of political trust adequately. As an — admittedly inadequate — surrogate, an indicator of generalized social distrust will be used.[62]

Similar problems do not arise with respect to the efficacy dimension. There we had six items altogether, among them being the traditional efficacy items which were used for the first time in the 1952 Survey Research Center election study.[63]

As was mentioned before, the theoretically important aspect of individual feelings of trust and efficacy is their quality of being a *general* frame of orientation for the citizen. It is precisely their lack of concrete political issue content, however, that necessitates the consideration of yet another dimension of general political orientation, the left-right continuum. This dimension, unlike the concept of trust and efficacy, also serves as a yardstick for the organization of attitudes on specific policy problems.[64] Furthermore, it is especially relevant that much of the recent research in political ideology has shown the left-right dimension to be the only ideological concept that can be meaningfully applied to a larger part of the mass publics in Western democratic societies.[65]

The last intervening variable I would like briefly to discuss is the perception of success of previous unconventional political behavior. The importance of this concept has been stressed by Gurr and Muller, who have also been able to show empirically its relevance for the explanation of protest potential.[66]

Unconventional Political Behavior

The work of Monica Blumenthal et al.[67] has made thoroughly clear the problems and ambiguities one must be prepared for in the empirical study of political violence. Nevertheless, the analyses reported by Edward N. Muller and, in particular, those by Alan Marsh[68] have led us to believe that we have been able to develop a valid Guttman scale of unconventional political behavior. The analysis of Marsh is particularly relevant for our research design, since he was able to show that the Guttman scale he developed is *not* sensitive to specific situational properties. This is a surprising result in the light of research on the relationship between attitudes and behavior.[69]

The research design contains evaluations of the following ten acts of unconventional political behavior (UPB) for the three dimensions of approval, actual or potential participation, and evaluation of effectiveness:[70]

a. Occupying buildings, factories, a.s.o.
b. Refusing to pay rent, rates, or taxes
c. Signing a petition
d. Damaging property
e. Personal violence (fighting with police, demonstrators)
f. Participating in a wild-cat strike
g. Obstructing traffic
h. Participating in an officially authorized demonstration
i. Writing slogans on walls
j. Participating in protest meetings

The Guttman scale analysis for the three dimensions came up with quite satisfactory results:

	Name	Coefficient of reproducibility	Percentage of cases that could not be classified
Scale 1	approval of UPB	0.966	3
Scale 2[71]	actual or potential participation in UPB	0.975	10
Scale 3	evaluation of effectiveness of UPB	0.981	15

The resulting scales look good enough to warrant their use as dependent variables (scales 1 and 2) or an intervening variable (scale 3) in the model for the explanation of unconventional political behavior.

RESULTS OF THE PRETEST ANALYSIS[72]

In the evaluation of the pretest analysis one must, in my opinion, consider two entirely different sets of problems that interfere in the process of theory testing. First, it seems only fair to point to the difficulties that any empirical test of a complex theory encounters with respect to the necessary data base. In particular, severe problems are posed by the requirements for longitudinal and crosslevel data. As far as this study is concerned, the lack of necessary resources will prevent any of these problems from being solved, in either the pretest or the main study.[73] Some of the consequences of these shortcomings have already been discussed in some detail.

The second set of problems is related to the preliminary character of the analysis, based only on a small data set of 67 pretest respondents. For one thing, the discussion of the key theoretical concepts should have amply demonstrated that the independent and intervening variables are not related to the dependent variables in a straightforward (i.e. linear and additive) way. Furthermore, there is reason to believe that more than one general, explanatory model is necessary to adequately account for *all* kinds of unconventional political behavior. Both these considerations put decisive limitations on any attempt to seriously test any such model on a poor empirical basis. What can be done with such pretest data, in addition to analysing scale properties, as well as the dimensionality of attitude items and the like, is to test whether the operationalizations of the key theoretical concepts in the study show at least the relationships to the dependent variables that one would have to expect on the basis of the theory behind them.

Before presenting the results of the analysis, a few remarks about the criteria for selection of the general life satisfaction variables are necessary. In the area of general life satisfaction, the results of analyses reported in the literature clearly point to the necessity for using indicators that take into account subjective perceptions of change over time. The two particular measures tested here are the perceived change in overall life satisfaction 1) over the last five years and 2) for the coming five years.

The first of these variables was selected on the assumption that mass publics do not evaluate their life situation according to abstract value opportunities, but rather according to their own, very much down-to-earth evaluation of their life achievements. A reinforcement of this attitude must be expected if the contention holds that political and social satisfactions and deprivations are not purely individualistic phenomena. It is precisely the collective character of subjectively perceived satisfactions that emphasizes the role of trade unions as the institutionalized interest representation of the working classes and, hence, authoritative interpreters of the achievements and deprivations of their members. Consequently, one would expect the unions to justify their incremental wage policies by continually attempting to convince their membership that there are – *in comparison with the past* – tremendous achievements indeed.

The second variable, perceived future change of life satisfaction, was chosen on the assumption that there might also be a segment of the population with high and permanent achievements (the 'post-acquisitives') for whom future improvement in life satisfaction is much more important than present improvement.

The following table contains the correlations between the independent, intervening and dependent variables.

TABLE 1

Correlations between key variables of the micro theory of unconventional political behavior

a) *Independent and intervening variables*

1. Change in general life satisfaction – five years ago and today
2. Change in general life satisfaction – today and five years from now
3. Average global political dissatisfaction
4. Selflocation on left-right continuum
5. Political trust
6. Political efficacy
7. Effectiveness of past unconventional political behavior.

b) *Dependent variables*

8. Approval of unconventional political behavior
9. Actual or potential participation in unconventional political behavior

Correlation Matrix (Pearson's r)

	1	2	3	4	5	6	7	8
2	−0.36							
3	0.00	−0.26						
4	−0.03	−0.27	0.20					
5	−0.06	0.10	−0.05	−0.05				
6	0.01	0.01	−0.15	−0.18	0.14			
7	0.01	−0.15	−0.28	−0.24	0.17	0.32		
8	−0.43	0.09	−0.35	−0.38	0.39	0.30	0.29	
9	−0.30	−0.08	−0.31	−0.33	0.32	0.21	0.47	0.85

The results of this bivariate correlation analysis are both extremely interesting and promising. First, there is only one of the independent and intervening variables that does not show substantial correlations with the two dependent variables: future-oriented change in general life satisfaction.[74]

Second, the correlations between independent as well as intervening variables are, on the average quite low. This is important because it points to a substantial amount of independence among concepts.[75]

Finally, and most satisfying, the correlations between the dependent and other variables are all in line with what one would expect on the basis of the theoretical discussion. It could be shown that

approval of unconventional political behavior and participation or potential participation in unconventional political behavior

are significantly related to:

- — a negative change of past-present overall life satisfaction
- — a high amount of average overall political dissatisfaction
- — a left position on the left-right scale
- — a sense of high political efficacy
- — a perception of effectiveness of past unconventional behavior

Neither of these results can already be accepted as sufficient confirmation of the theoretical approach developed for the explanation of unconventional political behavior. On the other hand, this first analysis, based on data from our 67 pretest respondents, has consistently yielded results that are in line with our theoretical expectations. This provides considerable encouragement for our future research.

NOTES

1. Adam Przeworski and Henry Teune, *The Logic of Comparative Social Inquiry* (New York: 1970), 51 ff.

2. Murray Edelman, *Politics as Symbolic Action* (Chicago: 1971).

3. Lester W. Milbrath, *Political Participation* (Chicago: 1965), 18.

4. Seymour M. Lipset, *Political Man* (New York: 1963), 445.

5. One noteworthy exception is the article by Edward N. Muller, 'A Test of a Partial Theory of Potential for Political Violence', in *American Political Science Review*, Vol. LXVI, No. 3, September 1972, 928 ff.

6. Charles Tilly, 'Collective Violence in European Perspective', in Hugh Davis Graham and Ted Robert Gurr (eds), *Violence in America* (New York: 1969), 4 ff.

7. Monica Blumenthal et al., *Justifying Violence* (Ann Arbor: 1972), 81, and Max Kaase, 'Demokratische Einstellungen in der Bundesrepublik Deutschland', in Rudolf Wildenmann et al. (eds), *Sozialwissenschaftliches Jahrbuch für Politik, Band 2* (München: 1971), 258.

8. Max Kaase, *Demokratische Einstellungen in der Bundesrepublik Deutschland*, op. cit., 326.

9. Monica Blumenthal et al., *Justifying Violence*, op. cit., develop the powerful distinction between violence for social control and violence for social change, and also show that the dissonance between favoring certain violent acts and the belief in the evilness of violence is resolved simply by defining these acts as non-violent.

10. Ted Robert Gurr, 'A Comparative Study of Civil Strife', in Hugh Davis Graham and Ted Robert Gurr, op. cit., 578; 'A Causal Model of Civil Strife', in *American Political Science Review*, LXII, December 1968, 1104 ff.; *Why Men Rebel* (Princeton: 1970), 232 ff.

11. William A. Gamson, *Power and Discontent* (Homewood: 1968), 163 ff., part. 190 f.

12. Murray Edelmann, *Politics as Symbolic Action*, op. cit., 4; William A. Gamson, *Power and Discontent*, op. cit., 42 ff.

13. B. F. Skinner, *Beyond Freedom and Dignity* (New York: 1971).

14. Murray Edelmann, *Politics as Symbolic Action,* op. cit., 3 ff.

15. The discussion about the end of the American party system seems to be a perfect case in point.

16. Ronald Inglehart, 'The Silent Revolution in Europe: Intergenerational Change in Post-Industrial Societies', in *American Political Science Review,* Vol. LXV, No. 4, December 1971, 991 ff.

17. Abraham Maslow, *Motivation and Personality* (New York: 1954).

18. It seems only fair to mention that there is very little empirical evidence for this theory, and that there is considerable scepticism about it in contemporary psychology.

19. Ted Robert Gurr, *Why Men Rebel,* op. cit., 13.

20. Ivo K. Feierabend, Rosalind L. Feierabend, and Betty A. Nesvold, 'Social Change and Political Violence: Cross-National Patterns', in Hugh Davis Graham and Ted Robert Gurr, eds. *Violence in America,* op. cit., 606 ff. It is not at all necessary to rely exclusively on the term 'relative deprivation'. John P. Spiegel, 'Theories of Violence: An Integrated Approach', in *International Journal of Group Tensions,* 1971, Vol. 1, No. 1, 83, speaks of the 'clash between the ideal value pattern and the actual or operative patterns', addressing the problem of the inconsistency between political ideals and practice as a motivating force to political violence. However, the decisive factor here is the discrepancy between expectations and reality.

21. See e.g. Robert K. Merton, *Social Theory and Social Structure* (Glencoe: 1949).

22. One of the rare applications is the study by Edward N. Muller. See also his article, together with Bernard Grofman, 'The Strange Case of Relative Gratification and Potential for Political Violence: The V-Curve Hypothesis', in *American Political Science Review,* Vol. LXVII, June 1973, 514 ff., and his paper 'A Nonalienation Interaction Theory of Political Protest', mimeo (Mannheim: 1973). The aggregate measures of relative deprivation by Gurr, 'A Causal Model of Civil Strife', op. cit., or Feierabend et al., 'Social Change and Political Violence: Cross National Patterns', op. cit., as ingenious as they may have been designed, appear controversial enough not to warrant any final conclusions from analyses that have been exclusively based on such measures.

23. Clark McPhail, 'Civil Disorder Participation: A Critical Examination of Recent Research', in *American Sociological Review,* 1971, Vol. 36, December, 1064.

24. The analyses of Edward N. Muller demonstrate that there is considerable pay-off if more time is used for the operationalization of theoretical concepts.

25. Leonard Berkowitz (ed.), *Roots of Aggression* (New York: 1969).

26. Leonard Berkowitz, ibid., 18, 107.

27. Martin Fishbein, 'Voyage into Darkness: The Search for Attitudinal-Behavioral Consistency', mimeo, 1969; Martin Fishbein, 'Attitude and the Prediction of Behavior', in Martin Fishbein (ed.), *Readings in Attitude Theory and Measurement* (New York: 1967), 477 ff.

28. This refers once again to the social context of the meaning of specific behaviors, the importance of which has been shown by Blumenthal et al., *Justifying Violence,* op. cit., for the meaning of violence. In technical terms, we have to consider the problem of scalability of items across sub-populations.

29. Edward N. Muller, 'A Test of a Partial Theory of Potential for Political Violence', op. cit., 933 ff., 955 ff.

30. Seymour Spilerman, 'The Causes of Racial Disturbances: A Comparison of Alternative Explanations', in *American Sociological Review,* No. 35, August 1970, 627 ff.

31. Bernard Grofman and Edward N. Muller, 'The Strange Case of Relative Gratification and Potential for Political Violence: The V-Curve Hypothesis', op. cit., 520 ff.

32. James C. Davies, 'The J-Curve of Rising and Declining Satisfactions as a Cause of Some Great Revolutions and a Contained Rebellion', in Hugh Davies Graham and Ted Robert Gurr (eds), *Violence in America,* op. cit., 671 ff.

33. I am grateful to Edward N. Muller for a comment related to the independent measurement problem. Undoubtedly, independent measurements over time are necessary to keep track of the changes over time. In addition to that, however, measurements about the *perceptions of*

the past and future at each interview point in time are absolutely essential in order to cope with the problem of changes in perception over time. This is particularly important in the light of the above mentioned macro-processes that can lead, depending on the conditions, to either revaluation or de-valuation of past and future. See also Bernard Grofman and Edward N. Muller, 'The Strange Case of Relative Gratification and Potential for Political Violence: The V-Curve Hypothesis', op. cit., 597 ff., and their reference to a paper by Charles Wolf, Jr., 'The Present Value of the Past'.

34. Abraham Maslow, Motivation and Personality, op. cit.

35. Ronald Inglehart, 'The Silent Revolution in Europe', op. cit.; it remains tó be seen, though, whether these differences in age and educational cohorts will remain over time or wither away because of life cycle influences.

36. Ted Robert Gurr, Why Men Rebel, op. cit.

37. This seems to be the story of the conflict between the conservatives and the new left.

38. See, e.g., William Kornhauser, The Politics of Mass Society (Glencoe: 1959); Neil J. Smelser, Theory of Collective Behavior (Glencoe: 1963); Ted Robert Gurr, Why Men Rebel, op. cit., and the able criticism of Joseph Firestone, 'Three Frameworks for the Study of Violence: A Critique and Some Suggestions for a New Synthesis', Research Paper No. 11, Center for Comparative Political Research (Binghamton: 1971).

39. Some of these factors would have to be classified into the facilitation (Gurr) cateegory, e.g. the fact that students are more flexible in their schedules and are very well integrated into networks of direct communication.

40. This is particularly important when one tries to keep in mind the dynamic aspects of the mobilization process, where the individual belief system is very important in screening in consonant and screening out dissonant information, hereby insulating the individual against overly immediate responses to external stimuli.

41. William A. Gamson, Power and Discontent, op. cit., 39 ff.

42. For an excellent empirical application of this type of conceptualization, see Edward N. Muller, 'A Test of a Partial Theory of Potential for Political Violence', op. cit.

43. Edward N. Muller, 'Cross-National Dimensions of Political Competence', in American Political Science Review, Vol. LXIV, No. 3, September 1970, 792 ff.

44. For detailed information see John P. Robinson, Jerrald G. Rusk, Kendra B. Head, Measures of Political Attitudes, (Ann Arbor: 1968), 459 ff.

45. This argument is more fully developed in Philip E. Converse, 'Change in the American Electorate', in Angus Campbell and Philip E. Converse (eds), The Human Meaning of Social Change (New York: 1972).

46. For a broad overview see Hubert M. Blalock, Jr. (ed), Causal Models in the Social Sciences (Chicago: 1971).

47. Monica Blumenthal et al., Justifying Violence, op. cit.

48. This case would fall under Gurr's category of normative justifications for political violence. See Ted Robert Gurr, Why Men Rebel, op. cit., 193 ff. It should be stressed again, though, that the rationale for giving up violence as a political means clearly lies in the presence of other, effective means of political exchange processes. There can be no rejection of violence simply on the basis of a priori moralistic grounds.

49. This is part of Gurr's Utilitarian Justification for Political Violence. One of the many facets of this problem is the relationship of mass media converage and political violence. For this point, see Gladys Engel Lang and Kurt Lang, 'Some Pertinent Questions on Collective Violence and the News Media', in Journal of Social Issues, Vol. 28, No. 1, 1972, 93 ff. For an operationalization of the concept, see also Edward N. Muller, 'A Test of a Partial Theory of Potential for Political Violence', op. cit., 944 ff., 959 ff.

50. William A. Gamson, Power and Discontent, op. cit., 59 ff., also 172 ff.

51. Philip E. Converse, Change in the American Electorate, op. cit., 336.

52. Edward N. Muller, 'A Test of a Partial Theory of Potential for Political Violence', op. cit., 950 ff.

53. Clark McPhail, 'Civil Disorder Participation: A Critical Examination of Recent Re-

search', op. cit.

54. See Bernard N. Grofman and Edward N. Muller, 'The Strange Case of Relative Gratification and Potential for Political Violence: The V-Curve Hypothesis', op. cit., 515.

55. Ronald Inglehart, 'The Silent Revolution in Europe: Intergenerational Change in Post-Industrial-Societies', op. cit., 991 ff.

56. All of these measures were obtained by using a Cantril self-anchoring scale with a range from 0 (worst possible situation) to 10 (best possible situation): For a detailed description, see Franklin P. Kilpatrick and Hadley Cantril, 'Self Anchoring Scaling', in *Journal of Individual Psychology*, Vol. 16, November 1960, 158 ff.

57. The measures of perceived change in satisfaction were constructed by subtracting two measures e.g. present from future satisfaction. The corresponding derived measures range from -10 (highest possible negative change) through 0 (no change) to 10 (highest positive change). In order to avoid outlier effects which can considerably influence regression analyses in a few cases, all of those variables were collapsed into ordinal variables with five categories:

1 = $-10 - -3$ (high negative change)
2 = $-1 - -1$ (slight negative change)
3 = 0 (no change)
4 = $1-2$ (slight positive change)
5 = $3-10$ (high positive change)

6 = Missing data

58. Lester W. Milbrath, *People and Government*, unpublished manuscript (Buffalo: 1971).

59. This preliminary analysis did not do sufficient justice to the potential interactive relationship between the three dimensions. Such detailed analyses require the full data set.

60. William A. Gamson, *Power and Discontent*, op. cit., 42.

61. Edward N. Muller, 'A Test of a Partial Theory of Potential for Political Violence', op. cit., 950 ff.

62. The item was: 'The worst in today's world is that most people don't believe in anything any more.' This item is close to the concept of anomie. Hans D. Klingemann and Franz U. Pappi, *Politischer Radikalismus* (München: 1972), 65, use it as part of a scale of authoritarian traditionalism. In the main study, we have now included genuine measures of political trust.

63. Angus Campbell, Gerald Gurin and Warren E. Miller, *The Voter Decides* Evanstown:-1954), 187 ff., 210 f.

64. The most interesting and consequential property of this concept for unconventional political behavior is that its power to develop an accordingly constrained belief system increases with increased education. For a detailed discussion see in particular Philip E. Converse, 'The Nature of Belief Systems in Mass Publics', in: David E. Apter (ed), *Ideology and Discontent* (Glencoe: 1964), 207 ff.

65. See Hans D. Klingemann, 'Testing the Left-Right-Continuum on a Sample of German Voters', in *Comparative Political Studies*, Vol. 5, April 1972, 99 ff.; Hans D. Klingemann and Franz U. Pappi, *Politischer Radikalismus*, op. cit., 17 ff.; Ronald Inglehart and Hans D. Klingemann, *Party Identification, Political Ideology and the Left-Right Dimension*, unpublished manuscript, (Mannheim: September 1974). In our study we used – like Klingemann – a ten-point, self-anchoring scale type instrument to measure the self-location on the left-right dimension.

66. The operationalization of this variable is described in the following section of this paper.

67. Monica Blumenthal et al., *Justifying Violence*, op. cit.

68. Alan Marsh, 'Explorations in Unorthodox Political Behavior, A Scale to Measure Protest Potential', in *European Journal of Political Research*, June 1974, Vol. 2, No. 2, 107 ff.

69. Martin Fishbein, 'Attitude and Prediction of Behavior', op. cit., I. Ajzen and M. Fishbein, 'The Prediction of Behavioral Intentions in a Choice Situation', in *Journal of Experimental Social Psychology*, Vol. V, 1969, 400 ff.

70. Alan Marsh, 'Explorations in Unorthodox Political Behavior, A Scale to Measure

'Protest Potential', op. cit., has elaborated on the rationale for this design.

71. For the Guttman scale analysis those respondents were scored 'yes' who had already actually participated *or* were willing to participate in a given form of unconventional political behavior.

72. All analyses reported here were performed with the version of OSIRIS II implemented at the Mannheim Siemens 4004/45 computer.

73. This is by no means a special characteristic of this study. Rather, it systematically reflects the lack of social science research infrastructure and lack of sufficient funds for social science research.

74. In terms of absolute coefficient magnitude and explained variance, the correlations may seem not particularly high. Compared with correlations usually reported in survey research, their magnitude is surprisingly high. For a comparison, see Clark McPhail, 'Civic Disorder Participation: A Critical Examination of Recent Research', op. cit.; Edward N. Muller, 'A Test of a Partial Theory of Potential for Political Violence', op. cit.

75. In a statistical sense, this result reduces the problem of multicollinearity, i.e. correlations between predictor variables in regression analysis which unstabilize the beta-coefficients as standardized measures of predictor importance. On the basis of these analyses, I felt sufficiently encouraged to try a straightforward multiple regression analysis which corresponds to an additive linear regression model. This kind of model, of course, does not represent the complex statistical model necessary to correspond to the theoretical part of the article. Nevertheless, the results are quite interesting. The two multiple regressions for approval of unconventional political behavior and participation or potential participation in unconventional political behavior as dependent variables have the following results:

7 Independent and Intervening Variables	Dependent Variable: Approval of Unconventional Political Behavior	Dependent Variable: Actual or Potential Participation in Unconventional Political Behavior
Multiple Correlation Coefficient	0.80	0.74
Explained Variance	63%	54%
Beta weights for independent and intervening variables:		
1. Change in general life satisfaction – five years ago and today	−0.54	−0.43
2. Change in general life satisfaction – today and five years from now	−0.34	−0.38
3. Average global political dissatisfaction	−0.33	−0.27
4. Self-location on left-right continuum	−0.39	−0.32
5. Political trust	0.15	0.01
6. Political efficacy	0.34	0.27
7. Effectiveness of past unconventional political behavior	−0.04	0.22

An inspection of the two sets of beta weights reveals considerable similarities. In the light of a correlation of 0.85 between the two dependent variables, this is of course not surprising. Also, the beta weights correspond quite well to the bivariate correlations, with one exception: the indicator for political trust. This result corroborates the suspicion that the pretest operationalization does, indeed, not adequately touch the dimension of political trust it was supposed to measure.

Union Consciousness Among Workers

Christel Eckart, Ursula Jaerisch, Richard Herding and Berndt Kirchlechner

IN THE PAST FEW YEARS, sections of the West German working class have gone on strike more and more often without — and, in a number of cases, against — the vote of their unions in order to support their material interests. After many years of union officials' complaints about apathetic union members who could not be activated, this fact poses again the question of relationship of organized and unorganized workers to the unions. The question of whether the autonomous readiness for conflict among these groups of workers is a result of changes in their attitudes toward their unions, or of changes in the articulated interests which they see as insufficiently or not at all represented by the unions, has become a central theme of union, political and industrial sociological discussion. The main point at issue is whether the latent conflict of interests which cooperative unions necessarily come into with their members will break out openly and affect the broad masses of workers, leading to a perceptible gap between members and organizations. Such a development would mean a considerable weakening of the unions as voluntary membership organizations. Their present political and economic function as disciplinary mediation authorities between the exigencies of the process of surplus production and the interests of wage-dependents would, in this way, be put in question.

In this article, we try to show on the basis of evidence from our material examinations that the relationship of different workers' groups to the union organizations is not uniform, and that it appears differently under different methods of analysis. Central to our considerations is the latent conflict of interests between organized and unorganized labor and the goals which leading groups of cooperative unions present as the goals of their organizations. Unions whose demands are oriented principally towards the existing economic situation, towards the given capacity of capital for making concessions, and which leave untouched the framework of the social system and therefore, also, the status quo of power and

Translation: Candace Suesskind

distribution, develop a logic of demands that is decided more in accordance with the rules of Keynesian economic policy than by being oriented toward members' interests. The active participation of members is, then, not necessary, and is in fact bothersome. Members' interests are not, however, meaningless for the unions, as they must ensure at least the passive loyalty of their members in order to maintain their bargaining power. In his article, 'International Organizational Processes of Cooperative Unions',[1] Bergmann analyses those mechanisms, starting with the goals of the organization, through which the process of forming the desires of the members is influenced to such an extent that the contradiction remains latent. The organization's function of interpretion and articulation is thus, for example in wage negotiations, turned against the interests of the active members in the name of the 'interest of the community'; the conditioned desire patterns of the members correspond to, or at least do not contradict the goals of the union leadership. The leadership can then rely on tendencies of conformity to the system and loyalty to the organization among members and officials. Only minorities which have rejected the prevailing interpretations develop demands that conflict with the unions' cooperative system of operation.

A POLL OF WORKERS INTERESTS

In a poll about the economic, union and political consciousness of wage earners and salaried personnel,[2] we raised the question of which demands workers make on unions. The answers given to these questions correspond to those taken in a poll of union officials.[3] This makes possible a comparison of the results.

The sample was presented with nine goals which outline the more or less system-conforming and more or less traditional union responsibilities. From these, the questionees were to choose the three most important objectives with which the unions should comply:

1. The unions should become an organization for class struggle and should struggle towards a basic rearrangement of state and economy. ('Class Struggle')[4]
2. The unions should have an active and militant wage policy and, when necessary, strike often in order that the worker get a bigger piece of the cake. ('Militant Wage Policy')
3. The unions should see to it that our total earnings are protected by wage agreements, and not merely a part of the earnings as is now the case. ('Assuring Actual Earnings')
4. The workers should co-determine all matters pertaining to their job. ('Worker Participation')
5. Equal co-determination of workers in management administration should be introduced into all firms. ('Worker Participation in Management Administration')
6. The unions should exercise more influence on state educational policy, in

order that the children of wage earners and lower-paid salaried personnel obtain equal opportunities in education. ('Educational Policy')

7. The unions should exercise more influence over housing policy so that rents no longer rise as they have until now. ('Housing Policy')
8. The unions should insist in the cities and communities that the public transportation system be improved and that it be used free of charge. ('Transport Policy')
9. The unions should work for the formation of financial assets in the hands of workers so that, in case of need, workers have greater financial security. ('Formation of Assets')

TABLE 1

The Most Important Union Goals

| | Wage-earners/ All | Salaried Personnel All | Wage-earners Unskilled and Semi-skilled | Skilled | Salaried Personnel | | |
					Lower-paid	Middle-paid	Higher-paid
	(1344) %	(719) %	(477) %	(724) %	(155) %	(366) %	(132) %
Assuring the actual earnings	24	20	24	24	16	23	14
Formation of Assets	17	18	16	17	17	17	22
Worker Participation on the Job	14	15	15	13	16	13	19
Worker Participation in Management Administration	11	10	9	13	12	10	7
Militant Wage Policy	10	5	12	9	5	5	2
Educational Policy	7	10	5	9	11	11	8
Housing Policy	7	10	8	5	12	10	11
Transportation Policy	4	4	3	5	2	4	8
Class Struggle	2	2	4	1	4	2	3

Table 1 shows the priority of demands in different sub-groups. In all, the concurrence of choice between wage earners, salaried personnel and their sub-groups is astounding; there are few differences. Almost all groups give first place to the demands 'Assurance of Actual Earnings' and 'Formation of Assets'; after these come the two demands for worker participation. From these priorities, it is evident that the majority of those polled demand from the unions that they look after their direct interests as wage-dependants: assurance of wages and salary as well as co-determination over their interests on the job. Both parts of these demands are restricted as far as economics are concerned, and do not question the system of working for wages. The union is not seen as an organization fighting for the interests of wage-dependants against capital and against the state, but rather — in agreement with the unions' present-day function — as a defensive representative of workers' interests against encroachments of management. Only a few of those polled — 12 per cent of the wage-earners, 7 per cent of the salaried personnel, 16 per cent of the unskilled and semi-skilled workers, 5 per cent of the salaried personnel in better paid positions — demand a militant, active wage policy and the use of the union as an instrument to reorganize society. Likewise, demands directed primarily toward the state and having to do with the domain of reproduction play a small part (Education, Housing, and Transport Policy). In the September strike investigation by SOFI, the situation was similar: Assurance of wage and on-the-job interests — 'Social Policy' — predominated over political demands on the unions.[5]

Just as there were hardly any differences worth interpreting between different groups of wage-earners and salaried personnel, a comparison between union members and non-members likewise shows no differences. One can well say that the demands on unions are strongly generalized and stereotyped. Members have the same preferences as non-members. Apparently, the interests that one supports through one's membership are general. In our opinion, this uniform response indicates that only those expectations are made of unions which can presently be fulfilled or at least presented in propaganda.

The employees' group that is most strongly represented in our investigations — the highly organized, skilled German wage-earners and salaried personnel — distinguish themselves, according to our findings, in that they find themselves in agreement with the unions and their cooperative policy oriented towards Keynesian economic models.

A comparison of the goal preferences of wage-earners and salaried personnel with those of union officials[6] shows likewise a high level of agreement (Table 2). The union officials' preference for worker participation in management administra-

TABLE 2

The Most Important Union Goals
(Percentage of the three goals mentioned most frequently)[1]

	Union Officials[2]	Wage-Earners	Salaried Personnel
	(601)	(1344)	(719)
	%	%	%
Assuring the actual earnings	43	53	45
Formation of Assets	39	47	49
Worker Participation on the Job	51	46	44
Worker Participation in Management Administration	62	38	38
Militant Wage Policy	24	24	15
Educational Policy	41	30	36
Housing Policy	17	25	29
Transportation Policy	4	14	17
Class Struggle	18	10	8

[1] The sum in each column totals 300.
[2] Data from the 'Union Study' of the Institute of Social Research.

tion is significant. This goal takes first place with them and only fourth place with wage-earners and salaried personnel. Assurance of actual earnings, formation of assets and co-determination on the job rank high with the workers. In this, a specific interest on the part of the union officials for the organization is suggested. For them, achieving this demand would directly secure more influence on the level of management relations; wage-earners and salaried personnel, on the other hand, are more interested in seeing that their financial situation is secure and that conditions on the job are improved. Interests in the domain of reproduction are emphasized rather more often by wage-earners and salaried personnel than by union officials.

The officials were also asked which goal preferences they supposed the members to have. On the whole, there was no great difference between their appraisal of their own and of the others' interests. However, there is a tendency to see the goals connected with wages and income as favored by the members, as is in fact the case, while union officials themselves more frequently emphasize goals which do not concern income. The conception of members formed by union officials is characterized by the priority of wage-interests. Some of the officials are aware that there are differences between their own interests and those which they suppose members to have. This is most clearly seen in the small group of officials who assign to the unions the task of effecting basic social change; only one-fifth are of the opinion that the members also hold their views. The ratio is the opposite with those who reject class struggle as the task of the union: This group feels that it is endorsed by four-fifths of the members. The most complete agreement is found among union officials who work above all for a militant wage policy, the majority of whom assume that the members are dissatisfied with the unions' wage policy.

The high incidence of agreement, on the whole, between the goal preferences of officials, members and non-members shows, on the level of investigation,[7] hardly any indication of the conflict potential between these groups. Since the priority of the most important goals also corresponds to the actual policy of the union bureaucracy of the DGB unions, with the exception of the stronger emphasis on wage policy towards the employer and worker participation on the job on the part of the workers, it can be assumed that the practical criticism of the unions which has flared up in the last few years through the strike movement has not settled into diverging verbally-articulated orientations of interest between members and bureaucracy. It could rather be assumed that it is the small degree of success in reaching these goals which is being criticized here. Because of this, there is often loud criticism when it comes to judging the outcome of union activities in pursuing their interests. In the September strikes of 1969 and the succeeding spontaneous strike movement up to 1973, the members made a practical criticism of the unions' policy, which was not oriented towards strongly pushing forward the workers' interests.[8] Also, in a number of sociological studies of the last few years, workers reacted with criticism on the question of whether or not the unions had really done as much as they possibly could in each case against management. In SOFI's September strike study,[9] 46 per cent of those polled judge this negatively. They are of the opinion that the unions presented particularly the wage policy in an overly cautious manner. In a poll of workers in the metal, textile and chemical industries taken at the beginning of 1971 by the Institute of Social Research,[10] 56 per cent were of the opinion that, in the last collective negotiations (1970), the unions could have 'gotten more out of them'. In the same study, when the workers were questioned about earlier collective negotiations, 63 per cent were critical, and, in certain firms where there was experience of strike action, far more than 70 per cent. Schumann and others point out in their study that the critical potential of this judgement should not be overestimated, since many of those polled are of the opinion that the reason for this lack of success is the minimal support that the 'basis' offers to the unions in pushing through their demands. Asked about the reason for the minimal balance of success, almost one-half of those who were dissatisfied with this considered the apathy of the workers themselves to be responsible for the present situation; only one-third felt that the unions alone were guilty.[11] Schumann and the others do not ask whether this withdrawal of criticism and its transfer onto the colleagues is merely a simple acceptance of union officials' favorite reasoning which excuses their own mistakes by blaming 'apathetic' membership. This reasoning masks their own failures and excuses the union, which was lacking an adequate analysis of the situation and had not done enough to mobilize the workers. The high quota of critics in the militant firms speak an entirely different language, as does the bitter criticism of many workers towards the role of union officials.[12]

In the last few years, there have been an increasing number of union ballot results in which the high quota of refusals after the wage settlement has warned of the dissatisfaction of members with the outcome of union bargaining strategy.[13] Thus, 57 per cent of the members with the right to vote in the metal industry of the Unterweser area refused the outcome of the IGM negotiations after a three-week strike (March, 1974); in the ÖTV during February, 1974, 38 per cent were dissatisfied with the settlement that had been designated by the ÖTV as highly successful.

Members' interests come into contradiction with the functions that the German unions have taken over within the framework of increased economic planning by the state; here, unions are to push for wage increases only within the boundaries of state planning figures. In the spontaneous strike movement of the past few years, this conflict broke out openly; this was, before all else, a practical criticism that had its roots in the minimal efficiency in implementing actual wage increases. It was not a basic criticism of unions and their policies. At the most, such factors are directly manifested in criticism towards individual people who expounded official union policy and thus set themselves against the activities of the employees who were trying to support their interests militantly. In the polls, no significant tendencies are to be found that would point towards an increasingly critical distance on an ideological and political level towards the unions. It is clear that the insight into the necessity for collective representation of interests is great among wage-earners and salaried personnel. It varies with their position in their firm's hierarchy, their understanding of their own situation as wage-dependants, and the dwindling of possibilities for individual representation of interests. These possibilities are narrowed down as the system becomes increasingly crisis-prone. The growing state intervention in the day-to-day struggles through political means, propaganda, and police – in contrast to the September strikes – and management's harsh threats of repression and dismissal make the aggravation of the situation clear. Union officials' policies at various levels will be of great importance in determining whether criticism of the unions develops further or decreases.

On the level of goal-perception, the results of our poll indicate that, at the moment, no relevant conflict potential is developing between members, union officials and union leaders. The agreement among them appears to be considerable. At most, there is a stronger emphasis on the part of the workers towards goals having to do with direct wage and on-the-job interests, while union management is more concerned with solving problems which they need to deal with only in a parliamentary way (workers' participation, education). Differences in demands which could lead to conflict develop here only to a limited degree.

WORKERS' INTERESTS IN SPONTANEOUS STRIKES

In this section, we are changing the method of examination and leaving the questionnaire results of representative, formalized polls to turn to the examination of conflicts that have taken place in firms during the last few years. This change of method brings with it a change, not of the subject of study – the conflict of interests between workers and unions – but rather a change in the random singling out of examples for study. We are here examining the interest-articulation of factory avant-gardes which are in combat situations, which bargain, organize strikes, carry through strike meetings, discuss and determine demands, etc. We are no longer examining the opinions of isolated individuals who have expressed these opinions only after being stimulated by certain questions, but rather, the behavior and activities of collectives. These collectives are no longer representative in a statistical sense, but they are politically and sociologically meaningful as the avant-garde of the factories, as leaders of social movements which express most clearly the tendencies of this movement.

The union strikes of the fifties and sixties were carried through mainly by skilled German workers. They had the greatest combat experience, had set up the best communication structures in the factories and attained the highest level of union organization. In the September strikes of 1969, it was still mostly these groups which led the strikes. However, the strike wave of 1973 clearly had the multi-national character of the broad masses of workers, especially in the long-lasting and more militant strikes (Pierburg, Neuß; Hella, Lippstadt; John Deere, Mannheim; Ford, Köln).

The social composition of this militant collective is not representative of the West German working class. Especially in the strikes of 1973, the groups of workers which were most active in carrying out the strikes were made up differently: they were the semi-skilled assembly line workers and wage-dependent women, in both cases, often foreigners. These are groups which are particularly disadvantaged in their social situation, in the factory as well as outside. As mobile workers doing mass work, they have no meaningful relationship to the work and no traditional, loyal attachment to the Social-Democratic unions. Their instrumental relationship to their work as well as to the organs of factory and union interest representation comes out, then, in spontaneous conflicts when disappointment over the results of union representation of interests sets in and actual possibilities of direct representation of interests are offered. However, in our opinion, a deeper contextual conflict is expressed in the struggles themselves.

Central to our comparative study should be the question of on which level (demands, forms of conflict) and through which content the conflict of interests is manifested in spontaneous strikes, where it often leads to open confrontation between strikers and the cooperative unions, since the logic of the workers' demands no longer follows the rules of Keynesian economic policy. The strikes that broke out shortly after the end of the collective negotiations of 1972-73 in the metal industry put in question, in a practical way, the commitment to state wage directives. The strike ballot results had already pointed out that the majority of IGM members were dissatisfied with the wage agreement reached by the union leadership. In most of the strikes, a cost-of-living allowance was demanded as a modification of the agreement. Here, there was no discussion as to how much more the industry or individual enterprise could pay, or of whether the wage increase corresponded to an increase in productivity, but only of the fact that the money demanded was needed to compensate for price increases in order to preserve the standard of living which had been attained.

In almost all the strikes, the cost-of-living allowance was linearly demanded (300 Marks, one Mark for each person). It was during the September strikes of 1969 that linear demands became prevalent for the first time in the BRD. Although linear wage-demands could also be set through in this time in collective negotiations — often in the modified form of a minimal wage increase for the lower-income groups — it is striking that clear linear demands were articulated in almost all non-union organized strikes. Several factors appear to be of importance here. Linear wage-demands are egalitarian, and their logic in the collective bargaining was: the cost of living has increased for all in the same amount; therefore, all need the same wage increase. Linear wage-demands stop the ever increasing disparity between wage groups. However, in our opinion they are seldom the expression of a general equality-norm among the workers. Tactically, a linear demand means that the partial interests of certain groups are not favored, and that all can support such demands if, of course, the amount of increase is high enough. However, the most important implication of a linear demand is the break — which is assumed in such a demand — with the ideological principle of the dependance of wages on individual productivity. The separation of the amount of wages and work-productivity is also included in demands for suspending wage-differences and in the demand for the same wage for all in part-time work. With this, the workers collide with principles that the German unions have always accepted in past years: that the total sum of wages is dependent on the increase of productivity, and that the internal distribution of differentiated wage increases should be calculated after individual measurable achievement. We do not mean that, when workers today make high linear wage-demands, they see through this break with past ways of thinking and consciously consider the ramifications, but that, basically, through their ad hoc legitimation, they have broken with the logic of capitalism.

The second important area of demands that came up in the wave of strikes in 1973 concerns the way in which the work is organized. Working men and women were, in many cases, no longer willing to accept the increase in work load. The worsening of working conditions is one of the answers of management to wage increases; through this means they compensate for the relative loss in profit, along with passing cost-increases onto prices. In a number of strikes, direct provocations for the conflict were increased work-intensity, changes in assembly line speed, piece work, wage-evaluation systems and dismissals. Until the union strike of the metal workers in Baden-Württemberg which was led under the slogan of 'Making Work more Human', unions in the sixties, on the whole, held the view that questions concerning general labor contracts should not be brought up in strikes without being coupled with changes in wage-rate agreements. The inclusion of demands concerning the organization of the work in the union-sanctioned strike demands appears to be a result of the fact that the starting-point for many of the spontaneous strikes was the protests of working men and women against the worsening of working conditions. It is, however, a fact that during the process of bargaining with management within the strike period, a degeneration of the list of demands can be observed. Very often, in order that any success whatsoever be obtained, a settlement concerning wages alone is finally accepted. The role that the union policies play in this process of degeneration remains to be more closely examined.

The demand for less work within the framework of capitalism is expressed in the demand for more breaks and longer paid leave, which is made most often by foreign working men and women.

A brief look at the demands articulated by workers in the spontaneous strikes of the last few years shows that the conflict which results from the unions' cooperative policies and the workers' interests has the following central points:

1. Regarding the question of wage increases and wage differentiation: The labor contracts obtained by the union are oriented more towards maxims of the Social-Democratic policies of stabilizing the society — procentual wage demands, among others — and towards the material interests of the skilled, better-paid German workers, who are overrepresented in the factory and union apparatus of interest representation rather than towards the needs and fighting strength of the masses of workers, which are scarcely fulfilled through the organized institutions but which find their outlet in spontaneous strikes.

2. Regarding questions of working within the framework of capitalism and the increase of work load, which also affect principally the disadvantaged sectors of the working class (unskilled workers, women, foreigners); For these groups, which keep increasing due to automation and rationalization — although, because of the rebellion of workers doing mass-work in Western

Europe, capitalist counter-strategies to restructure the labor force are indicated (for example, barring foreign workers, the Fiat Plan, Volvo experiment) — there exist hardly any possible compromises with capitalistic forms of work, such as those envisioned in the union project 'Making Work more Human'.

3. Regarding the legalism of unions, which have their actual power through the courts: The spontaneous strikes and the actual occupation of factories during the strike campaigns show that workers' interests cannot be held in check by legalistic concerns when the workers see chances for the actual collective setting through pursuit of their interests. Here, also, it is the unskilled, mobile masses of workers who have taken the initiative in the last strike movements.

To what extent the three above-mentioned main areas of conflict will become stronger or weaker will be dependent on several factors: on the strategies from the side of capital and the state, on the effect of the crisis and on the repression inside and outside the factories against the newly-awakened militancy. The development of the conflict will depend on how effective these factors are over a long period of time in limiting the chances of realizing the workers' needs and of increasing the unions' capability of coopting those interests of the workers which do not follow the logic of capitalism, and of realizing these, at least in part, after the pattern of 'Making Work more Human'.

NOTES

1. J. Bergmann, *Organisationsinterne Prozesse Kooperativer Gewerkschaften,* in: Lev., 1973, 242-253.

2. A poll of wage-earners and salaried personnel about the problem of evaluating and interpreting social inequality, Ch. Eckart et al.: 'Soziale Ungleichheit und materialle Erwartungen'. Institut für Sozialforschung, mimeo (Frankfurt: 1974). In 1971, nearly 3000 wage-earners and salaried personnel living in densly populated areas of the GFQ and working in firms employing more than 1000 were polled. A summary of this study was published in 'Gesellschaft, Beiträge zur Marxschen Theorie 4,' Frankfurt, 1975.

3. Poll of union officials for the purposes of the union study of the IFS; in 1970, 601 union officials of the unions IGM, IC, CH, PK, CTB, were polled, of whom 45 held high positions in their unions. ef. J. Bergmann/W. Müller-Jentsch, Lohnpolitik im Bewußtsein von Funktionären mimeo (Frankfurt, 1974).

4. Key-words that will be used in the text as abbreviations.

5. M. Schumann et al., Am Beispiel der Septemberstreiks, (Frankfurt: 1971), 60.

6. W. Müller-Jentsch, *Mitgliederinteressen und Funktionärspräferenzen,* in: Note 2, 7.

7. A questionnaire with standardized form questions.

8. S. E. Schmidt, 'Spontane Streiks 1972/73', in: *Gewerkschaften und Klassemkampf, Kritisches Jahrbuch* (Frankfurt: 1973).

9. M. Schumann, op. cit., 1971, 66.

10. E. Teschner et al, *Aspekte betrieblicher Lohnpolitik,* 1973, 203.

11. M. Schumann, op. cit., 66.

12. M. Schumann, op. cit., 67.

13. Compiled from Bergmann, J. et al: *Gewerkschaften in der BRD,* Gewerkschaftliche Lohnpolitik zwischen Mitgliederinteressen und ökonomischen Sachzwängen. (Frankfurt Cologne: 1975).

The Development of Political Planning in the Federal Republic of Germany

Heribert Schatz

PLANNING AS THE SUBJECT OF SCIENTIFIC RESEARCH

POLITICAL PLANNING, understood as 'systems politics'[1] with the objective of overcoming the customary reactive, piecemeal process of formulating intentions and decisions, first became the subject of scientific consideration and public discussion in the Federal Republic of Germany during the early sixties. The incentive for this discussion did not come, as in other western countries, from the potential area of application for political planning, the central government and administrative apparatus, but rather from the supra-national level. In October 1962, the EEC Commission published a memorandum concerning the programme of action for the second stage of the Common Market, which, modelled on the French 'planification' contained among others, recommendations for an indicative programming of economic development based on a longer-term forecast.[2] Because of the dogmatic animosity towards planning during the Adenauer/Erhard era (to be dealt with later), this initiative at first remained without any extensive effect in the politico-administrative system of the Federal Republic,[3] but the echo was considerably stronger in the press and in scientific circles. For example, in the middle of 1963 the distinguished List Society dealt with these new problems during a conference entitled 'Planning without a Planned Economy'.[4] The selection of the conference topic was no coincidence. On the contrary, it was a direct endeavour to free the term 'planning' of the odium associated with communist planned economy, as one of the horror-evoking terms of the Cold War.

During the following years, scientific discussion about political planning remained strongly determined by this not infrequently almost neurotic compulsion to differentiate between the two terms. At the same time, however, questions of constitutional and procedural legality came increasingly to the fore. Due to the lack of practice in political planning, no field of activity presented itself during this phase to the empirical social sciences, which in any case, at this time, were only in

41

the early stages of their development in the Federal Republic. Therefore, the normative theory of constitutional law and a prescriptive/descriptive theory of government and administration dominated the academic scene into the second half of the sixties.[5]

This situation changed when, after the collapse of the Erhard Government in 1966, political planning became 'respectable' even in the governmental and administrative practices of the Federal Republic of Germany. With the commencement of planning at Federal and Land levels, starting in 1967 (as described in detail in the following sections), a rapidly growing demand for scientific consultation about planning developed in the politico-administrative system. As a reaction to this demand, a practice-oriented line of thought in the political sciences developed relatively quickly within the established constitutional and administrative sciences. Increasingly, theoretical approaches and research methods of the social sciences were employed and were promptly requisitioned by the government and administrative apparatus for surveys.[6] As a result of this practice-oriented research, there is available today a relatively broad range of publications referring both to such problems as planning organization, planning methods and techniques (including programme budgeting) and to questions of personnel and information.[7]

However, due to the strong alignment towards ministerial bureaucracy, especially that of the Federal Government, problems of planning-execution in the field of subordinate administration were neglected. Not until recently has there been an increase in the number of projects concerned with planning on regional and communal levels and also dealing with the problem of participation by those affected by planning. A further type of investigation seldom found up to now is the overlapping, macrosociological investigation of the planning process. Renate Mayntz, in her Trend Report for the 'Deutsche Gesellschaft für Soziologie' (German Sociological Society) for 1974, attributes this to the 'fragmentized' attention paid to the politico-administrative system by sociologists, the consequence of which is to this day 'that partial questions have been treated scientifically as to a relatively large extent independant issues and that questions related to the internal dynamics of the politico-administrative system, to the interplay between its individual components, are very difficult to come to grips with'.[8]

Research gaps of the latter type, but especially the disregard of the actual 'function of political planning for the domination and survival of the capitalist system',[9] provoked increasing numbers of neo-Marxist researchers towards the end of the sixties to concern themselves with the new phenomenon of planning. Further stimulated by the unexpected functional deficiencies of the first generation of planning systems which they regarded as reflecting the 'contradictions of the capitalist system', they dedicated themselves to discovering the laws of motion governing the bourgeois state in a developed stage of capitalism.

Despite their differences in perspective and the analytical categories applied, these examples of politico-economic research share the common basic assumption that the change in the state's functions observed in reality is ultimately due to alterations in the functional conditions of the economic system.[10] The impulse setting off modifications of the state's structure and functions is regarded by the majority of these authors as emanating from concrete developmental difficulties in the economic field which manifest themselves in acute crises of the whole system.[11] The adjustment reactions are directed towards the objective of preserving and stabilizing the capitalist system. 'The highest functional imperative . . . for the state's activity consists . . . in an optimal utilization of functioning capital . . . The system-immanent and bourgeois reflex of this law of development is the imperative of quantitative growth according to value'.[12] In the more differentiated theoretical approaches along these lines, such as those of Habermas, Offe or Naschold, this premise does not however contain the assumption that the state itself is the 'executive agency of economic and industrialist interests'; for them it acts more as an 'ideal collective capitalist'[13] reacting relatively autonomously towards the political demands articulated by the economy.

Until very recently, the politico-economic planning theories remained unconnected with the non-Marxist approaches in the field of decision-making and action theory, due to their completely different assessment of the importance of exogenic and endogenic conditions for the planning process. The right-wing/left-wing polarization of the political scene in the Federal Republic of Germany from 1967 to 1968 onwards doubtlessly contributed to this mutual isolation. Today however, a tendency is emerging among individual authors of both camps to move closer together in their theoretical conceptions − although without surrendering their basic positions − and to attempt to combine macroscopic and microscopic approaches.

After this necessarily very abbreviated survey of the development of planning research in the Federal Republic,[13a] an attempt will be made in the following sections to describe the practice of planning at Federal and Land levels in more detail. Our starting point is the domestic political situation at the beginning of the sixties which, as a result of a variety of cumulative crisis tendencies, finally led to the collapse of the government's official anti-planning dogma. The following description is structured according to individual types of planning, i.e. functional aspects. The historical course of this process of development is taken into account inasmuch as the various types of planning are treated as far as possible in order of their introduction into politico-administrative practice.

THE DEVELOPMENT OF PLANNING − PRACTICE

Misdevelopments in the Politico-Administrative System of the German Federal Republic in the 'Pre-planning' Phase (up to 1966)

After the years of the 'German Economic Miracle', the successful restoration of the bourgeois society and the safeguarding of the new Federal Republic of Germany in its foreign- and security-policies, the first signs of a backlog of unsolved social and economic problems began to be apparent at the beginning of the sixties. The rapid recovery of the West German economy after the currency reform in 1948 had been regarded up to then as a confirmation of the principle of Social Market Economy. The Minister of the Economy, Ludwig Erhard, had made the neo-liberalism of the

'Freiburg-School' the official doctrine in economic and social policies. As a result, the almost unlimited faith in the self-regulating capacity of the market charac- teristic of this school of thought led to a systematic neglect of Federal growth policy. 'Other nations might practice 'planification' . . . but Germany relied on the proven free development of market forces and forgot the infrastructural basis',[14] especially in the fields of education and the development of technology. The result was an at first hardly noticeable, but after 1960 more and more drastically apparent decline in the growth rates of the gross national product[15] and a corresponding levelling-off of increases in the tax-income of the government.

The negative consequences of the hostility to planning during the Adenauer/Erhard era were increased by a creeping deterioration of power in the control-centre of the politico-administrative system, the Chancellor's Office. After losing their absolute majority in the 1961 Federal elections, the CDU/CSU were forced to conclude a coalition agreement with the substantially strengthened FDP, which considerably reduced the previously existing ability of the Chancellor's Office to exercise a 'directing coordination' (Böckenförde) of departmental activities, especially since Adenauer's position in the Cabinet and Parliamentary Party had not remained unaffected by this development. The trend towards independence of the departments continued to increase after Erhard became Chancellor. In their efforts to secure the goodwill (and votes) of the pressure groups 'most important' for their departments, many Ministers, with the active support of the parliamentary lobby, undertook to an increasing degree, financial obligations extending over several years. Although unintended by their initiators, these fre- quently developed into considerable burdens on public budgets as a result of technical deficiencies in the relevant legislation and a lack of coordination with other measures. Examples are found particularly in the immensely expanding payments for agricultural and mining subsidies and in the legislation on savings- and house-building premiums designed, not least of all, to promote the building in- dustry. In the latter case, the payments to be made from the Federal budget were at first estimated at a few hundred million Deutschmarks, but then − between 1955 and 1970 − led to expenditures of no less than 28 milliard DM in premium claims.[16]

The departments' main orientation towards the interests of the established economic and social pressure-groups corresponded to a neglect of newly-arising social demands, which were less articulate and less able to enter into conflict. Thus, unsolved problems and conflict situations accumulated in many areas during this period. Dahrendorf referred to this loss of intake into the politico-administrative subsystem − according to Deutsch a central feature of pathological learning processes − appropriately as follows: 'The State subsidy and social policy . . . still boil down to having the effect of hindering people from rational, modern behaviour by constantly providing them with security in whatever position they happen to be in: the farmer as a farmer in an increasingly backward agricultural system, the miner in his job in an obsolescent trade, the refugee as a refugee and the pensioner as a pensioner'.[17] This internal political situation provided the fertile soil for the political radicalization in the mid-sixties, which temporarily brought on the startling election successes of the radical right-wing National Democratic Party (NPD) and, on the other hand, led to the creation of a neo-Marxist Left which is still virulent today.

Other political institutions, such as the Lower Chamber of the Federal Parliament (Bundestag), parties or Land governments, were powerless, for reasons which cannot be explained here in detail, to stop the disintegration process in the field of government and administration or to mitigate the concomitant particularization tendencies of the political decision-making process. Nevertheless, a few attempts were made to counteract these misdevelopments, the most important initiative being the setting up of a Commission for Finance Reform ('Troeger' Commission). Before these measures could become effective, however, the behaviour pathologies of the politico-administrative system had already come to a head in the economic, financial and legitimation crisis of 1966 which toppled the Erhard Government and opened the way for the Grand Coalition ('Große Koalition') of the two major parties.

The introduction of General Economic Framework Planning, Medium-Term Finance Planning, and their further development up to the present

Very soon after taking up its official duties, the Government of the Grand Coalition introduced a number of functional-structural innovations under the heading of 'General Economic Framework Planning' ('Gesamtwirtschaftliche Rahmenplanung') and 'Medium-Term Finance Planning' ('Mittelfristige Finanzplanung'), which are rightly referred to in the literature on the subject as the starting point of political planning in the Federal Republic. Planning was thus 'a child of the crisis' (Kaiser).

The spectacular collapse of the previously valid economic and socio-political doctrine cannot, however, be regarded as a precondition sufficient to determine the transition from the previous hostility towards planning over to a new willingness to plan. On the contrary it was at least of equal importance that, at the climax of the 1966-67 crisis, a practicable alternative course of action was available. Disregarded by the official economic policy of the Federal Republic, international economists had developed a strongly interventionistic theory of growth during the previous years which, in its various forms, had been applied with some success in political practice (for example, in the USA, France and Japan). Similar orientation aids, particularly in the field of finance-planning, were supplied by the Planning-Programming-Budgeting-System (PPBS) which was introduced officially in the USA at Federal level in 1965.

The crisis managers of the Grand Coalition found, therefore, a personnel potential and an economic-financial political concept which they could introduce almost directly. The new trade and growth policies thus bore all the signs of the 'new economics', above all the central concept of global direction of the macro-economic coefficients by long-range State finance, credit, structural, income and currency policies, and precise direction of behaviour on the private, individual level of industry by means of the market mechanism. Within the apparatus, the activities of the departments were to be much more extensively coordinated than before with the requirements of economic policy and with what was feasible financially. To this end, under the 1967 Law for the Development of Stability and Growth of the Economy ('Stabilitätsgesetz': stability Law), a whole range of new committees were formed, existing ones upvalued in function and new planning-processes introduced. In the course of this reorganization, the 'Council of Experts for Assessing General Economic Development' ('Sachverständigenrat zur Begutachtung der gesamtwirtschaftlichen Entwicklung'), which had been established in 1963, was foremost among the extra-governmental institutions in acquiring considerable political weight. This five-man council of experts, the members of which are suggested by the Government to the Federal President for appointment in a rotating system, produces an Annual Report by 15 November every year on the general economic situation and the anticipated development of the German economy in the context of the economic development of the European Community and world economy. The Stability Law specifies that the Government must publish this report without delay but may comment directly upon it. As a rule, however, a detailed commentary is not made until January of the following year in the 'Annual Report on the Economy' presented by the Federal Government to the lower chamber of the Federal Parliament.

The 'Five Wise Men' are expressly required not to give concrete economic or socio-political recommendations as to how the targets prescribed in the Stability Law of full employment, price stability, balanced payments and steady economic growth can best be achieved. However, the method applied in their report of submitting several alternative developments and the directive measures pertaining to each is, in political reality, usually taken as a vote for action in a particular direction. The politically explosive nature of the Annual Report can thus be high, depending upon the economic situation and the current position of the negotiations between labour and industry. Similar political repercussions, often equally unwelcome in the eyes of the Federal Government, are also aroused by publications on the report by the Economics Institute of the trade unions or by the reports published half-yearly by the Working Committee of the Economics Research Institutes on 'The State of the World Economy and the West German Economy'. This politically independent working committee was formed as early as 1949, but did not acquire any great degree of significance until after the introduction of the new concept of economic and finance policy. Today it plays an important role in economic diagnosis, as well as being commissioned to carry out research and evaluation projects for the Federal Economics Ministry and other State institutions.

Within the government apparatus, further committees were founded on the basis of the 1967 Stability Law for the formulation of opinions and for coordinating the various statements on the respective economic situation and further economic developments. From already existing forms of cooperation the inter-ministerial Working Committee on 'General Economic Forecasts' was formed, whose members represent – apart from those of the Federal Ministries concerned with economic questions – the Federal Statistics Office ('Statistisches Bundesamt') and the Federal Bank ('Bundesbank'). The Chairman is the President of the Federal Statistics Office; the conduct of business is in the hands of the Federal Economics

Ministry. As a rule, this working committee meets in the spring and autumn of every year in order to consult about the latest data from the Federal Economics Ministry and supplementary reports from non-official institutions concerning economic developments. The results of these deliberations form the most important basis for a further inter-ministerial group, the Working Committee for Tax Estimates, which belongs to the Federal Finance Minister.

Apart from the short-term forecasts already mentioned, the Federal Economics Ministry, in cooperation with other departments and inter-ministerial committees, produces long-term 'Perspective Projections' every two or three years. These calculations covering a period of 10 to 15 years, are intended to reveal possible bottlenecks in the general economic development and permit an assessment of long-term specialized plans, particularly those of the education, transport and defence programmes and of social policy (Pension Adjustment Laws, Health Insurance). The medium-term 'Objectives Projection' has its place between the short and long-term forecasts. It covers a period of five years and is extended annually by one year. As the name implies, this report already contains assumptions about the effects of current economic and financial measures taken by the Federal Government. At the same time, the medium-term 'Objectives Projection' is geared to the medium-term Finance Plan and the 'Social Budget', which are also formulated for five years. Simultaneously, data also flow into these projections from the long-term 'Perspective Projection', which thus represents an interpolation between the current general economic situation and the desired long-term economic development.

Apart from the already-mentioned Federal level work committees, new committees were formed after the Stability Law came into force for the coordination of the various Federal-Land levels. These were, in particular, the 'Economic Council' and the 'Finance Planning Council', as well as further joint Federal/Land working committees. The task of the Economic Council, which meets three to four times annually, consists principally in consulting on the economic measures necessary to achieve the 'data bases' (growth rate, inflation rate, level of employment and application structure of the gross national product) established in the 'Objectives Projection'. In addition, it discusses the possibilities of meeting the demand for credit on the part of the Federal Government, the Länder and local governments in a way compatible with the above objectives.

These discussions are based on documentation supplied by the Federal Economics Ministry, plus the report of the Council of Experts and the Annual Economic Report of the Federal Government. The results of the deliberations of the Economic Council are reported as recommendations and statements addressed to the Federal and/or Land governments, but the Council as a body cannot formulate binding resolutions. This also applies to the Finance Planning Council, which usually meets simultaneously with the Economic Council and is as a rule concerned with a discussion of the data presented by the Federal Finance Ministry on the development of income through taxes, and the conclusions to be drawn from this data regarding growth-rates of the public budgets.

To coordinate the behaviour of Federal, Land and local governments on the one hand, and industrial federations and trade unions on the other, a further institution was created under paragraph 3 of the Stability Law, the 'Concerted Action'. This discussion group, which also meets several times annually with the participation of the Council of Experts, is intended to ensure that all participants in the economic process base their actions on the same 'Orientation Data' for future economic development supplied by the Federal Government, and furthermore, that they agree on simultaneous coordinated strategies during times of crisis. Finally, a range of committees in connection with these organizations which have been created on an international level during the course of recent years must be mentioned. Within the framework of the European Community, the 'Economic Policy Commission' must be mentioned above all, and within the OECD the 'Economic Policy Committee', both of which in turn have formed various sub-committees. Similar to the national committees already mentioned, their basic task is to discuss the various general economic analyses and forecasts together with the conclusions to be drawn from them. Binding recommendations for the respective member states cannot, however, be formulated by these committees. With the above described complex planning system — which has become more and more highly differentiated during recent years — the initiators of General Economic Framework Planning and Medium-Term Finance Planning believed that two objectives could be achieved:

1. A steady continuity of economic growth and tax income.
2. Integration of the planning of the specialist departments at Federal and Land levels into a coherent, overall political plan.

The medium-term finance planning was programmatically described as a 'Government programme clothed in numbers', in which the time-priorities and the positive and negative emphases are shown in the light of the views of the Government.[18]

These hopes, however, remain largely unrealized. After the indubitable initial successes of the new planning system (in overcoming the economic recession and reorganizing public finances etc.), the first difficulties in achieving the high objectives that had been set appeared towards the end of the period of office of the Grand Coalition. Despite constant attempts to improve processes and methodological instruments for global direction and medium-term finance planning, growing efficiency losses occurred in both planning systems the farther the climax of the 1966 crisis was left behind. Apart from the information deficits inherent in the system during the production of the bases for the forecasts of the various projections, the main cause of this efficiency loss was to be found in the decreasing reliability of the data bases of the medium-term objectives projection for the wage and price policies of the pay negotiators. It became obvious that, in a growing economy, the union leadership did not possess the necessary support of its membership in keeping wage demands within the framework of the guide-lines sketched by the Federal Government. In the meantime, it was demanded at several union area committee meetings that union leaders stay away from future meetings of the 'Concerted Action' because these talks led to 'an extensive integration into the capitalist system'.[19] There was a similar development among the employers' associations.[20] Here too it proved impossible over any length of time to influence the profit-orientation and investment-inclination of individual industrialists in such a way as to achieve the desired overall economic data bases. Due to this 'exposed flank' of the system, general economic framework planning has remained largely non-obligatory during recent years, so that the inflow of financial resources for the politico-administrative system has remained to a large extent determined by relatively autonomous economic and growth processes.[21] Only recently has the new interruption of the course of the economy in the wake of the 1975 'oil crisis' effected among the pay negotiators a return to the measure of discipline originally intended to be concommitant with 'Global Direction'. Irrespective of the fact that these functional weaknesses are inherent in the system, efforts are currently being made in the Federal Economics Ministry to supplement Global Direction of the market economy with a set of instruments for directing the sectoral structure policy (i.e. applying to branches of industry).

Due to the above-outlined insufficiencies of general economic framework planning, the objectives projection of the general economic development was unable even within the Federal Government to develop the measure of instrumental effectiveness that the fathers of the new planning process had hoped for. Because the data bases of the objectives projection continually had to be adjusted to the latest economic developments more frequently than had been expected, it was practically impossible to establish a reasonably reliable ceiling for State expenditures beyond the one-year budget plan. Thus, the Finance Plan could never properly fulfill the function for which it had been intended, namely to relieve the annual budgeting conflicts by means of important prior decisions and, in this way, to rationalize the programme-planning of the departments. As before, decisions concerning the short-to-medium-term priorities of Government policy are concentrated within a few weeks of the year, with the result that there are regularly rigorous forms of complexity-reduction during the consultations in the Finance Cabinet and prior rounds of conferences concerning the allocation of funds to the departments. Instead of a concept-based adjustment of departmental allocations within the staked-out financial framework, the customary formal, fiscal budget practices continue to dominate unchanged,[22] and it is often only at the end of the discussions that it becomes clear what action government policy actually emphasizes for the coming period. Under these circumstances, finance planning tends to cement existing budget allocations rather than to adjust the current programme to changed social and political conditions. In the relationship between the Federal Government and the Länder, medium-term finance planning has also proved to be unsuitable up to now in coordinating the expenditure conduct of the various public agencies in accordance with uniform objectives-criteria applying to society as a whole. The absence of a uniform debt administration alone leaves the Finance Planning Council deprived, in practice, of the possibility of effectively steering the capital-market debit and other economic and growth-related effects of political decisions at the State and local government levels. Also, the attempt of the Finance Planning Council to pre-insert a longer-term expenditure plan before the medium-term finance plan must be written off as unsuccessful. The 'Working Committee for

Requirement Estimates' ('Arbeitskreis Bedarfsschätzung'), instituted for this purpose in 1970, was very soon forced to give up its aim of estimating the total public expenditure requirements up to 1980 and of making recommendations for the establishment of areas to be given political stress;[23] this was not merely because of methodological and information difficulties, but mainly because of growing fears on the part of the Federal Finance Ministry that the Länder might make use of a projection of this kind to derive claims for the periodically decided redistribution of turnover-tax. For these reasons, the Working Committee was dissolved during 1973. The activities of the Finance Planning Council for periods beyond the five-year horizon of medium-term finance planning have since been limited to individual measures, such as reducing the envisaged volume of finance for the general education plan.[24]

The Extension of Planning Capacities in the Federal Ministries and Between the Federal Government and Länder

Regarded historically, the development of the programme-planning capacities of the specialist Ministries at Federal level showed a distinct increase during the years 1966-67. This is not a coincidence, but, on the other hand, cannot be attributed simply to the greater enthusiasm of the Grand Coalition for planning. As with the introduction of Global Guidance and Medium-Term Finance Planning, the changed economic-technological conditions of the environment played a decisive role here. This becomes particularly clear in the case of defence planning. As a reaction to the exponential growth of development and acquisition costs for new weapons system, a compulsion towards increased rationality of the decision-making process was felt relatively early. During the early years of building up German Armed Forces, the German defence planning was oriented exclusively to the long-term strategic concept of the USA or NATO which was current at the time. A medium-term programme for the national defence budget based on this did not exist; funds for the next defence budget had to be negotiated anew each time by a traditional inductive budgeting process based on short-term considerations. The result was that the adjustment of the funds requirements of the Defence Ministry within the sanctioned ceiling produced a different financial margin every time, so that long-term acquisition projects had to be stretched in one year and forced through the next, frequently to the detriment of an efficient armaments policy. When Medium-Term Finance Planning was introduced, this situation changed. Required – as were all the other ministries – to present a medium-term expenditure plan, the Defence Ministry developed a task-planning system of its own. It was based on the Planning-Programming-Budgeting System (PPBS) introduced by McNamara into the US Defence Department in 1961, and was introduced under the jurisdiction of the Defence Ministry through the 1968 'Planning Derective'. One year previously, a medium-term plan for the extension of the Federal transportation system had been developed, also for the first time; this was called the 'Leber Plan', after the Transport Minister of that period.

After the end of the Grand Coalition, this development continued in other areas of the infrastructure. In general, the personnel fluctuation in the ministerial bureaucracy (caused by the change of Government in 1969) and the self-committment of the new Government to a 'Policy of Internal Reforms' led to a new peak in planning thinking and to the creation of corresponding planning capacities.[25] If the acknowledgement of planning at the time of the Grand Coalition was in many ministries at first no more than a concession to the spirit of the times, there now seemed to be a serious willingness to break hardened interest and power structures and to rationalize the political decision-making process with respect to its capacity for value consideration and information processing on a broad scale (s.u.). Previously neglected fields of policy were formulated as problems from a reform-oriented, socio-political position and new solutions were tackled, for example in the fields of urban development, research policy, the health services, conservation of the environment and regional structure. The official reports issued by the individual departments during 1970 and 1971 clearly display this new orientation. Concrete and binding programmes of action have, however been drawn up only in a few cases. The 'Environment Programme' passed by the Federal Government in 1971 does contain a Programme of Action for the next five years and, beyond that, more extensive objectives for a period of 10 to 15 years, but only a minimal proportion of these have been operationalized and even these are not yet bound to any firm deadlines. Financing does not appear to have been clarified either. Similarly non-binding is the Federal Regional Structure Programme ('Bundesraumordnungsprogramm') passed by the Federal Cabinet in 1974 after lengthy preparation and negotiations between the Federal Government and Länder.

The Division of the Federal area into 38 area units proposed in this programme is intended to provide a frame of reference for the coordination of measures affecting regions taken by all the decision-making centres on Federal Government, Land or local government levels. It is precisely for this reason that the Länder regard it as a potential danger to their autonomy.

In the field of transportation planning a 15-year plan, sub-divided into three 5-year plans, was passed as a law in 1971.[26] This plan, based on a corresponding estimate of requirements, structures the planning for Federal motorways and Federal roadways in three stages of priority and establishes roughly the location of the new roads. However, the plan contains no firm financing arrangements. The allocation of funds is a continuous procedure within the framework of the annual extension of the Finance Plan. The same applies to the 'Social Budget', which now exceeds 250 milliard DM, i.e. more than a quarter of the Federal Republic's gross national product. The nature of this budget is, however, less that of an integrated programme of action than 'a comprehensive, quantitative inventory of all the social achievements and their projection for the next (4) years on the basis of the valid legislation and the draft legislation passed by the Cabinet'.[27] In addition to the extension of capacities within the departments themselves, new planning institutions between the Federal Government and the Länder were also established after the change of Government in 1961. Worthy of particular mention here are 1) the planning Committees for the framework-planning of what are termed 'common responsibilities' of the Federal Government and Länder ('Gemeinschaftsaufgaben') according to Article 91a of the Basic Law (the extension of and new building of universities, the improvement of the regional economic structure, the improvement of the agricultural structure and of coastal protection); and 2) the 'Joint Commission for Education Planning' according to Article 91b of the Constitution. While the five-year plans of the first-mentioned committees are binding within the Finance Plans of the Federal Government and the Länder, the 'General Education Plan' passed by the Commission for Education Planning of the Federal Government and the Länder in the autumn of 1973 has not yet achieved this degree of binding force. Nor has agreement yet been reached on the plans for the first medium-term stages to fill out this framework-plan. In particular, there has been a lack of success in coordinating the contents of these plans with the Finance Plans of the Federal Government and the Länder in such a way that, at the time when the 'Federal Government and Länder Commission' reached a decision, it would already be clear whether the respective plans for the stages could be financed. Taken as a whole, the gains in rationalization produced by programme planning in the Federal Departments and between the Federal Government and the Länder, despite a multiplicity of efforts, clearly lagged behind those anticipated by their initiators and eventually, as a result of appropriate propaganda, behind those anticipated by the public as well. As education-planning illustrates particularly clearly, many a grand-scale plan — after passing through the millstones of the allegedly 'cooperative' Federalism — was reduced to little more than a mixture of only very partially coordinated individual measures. In other fields, such as in the case of Common Responsibilities according to Article 91a of the Basic Law, the vertical coordination between the participating specialist departments at Federal and Land levels did function to some extent, although it lacked horizontal coordination with neighbouring problem areas.[28] The causes of this are not only the almost unchanged, continuing pluralistic interest and power structures in the political system of the BRD, but also the differentiating and competitive mechanisms immanent within the politico-administrative system itself.[29] Their centrifugal dynamics have so far defied every attempt at integration, either in the form of finance planning or other 'cross-section plans', such as the Federal Regional-Structure Programme, or even the initial attempts at inter-departmental planning which will be described in the section after next.

On the State of Development of Task and Programme Planning in the Federal Länder

The planning organization of the Federal Länder is currently at distinctly varying stages of development.[30] The first attempts at Land-level development planning were made as early as the beginning of the sixties, but this was exclusively planning referring to specific fields such as construction, urban development and area utilization, roadways, etc. Planning with a directive character for the general investment activity and fiscal conduct of a Federal Land, however, is all of a more recent date. Of the large-area Länder, Hessen has the most extensively developed planning system up to now, followed by North Rhine-Westfalia, Rhineland-Palatinate and Lower Saxony. The Hessian Land-Development Plan, by operation of the Land Planning Law, constitutes an obligatory framework for planning by the specialist departments and local governments and is procedurally fully integrated with Medium-Term Finance Planning. In the other three above-mentioned Länder, no functioning connection appears to have been established yet between Land, finance and inter-departmental development planning.[31] At all events, the fact that the plans for extending the 'North Rhine-Westfalia Programme '75' for the period up to 1980 were recently abruptly halted by Minister President Kühn indicates that, at least in North Rhine-Westfalia, extensive differences of opinion still exist regarding the functions and procedures of Land-development planning.

The directive function of this planning is correspondingly low at local government level. For the other large-area Länder (Schleswig-Holstein, the Saar, Bavaria and Baden-Würtemberg), this holds true to an even greater extent because in these Länder there are practically no procedural connections between Land area-planning and finance planning. In the case of the City Länder, too, inter-departmental area-planning is at different stages of development. While Berlin has no area-development plan, Bremen and Hamburg have City-Development Programmes for a period of 10-15 years. The plan for the City of Hamburg represents the first stage in the realization of the Development Model for Hamburg and its surrounding area up to the year 2000.[32] However, this development model does not yet contain any obligatory establishment of priorities. Accordingly, as in the case of Bremen, the question remains open as to the extent to which the plans developed up to now will lead to an increase in rationality of any significance for the actual course of development. As long as the development plans of the neighbouring Länder are so little consolidated in respect to substance and finance as is in the case at present, it remains impossible to make a sensible forecast of important basic data for the planning of the City Länder. The risks of long-term investments are correspondingly large.[33] Similar problems exist in other agglomeration areas overlapping Land borders, such as in the cases of the Mannheim-Ludwigshafen and Rhine-Main areas.

Attempts at Central Task-Planning at Federal Level

After the previously mentioned introduction of General Economic Framework-Planning and Medium-Term Finance Planning in 1967, it was believed in the Chancellor's Office that a planning system was within reach which would fulfill not only the function of planning resources but also that of central task-planning, particularly the development of a framework programme for departmental plans which would be oriented to current and future social needs. What was overlooked was that this planning system, if only because of its lack of an information basis independent of the specialist departments, could not be in a position to develop a general political concept which was more than an extension of the programmes planned by the specialist departments, which were of necessity selective in their problem perspectives. This lack of problem-consciousness largely explains why, after the formation of the Grand Coalition, the Federal Chancellor made no sustained effort to develop the instruments at his disposal for exercising directive jurisdiction. It is true that, in 1967, a small planning staff was formed in the Chancellor's Office and a committee of political experts was called in, but both bodies had largely decorative functions and, in practice, exercised practically no influence on the Chancellor's decisions.

Not until after the fresh change of Chancellor in 1969 did the government systematically set about developing capacities for central task-planning. The result of the Federal elections in the autumn of 1969 was regarded by the new 'Government Team' as a challenge to implement the long overdue socio-political innovations, within the framework of a 'Policy of Internal Reforms'. Against this background, the development of a set of central directive instruments appeared more important than ever, since it had to be anticipated that, without instruments of this sort, the ministerial administration which had been formed by the hierarchy of 20 years of CDU rule could impede innovations, thus affecting the substance of the political decision-making process.

For the realization of reorganization plans within the domain of the Federal Government, Ehmke, as the new head of the Chancellor's Office, was able to fall back on preliminary work by the 'Project Group Government and Administration Reform', an inter-ministerial working group which will be referred to again later. The major organizational innovations decided upon shortly after the assumption of office by the Brand/Scheel Government were the expansion of the Chancellor's Office Planning Staff to a Planning Department, soon comprising more than 50 members, the establishment of a committee of 'Planning Delegates' from the Federal Departments, and the introduction of a computer-aided process for recording and evaluating the 'reform plans' of the departments. This 'Early Coordination System of the Federal Government' was intended to serve the purpose of changing the traditional interministerial decision-making process in such a way that the Chancellor and Cabinet would receive earlier and fuller information about important proceedings in the spheres of action of the specialist departments. They would thus be able to formulate the political guide-lines for achieving the desired solution in each case, instead of having to accept the preliminary decisions of the ministerial bureaucracy more or less without real alternatives. To this end, the new Task-Planning Procedure was to precede the Finance-Planning Process, the efficiency of which was assessed very critically by the new leadership of the Chancellor's Office.[34] The fortnightly meetings of the Planning Delegates, mostly civil servants with the rank of Departmental Director, were intended to organize and check the early coordination within and between the departments and, if necessary, to initiate planning themselves. Above the Committee of Planning Delegates, there was a Standing Conference of the Permanent Secretaries of State from the Federal Departments, which met every Monday under the chairmanship of Ehmke.

The new planning procedure, after overcoming the initial difficulties of getting under way, soon led to a considerable increase in the transparency of current departmental activities. With the aid of formalized questionnaires (Data Sheets), information was obtained from the departments in several questionnaire surveys on nearly 500 individual projects, classified according to fields and compiled into 'Major Reform Objectives'.[35] However, attempts around the middle of 1970 made by the planning Department of the Chancellor's Office with the purpose of developing for the first time its own recommendations for the setting of political priorities on the basis of the data obtained brought forth reactions which startled the departments. What had at first been offered to them as an information service now turned out to be, in their view, an attempt to reduce their decision-making autonomy. The reaction was a 'politicization' of the input-data in the 'Early Coordination System' i.e. a filtering by the leadership level according to political tactical aspects, such as had been typical of the previous information flow between the Departments and the Chancellor's Office. It thus proved impossible to achieve the original objective pursued by the Chancellor's Office, namely to shift the emphasis by means of this planning system from the departmental to the Chancellor and Cabinet principle, and thus to combat the process of fragmentation in the government apparatus. Today this planning procedure, now referred to more modestly as a 'Project Planning System', serves principally as an instrument to improve the work and timing-planning of the Cabinet and similarly for the international procedural planning of the Federal Departments. At its present stage of development,[36] the 'Information System for the Project Planning of the Federal Government' functions in such a way that, by the middle of each month, all the Federal Departments, using the repeatedly improved Data Sheet, report to the Planning Department of the Chancellor's Office all those projects (legislation, decrees, administration regulations etc.) which are to be dealt with within the foreseeable future by the Cabinet and its committees, as well as the Lower or Upper Chambers of the Federal Parliament, and/or organs of the European Community, or which are otherwise of 'essential political and financial consequence'. The description of these projects is given in 40 categories, such as information about the initiating and participating departments, about content (subject, group in reference to the Government Programme for the Legislative Period etc.), about anticipating deadlines for the various phases of decision, funds required, any potential effects on the environment, spatial development, international relations and, not least, about the reaction to be expected from the Opposition in the Lower or Upper Chambers of the Federal Parliament or from the public.

Currently, about 50-70 new projects are reported monthly. During the first two years of the current legislative period, more than 1700 projects were recorded and stored in the data bank of the Chancellor's Office, where there are roughly 800 projects at present. In about 300 cases a month, the departments report changes (mostly concerning the timing); 30-50 projects a month are reported concluded, in the sense of a regular completion (defined as conclusion of the decision-making phase in the respective committee of the executive or legislative body.)

Recently, the information system of the Federal Government was procedurally connected up with the similarly conceived 'Information System GESTA' ('Gesetzgebungsstand' – State of Legislation) of the Lower Chamber of the Federal German Parliament. Using largely identical categories, this system records all the projects to be dealt with in the Lower and Upper Chambers of the Federal Parliament. In addition, GESTA stores for every project all the stages in the parliamentary decision-making process which actually have to be passed through (the plenary assembly, committees etc.). At present, these consist of about 80 possible stages, including repeated passage through the Meditation Committee. To avoid double labour, a data-exchange was installed between the Planning Department of the

Chancellor's Office and the Federal Parliamentary Administration, so that the Federal Parliament now receives from the Chancellor's Office a list together with a corresponding tape recording outlining the overlapping features contained in the 'Legislative Projects and Reports' which, 'while not firmly so committed, are expected to be dealt with by the Federal Cabinet during the next few weeks'. Since December 1974, the Chancellor's Office has received in exchange weekly information from the Federal Parliament. By comparing this information with its own schedule, the Chancellor's Office can use the data to establish on a continuous basis if and where delays have occurred in the parliamentary processing of individual projects. In a further extension to this, the data stored in the Chancellor's Office and the Federal Parliament are in future to be made utilizable in direct conjunction with each other.

Within the Federal Government, the data stored in the Project Planning System are, as has already been mentioned, used principally for schedule planning. Contrary to the practice in the period 1970 to 1971, when all the departments received the whole stock of data as a computer print-out monthly classified according to three main criteria, today the data are evaluated only when a specific order is received. At the present time, the departments have about 120 standing-orders running. To these can be added a further 20-30 special orders a month for single evaluations. The standing orders concern, for example, the compilation of all projects for which a certain department is responsible or is involved in as a participant in the decision-making process of other departments, the listing of all projects which are to be dealt with in the Cabinet during the next few weeks, etc. Among the special orders are for example, listings of all projects in connection with the population groups 'youth', 'women' or 'employees', or those which have got held up in a particular Federal Parliamentary committee and the like. In some departments, the analyses produced by the Chancellor's Office serve as starting data for internal departmental planning processes, such as in the Federal Labour Ministry, the Federal Home Affairs Ministry and the Federal Ministry for Research and Technology.

In the Planning Department of the Federal Chancellor's Office, information is obtained from the stock of the project-recording system for extending the legislative-period programme known as the 'Working Programme of the Federal Government'. For this purpose, those projects which are considered to have particular political relevance are filtered out from the mass of projects. The criteria for this classification are the rank assigned to a project in the Government Programme given at the beginning of the legislative period, its anticipated conflict content in the parliamentary decision-making process, and also its probable effectiveness among the electorate. The projects thus designated as being of major importance are given particular attention by the Chancellor and Cabinet. Relatively high demands are made on the departments voluntarily keeping to the schedules and costs they have specified, and explicit limitations are set on the public activities of the individual Ministries. The later provision serves the purpose of avoiding uncoordinated 'announcement effects' so as not to repeat what happened at the beginning of the period of office of the Social Democratic Liberal Coalition, namely to awaken expectations among the public which cannot then be fulfilled.

For the precise timing of the Major Projects, the Planning Department keeps a calender containing all the forseeable, politically important deadlines for the following year (e.g. Federal and Land elections, the Chancellor's trips abroad, the beginning and end of the sessions of the Upper and Lower Chambers of the Federal Parliament etc.). With its aid, for example, the timing proposed by the departments for the procedural treatment of their projects by the Government and Parliament are corrected, where necessary, so that legislation, legal regulations etc., which will have a positive effect on the electorate are finalized *before* an important election, whereas projects likely to be unpopular or cause conflict are left for the phase *after* such a deadline. Wherever politically sensitive projects require decisions regarding timing or content, the Head of the Chancellor's Office is informed of this at least every two months by the Planning Department. Such decisions are usually made at the level of departmental directors in contact between the specialist departments of the Chancellor's Office and those of the respective Ministries concerned. In the case of more important problems, the decision is arrived at via the 'Standing Conference of the Permanent Secretaries of State', the previously mentioned committee of all the permanent Secretaries of State of the Federal Government. If necessary, a discussion between the coalition partners will be organized as well. Strangely enough, the Committee of Planning Delegates founded in 1969 no longer has any function in this procedure. According to reports, this committee proved problematic from the point of view both of technical competence and of informational 'leakproofness'. At present, the Planning Delegates meet only sporadically. Only the 'Technical Delegates' among the Planning Delegates meet regularly in the Chancellor's Office to discuss current problems and further developmental stages of the project-recording system.

Even without the retrogression described above from an instrument for medium-term task-planning to one for short-term operative planning, the 'Early Coordination System' would not have produced the directive effect that had been hoped for at its conception in 1969. The main reason for this was that the plans for various programmes had meanwhile extended into longer-term horizons, such as the already mentioned defence programme and, above all, the transportation and education programmes. With its set of instruments designed for a legislative period or four-year term, the Early Coordination System was unsuitable to keep this planning under control, both in volume and content. As early as 1970, the nature of this problem caused the Planning Department of the Chancellor's Office to start considering a model for longer-term planning. This was accelerated when the previously mentioned Working Group for Requirement Estimates ('Arbeitskreis Bedarfsschätzung') of the Financial Planning Council became active. In the Federal Chancellor's Office it was feared that this would lead to an extension of the 'cementing' effects of medium-term financial planning into long-term time dimensions, and that the need for political programmatic decision-making in long-term planning would not be recognized in this procedure. In the autumn of 1970, the first alternative concept for longer-term task planning was presented in the Committee of Planning Delegates. This provided for a rough but all-round inventory of public tasks and anticipated available resources for the period 1976-1985. A supplementary 'gap analysis' was intended to define the problems of policies already initiated and to ascertain future social needs now beginning to reveal themselves, but not yet considered. To deal with these tasks, seven interministerial working groups under the Planning Delegates were formed, each with five to eight senior-grade civil servants, all of whom took up their work in March 1971.

The departments reacted to this new initiative on the part of the Chancellor's Office mostly with reserve, even though their motives varied. Frequently, the strained personnel situation played a part. Under these circumstances, the Chancellor's Office found itself forced, after the presentation of an interim report by the working groups, to drastically reduce the objectives of the project. Nevertheless, the Federal Länder were successfully prevailed upon during the second phase to participate in the project, subsequently known as 'General Problem Analysis' ('Gesamtproblemanalyse'). The Preliminary Report ('Sachstandsbericht') presented in May 1972 revealed a large number of deficiencies in the data used as bases for the planning of the Federal Government and the Länder, as well as in the procedures, methods and techniques applied. A decision could not be reached to continue the project at the same level of activity because, apart from the notorious shortage of personnel in the participating departments linking the Federal Government and the Länder, the intensified confrontation between the SPD and CDU/CSU was becoming a more and more apparent obstacle. Today, the 'longer-term task planning' is practically back to the form practiced in 1968, namely that of an informal, sporadic exchange of views between the Chancellor's Office and the State and Senate Chancellories of the Länder.

If one regards the development of the above described initial moves towards medium- or longer-term planning as a related whole, it can be said that the Chancellor's Office has not yet succeeded in giving its directive capacity towards policies of the various departments a conceptional basis. Since the 'Working Programme of the Federal Government' is obtained inductively from the specialist planning of the Departments, the possibilities for the Chancellor to exercise his directive competence in a manner oriented to general social objectives still remain largely dependent on the interest and power constellation concerned in each individual case. If an evaluation of programme-content is carried out at all, it is confined within this framework. What is quite efficient, however, is the timing of the decision-making process within the Federal Government and, as a result of corresponding procedural improvements, the subsequent final parliamentary phase. In this respect, the Project-Recording System has become an indispensable aid.

Up to now, it has not yet been possible to compensate for the lack of inter-departmental concepts by corresponding planning capacities of the governing parties or their parliamentary representatives (in the Lower Chamber). The SPD has made the most progress in its moves to develop an integrated medium- to longer-term programme of action at this time. The 'Long-Term Commission', formed by a resolution of the Party Congress in Saarbrücken in 1970, presented an interim report in 1972,[37] which is currently being revised. The revised version is to be submitted to broad-scale discussion within the Party after the end of 1974. It remains to be seen what effect the programme will ultimately have on the societal rationality of government and administrative action. What is also uncertain in this respect at present is the outcome of current efforts by both the FDP and CDU to give planning and management competence to their respective general secretaries.

Planning the Organizational, Personnel and Information Decision-making Premises

It appears to be characteristic of the ministerial bureaucracy of the Federal and Land governments that capacities for the rational establishment of internal premises for the politico-administrative decision-making process (organization) of development and procedure, information and personnel systems are notoriously under-developed. Changes in the decision-making structure of the system thus normally take place in the form of an incremental growth in size, in which the existing structures are merely extended by similar elements, e.g. by the installation of a new section in a department or of a new inter-departmental committee, by the employment of more personnel with the customary education and training etc. Larger-scale structural innovations apparently occur only if the efficiency of the existing organization (in absolute or relative terms) is dramatically reduced[38] or if, due to changes on the political scene, the subject of structural reform itself becomes a political issue.

At Federal level, the competence for routine adjustment of organizational, personnel and information premises for decision-making is in the hands of the 'Central Sections' of the specialist Federal Departments. The Finance Ministry participates in decisions of this nature only where financial aspects are concerned. A centralization of these functions, such as in the Civil Service Department of the British Government, does not exist. For dealing with organizational problems that involve more than one department, there is the inter-ministerial 'Committee for Organizational Questions', but up to now this has concerned itself excusively with problems of detail (e.g. uniform regulations for the typing service or the exchange of mail etc.). It is indicative of its role that it did not participate in the conception of the decision-making structures of the general economic framework planning, medium-term finance planning or medium- longer-term task planning. Limited effectiveness was also the lot of the President of the Federal Audit Office ('Bundesrechnungshof') in his capacity as Federal Delegate for Economy in the Administration (BWV), not least of all because the occupant of this office, which was created under Chancellor Erhard, can act only in an advisory capacity and has no sanctioning powers of his own. Under these circumstances, it required a relatively crisis-like development of the internal political situation in the Federal Republic of Germany before the prerequisites were given for the establishment of specific planning capacities which had as their goal a reform of the decision-making structures of the government apparatus. This situation occured very soon after the formation of the Grand Coalition. After the economic recession of the years 1966-67, the majority of the population, whose resistance had been overcome, soon showed its usual measure of 'loyalty to the system' and a simultaneous general lack of interest in politics. This development was, on the other hand, accompanied by a growing tendency to move away from the 'establishment', which could be observed

above all in the 'extra-parliamentary opposition' ('außerparlamentarische Opposition'), a collective term for various groups of intellectuals in the field of journalism
and in the universities, as well as in a series of new, radical splinter groups. The
international political disturbances, which were increasingly led by student groups,
reached a climax in 1968 and spread to other groups of the younger generation. Of
particular relevance as starting condition for the context to be analysed here was
the raising of the topic of structural problems of 'late capitalist' systems by the
New Left. The latter went far beyond the value consideration capacity of the
politico-administrative system, however, with their concept of strategies for 'overcoming the system' or their call for a 'march through the institutions'.

For the politico-administrative system, this development did not represent, on
balance, a direct threat to its legitimation basis which would have forced immediate
functional-structural changes, as did the crisis situation of 1966. On the other hand,
the echo that the problem of the structure and efficiency of State institutions —
raised by the Left with the help of the mass media — began to produce among the
politically interested public signalled a 'reform climate' to the political parties
which gave them the opportunity to mobilize certain groups of voters for themselves by announcing reforms. Particularly for the SPD, this was a prerequisite for
the further improvement of its prospects for the approaching Federal election of
1969.

Against this background, the topic of 'government and administration reform'
became an object of party competition between the SPD and CDU/CSU. As a result
of a corresponding initiative by the then Vice-Chancellor Brand, who was able to
rely on the preliminary work done by an internal Party working group under the
leadership of Ehmke about the problems at the beginning of 1968, Chancellor
Kiesinger instructed the Secretaries of State in the Ministries of Justice and Home
Affairs to prepare a procedural draft. After disputes about competence lasting
several months between the Home Affairs Ministry and Chancellor's Office, finally,
in December 1968, the 'Cabinet Committee for the Reform of the structure of the
Federal Government and Federal Administration' was formed. The Federal Home
Affairs Minister and five other Federal Ministers were members of the committee,
which was chaired by the Federal Chancellor. The 'Project Group Government and
Administration Reform', a committee of nine senior civil servants from the same
ministries, was assigned to this 'Reform Cabinet'.

The Project Group was directed by the 'Reform Cabinet' to put the 'Federal
Government and Administration in a structural and functional position to fulfill
their tasks with the least possible expenditure but with optimum efficiency, at the
same time doing justice to the needs of the State Community and its future
problems'.[39] The first reform recommendations were to be prepared by the
approaching Federal election in the autumn of 1969.

The Project Group did, in fact, present its first report after six months, in
August 1969.[40] It contained concrete recommendations for a new delimitation of
the scope of competence of the Federal Ministries (dissolution of five Ministries),
for the general introduction of the office of 'Parliamentary Secretary of State' as
link between Government and Parliament, and for the development of a central

task planning system in the Chancellor's Office. The last mentioned of these recommendations formed the most important basis for the development of the 'Early Coordination System of the Federal Government' described in the last chapter, the further development of which was transferred to the direction of the Planning Department of the Chancellor's Office.

After the Federal elections, which were successful for the SPD and FDP, and the formation of the Social Democratic Liberal Coalition at the end of 1969, the Project Group continued its work. It received a new directive from the 'Reform Cabinet' to prepare comprehensive reform recommendations and to carry out or commission the investigations necessary for that purpose. It was to be the aim of these efforts 'to create a better personnel and organizational basis for the preparation and successful execution of a comprehensive political concept'.[41] To comply with this directive, the project group, in cooperation with an inter-disciplinary group of social scientists, developed a differentiated theoretical frame of reference which was intended to render it possible to make a causal analysis of the existing system-deficiencies. Simultaneously, a catalogue of deficiency hypotheses was produced. On this basis, the following 'Main Reform Objectives' were finally formulated:

1. Democratization of the political objective-finding process through a broadened consideration of interests and the utilization of all possibilities for increased participation by the citizens, by an increased transparency of conflict regulation and the establishment of consensus, and by the reduction of hierarchical structures within the politico-administrative system.
2. 'Politicization' of the internal government and administration decision-making process with the object of breaking through the routinely bureaucratic, innovation-resistant methods of determining and realizing objectives and, finally
3. Improving the 'intelligence' of the government and administration organization by improving the capacities for obtaining, registering and processing information about the state and development trends of the environment and of the politico-administrative system itself.

The preparation of this reform concept, only briefly sketched here, took a period of nearly six months, not least because the members of the Project Group (and their advisers), initially had strongly diverging views concerning the content-orientation and the necessary theoretical foundation of the project. When the group had finally come to an agreement in a series of conflict-ridden decision-making procedures and had presented its proposals in a report to the Cabinet in May 1970, it was too late for the originally-intended influencing of the 'Reform Cabinet's' expectations — the reform impetus of the new Government's first months in the office had already dissipated. A further factor was that the members of the 'Reform Cabinet', impressed by the initial successes that the Planning Department of the Chancellor's Office had achieved in a very short time in developing the 'Early Coordinating System of the Federal Government', subsequently showed very little understanding for the time-consuming process of searching for objectives proposed by the Project Group Government and Administration Reform. The members of the Cabinet Committee seemed to fear that the Project Group would not be able to develop any more recommendations which would be ready for implementation and which could also be used in the government's public work before the end of the legislative period. Because, in addition, there was for various reasons little prospect that the relatively short-term success orientation of the 'Reform Cabinet' could still be influenced, the Project Group was forced to limit drastically the object area to which the planned changes in the system structures were to apply and to reduce the level of the pretentions of their reform concept to that of a structural adjustment accepting the existing status quo.

This reduction took place in several stages. First, there was the renunciation of the development of specific strategies for increasing readiness for reform within the politico-administrative system. The direct and intensive feed-back from all decision-making levels within the government apparatus which would have been necessary for this purpose would have, in any case, been possible only to a limited extent, as the Project Group, by the very nature of the situation, was mainly dependent on the usual hierarchical lines of communication. Therefore, the group adopted a work-form which, in its lack of feed-back to the occupants of the 'planned' existing positions did not differ essentially from that of the traditional commissions, and thus could not contribute to the improvement of the conditions for implementing the reform recommendations to be developed.

Step by step, the areas to which reform deliberations applied became increasingly limited, especially because there was little chance that the working capacity of the group could be increased to the extent required. Whereas questions of procedural techniques in the decision-making process were initially of equal importance to information and personnel problems, the former now began to come more and more to the foreground. Furthermore, the Project Group concentrated increasingly on the internal conditions in the sphere of Federal Government and administration, although problems of direct citizen and parliamentary participation in political planning had at the outset been regarded as central issues. It is true that orders were placed for experts' reports in these problem areas, but they were not dealt with any further. As a result of this reduction, which had in the meantime modified the original concepts, the mainly conventional recommendations of the Third Report of the Project Group for Government and Administration Reform – completed in November 1972 – stand in distinct contrast to some of the experts' reports produced for the Project Group, which still reflect the reform objectives of the initial phase in 1969-70.[42]

The substance of the 'Third Report'[43] contains recommendations for the step-by-step introduction of a programme budget on the Federal level, for the redesign of the internal organization of the Federal Ministries and for the re-definition of their ministerial responsibilities, and finally, for the creation of a Cabinet Office for Planning and Organization.

These recommendations have largely still not been realized in Government practice. However, the Project Group did subject some of the conceptional ideas developed in the report to a reality test in the course of their participation in the reorganization of the Federal Agriculture Ministry, which began in October 1971.

Partly in causal connection with the reduction of the field of activity of the Project Group for Government and Administration Reform, a number of other inter-ministerial ad hoc committees became active in 1969-70 in the field of ministerial organization or planning of the informational and personnel decision-making premises.[44] Most of these have completed their tasks in the meantime or passed them on to the line organizations. Among the inter-ministerial groups, the 'Study Commission for the Reform of the Civil Service Regulations' summoned in 1970 is worthy of particular mention here. In the spring of 1973, it presented a report containing extensive recommendations for increasing the 'functional adequacy of the Civil Service Regulations'.[45] Deliberations for the realization of these reform conceptions are in progress. In the Federal Home Affairs Ministry, a report to the Cabinet on this subject is currently in preparation.[46]

Comparatively less important reform impulses were generated in the inter-ministerial 'Working Group for Information-Banking Systems' founded at the Federal Home Affairs Ministry in April 1970. The Federal-wide data-banking system recommended in the report of this group in May 1971[47] is no longer being considered, not least of all because of its immense development and operating costs. Most of the current activities for extending information systems based on electronic data processing are to be found in the spheres of action of individual Ministries, such as the Federal Ministries for Home Affairs, Research and Technology, Defence, Labour, and Transport.

Another set of recommendations to have remained unrealized up to now are those proposed in 1972 by the 'Commission for Restructuring the Area of the GFR' ('Neugliederungskommission') set up by the Federal Government in 1970.[48] One of the few inter-ministerial reform bodies still active, the 'Working Group for Constitutional Reform' which was also set up in 1970, is still concerning itself with the preparation of statements of the Federal Government in reply to questions and recommendations of the 'Inquiry Commission for Constitutional Reform' of the Lower Chamber of the German Federal Parliament which continued its activities after 1972.[49]

The restriction of the problem areas treated by the Project Group and their successive distribution among various reform committees had important consequences for the general process of introducing structural change in the sphere of Federal Government and administration. One of these was that after 1970, there was no organization unit in the government apparatus which was responsible for the development of a general concept which could have been used to direct the content of the creation and embarkation on activity of the various structural planning committees in the spheres of action of the Chancellor's Office and the Ministries. Thus, the 'Reform Cabinet' and the Committee of Departmental Directors assigned to it in 1970 lacked a 'target-model' as a basis for exercising their coordinating competence in respect to Government and administration reform. A coordination of the content of the various individual structural planning activities was, therefore, only possible in the traditional form of a customary 'negative coordination'

('Scharpf') with the result that important problem interdependencies were not taken into consideration. Since, simultaneously, there was no coordination of timing, the ministries were inundated for a time with numerous empirical surveys, some of which were identical to each other, as well as with the most widely differing recommendations for modifying their decision-making structures. Thus, the limited 'learning capacity' of the Ministries could not be utilized systematically for such structural changes as could have been expected to be most likely to lead to progress in the direction of the objective that was being pursued, namely, the increase in the rationality of the politico-administrative decision-making process.

SUMMARY AND OUTLOOK FOR THE FUTURE

In a comparison of the development of the various partial planning systems in the period described, two peaks become apparent in the functional-structural modifications of the politico-administrative system. The first coincides with the introduction of General Economic Framework Planning and Medium-Term Finance Planning in 1966-67. The second occurs during the years 1970-71 and is marked by the various initiatives for the introduction of central task planning by the Federal Government and the emergence of a system of committees for planning decision-making structures.

Although none of the types of planning dealt with remained unaffected by these boom-phases, the dominant position of decentralized specialized planning by the Federal Departments as compared with central task planning has developed more to the disadvantage than to the advantage of the latter. Although the coordination of the timing of specialized departmental planning was extensively improved by the 'Project Recording System' of the Chancellor's Office, the criteria for content coordination of such planning are still obtained almost exclusively through induction from the plans themselves rather than from a general analysis of economic and social developments which would be independent of the specific interests of the existing departments and their clientele. Therefore, it is only with reservations that one can still speak of a conceptual direction of departmental planning on the part of the Federal Government. To what extent this situation will change in time through the further extension of the planning capacities of the political parties cannot be foreseen at present.

Taken by itself, the programme planning in the Federal and Land Departments has gained in internal rationality in many fields. Due to the barely changed environmental dependence of the politico-administrative system, the possibilities of changing the content of the decision-making process by the introduction of new procedures and the opening up of new sources of data and information have, without exception, remained limited. Strategies which could have increased the value consideration capacity of the specialist departments, such as the political mobilization of previously under-privileged groups, were consciously avoided. The result of this development is a 'mixed bag' of individual plans, which diverge widely where time horizons and the spectrum of social interests considered are concerned.

For similar reasons, General Economic Framework Planning (Global Direction) and Medium-Term Finance Planning have not developed the efficiency originally anticipated when these planning procedures were introduced. The possibilities of achieving a stabilization of Federal income and expenditures, which would be desirable in many respects, thus continue to collide frequently with the demands from the spontaneous dynamics of the economic and growth processes.

In the use of planning in creating international premises for the political decision-making process, the only fields in which a few advances have been made in recent years are those of the information and advisory systems. On the other hand, the recruitment, training and employment of personnel in the various Ministries is still largely conducted without a guiding concept, with the possible exception of the planning efforts in the fields of defence and education. Organization planning, too, remained underdeveloped. The planning capacities which had in the meantime become differentiated for this purpose have already been largely reabsorbed by the line organization. The Project Group for Government and Administration Reform today operates 'on a low flame', without great prospects of spectacular results.

Taken together in context, these findings reveal that the politico-administrative system of the Federal Republic of Germany, as a result of the above described failures of many reform efforts in recent years, is still in great need of rationalization. To meet this need, which is likely to increase in the future, remains under the existing circumstances one of the most urgent tasks of the applied administrative sciences and of political practice.

NOTES

1. A. Schick, *Systems Politics and Systems Budgeting,* in: F. J. Lyden and E. G. Miller (eds), *Planning, Programming and Budgeting* (Chicago 2 1972), 78 ff.

2. More details in N. Kloten and R. Vollmer, 'Stabilität und Wachstum in der Wirtschaftspolitik' and R. Jochimsen and P. Treuner, 'Staatliche Planung'; both articles in R. Löwenthal and H. P. Schwarz (eds), *Die zweite Republik* (Stuttgart: 1974), 703 ff and 844 ff.

3. Nevertheless, the German Federal Parliament did pass a law on 14 August 1963, to found the 'Sachverständigenrat zur Begutachtung der gesamtwirtschaftlichen Entwicklung' (Experts Council for Assessing General Economic Development).

4. Compare with Cf. A. Plitzko (ed), *Planung ohne Planwirtschaft* (Publications of the List Society) Vol. 34 (Basel: 1963).

5. As evidence see, for example, the subjects treated in the first two volumes of the series edited by J. H. Kaiser, (ed), *Planung* (Baden-Baden: 1965 and 1966); also the literature used in the contribution by D. Oberndörfer et al., Politische Planung', in: *Erster Bericht der Projektgruppe Regierungs- und Verwaltungsreform* by the Federal Home Affairs Minister, supplement (Bonn: 1969), 316 ff.

6. The most prominent representatives of this line of thought are T. Ellwein and F. W.

Scharpf; also compare the information in: V. Ronge and G. Schmieg, (eds), *Politische Planung in Theorie und Praxis* (Munich: 1971), 7 f., and the volume *Planungsorganisation* (Munich: 1973), edited by R. Mayntz and F. W. Scharpf.

7. Cf. also this with the documentation in H. Schatz, 'Probleme politischer Planung im Regierungssystem der Bundesrepublik Deutschland', a publication in preparation for the documentary series of the 'Kommission für wirtschaftlichen und sozialen Wandel' (Commission for Economic and Social Change), Bonn: 1975); also, the same results in the 'Trend Report' prepared by R. Mayntz for the conference of the 'Deutschen Gesellschaft für Soziologie' 1974, 'Staat und politische Organisation', manuscript (Cologne: 1974), 22 f.

8. R. Mayntz, *Trend Report, op. cit.* 2.

9. V. Ronge and G. Schmieg, *op. cit.* 25.

10. Cf. also the review in F. Naschold and W. Väth, 'Politische Planungssysteme im entwickelten Kapitalismus', in: (by the same editors) *Politische Planungssysteme* (Opladen: 1973), especially 33 f.

11. Cf. for example, with V. Ronge and G. Schmieg, *Restriktionen politischer Planung* (Frankfurt: 1973), 20.

12. Same authors, *op. cit.*, 21.

13. Same authors, *op. cit.* 20.

13a. For more details see U. Thaysen, Staatsaufgabe 'Planung'. Zeitschrift für Parlamentsfragen, 2/1974, 280-290.

14. Prognos A. G., *Gesellschaftspolitische Grundlagen der längerfristigen Sicherung des wirtschaftlichen Wachstums* (Basel: 1969), Vol. I., 18.

15. Cf. N. Kloten and R. Vollmer, 'Stabilität und Wachstum in der Wirtschaftspolitik', in: R. Löwenthal and H. -P. Schwarz (eds) *Die zweite Republik* (Stuttgart: 1974), 708 f.

16. Cf. also D. Zavlaris, 'Die Subvention in der Bundesrepublik Deutschland seit 1961, DIW, *'Beiträge zur Strukturforschung'*, No. 14 (Berlin: 1970).

17. R. Dahrendorf, *Gesellschaft und Demokratie in Deutschland* (Munich: 1965) 466.

18. Cf. *'Erste Finanzplanung des Bundes 1967 bis 1971'*, Bundestags-Drucksache, V/2065, 97 and 106 f.

19. Quoted from: 'Der Spiegel', 'Aus der Mottenkiste', No. 39, 1972, 70.

20. Compare Cf. with H. Adam, *Die konzertierte Aktion in der Bundesrepublik* (Cologne: 1972), and Eike Hennig, *'Zur Kritik der* konzertierten Aktion', in: *Blätter für deutsche und internationale Politik* (1970) 508.

21. Cf. on this F. Naschold, 'Gesellschaftsreform und politische Planung', in: F. Naschold and W. Väth (eds), *op. cit.* 69 f.

22. Cf. also for the situation in the USA before the introduction of the PPBS, A. Wildavsky, *The Politics of the Budgetary Process,* (Boston: 1964), especially 130 ff.

23. Cf. also 'Bundesministerium der Finanzen, Finanzbericht 1970', especially 155.

24. Compare with, among others, H. Hamm-Brücher, 'Reform in Handschellen', in Die Zeit, No. 40, 27. 9. (1974) 18.

25. Before 1969, the planning capacities of the departments were comprised almost exclusively of new staff posts. According to a survey produced by the Home Affairs Ministry in mid-1968, there were planning staffs of this type in the Chancellor's Office and in five other Federal Ministries. After 1969, on the other hand, most Ministries endeavoured to expand the planning capacities down the line, i.e. in the individual sections of their departments, by assigning the necessary coordinators to a section, sub-section, or planning group as required. According to the answer of the Federal Government to a 'small interpellation' ('Kleine Anfrage') on this matter by the CDU/CSU (Bundestagsdrucksache 7/2490 of 16.8.74), there are currently only four remaining planning staffs outside the line organization, namely, in the Foreign Office, the Federal Defence Ministry, the Federal Post and Telephones Communications Ministry and the Regional Planning, Construction and Federal Urban Development Ministry. These staffs contain between two and twelve academically fully trained members.

26. Compare with the 'Gesetz über den Ausbau der Bundesfernstraßen in den Jahren von 1971-1985', of 30.6.71 (Bundesgesetzblatt I, P. 873).

27. *Sozialbericht der Bundesregierung* 1973, Bundestagsdrucksache 7/1167, 25th.10.1973, 35.

28. A survey of the most important terms of joint specialist planning by the federal and Land Governments is contained in the investigation carried out by Prognos, A. G., 'Entwicklung alternativer Instrumente zur Verbesserung der Koordinierung der Raumordnungspolitik' (Basle: 1974), 26 f.

29. Cf. also F. W. Scharpf, *Politische Durchsetzbarkeit innerer Reformen im pluralistisch-demokratischen Gemeinwesen der Bundesrepublik*, manuscript (Berlin and Constance: 1973), 28 ff. (Publication in preparation for 1975).

30. Cf. on the following among others, R. Waterkamp, *Interventionsstaat und Planung* (Cologne: 1973), 35 ff. and 111 ff. and F. Wagener, *Für ein neues Instrumentarium der öffentlichen Planung*, in: WIBERA-Sonderdruck No. 39 (Düsseldorf: March 1973), 3 ff.

31. Thus F. Wagener, op. cit. 22.

32. Compare with the Senate of the Free Hanseatic City of Hamburg, 'Das Entscheidungs-modell für Hamburg und sein Umland', in: *Berichte und Dokumente*, No. 186, 18.7.1969.

33. Cf. also the 'Bericht über die Industrialisierung der Unterelbe', in *Der Spiegel*, No. 44/1974, 49 ff. A similar development is emerging in the Bremen-Lower Weser area.

34. Cf. also R. Jochimsen, 'Zum Aufbau und Ausbau eines integrierten Aufgabenplanungs-systems und Koordinationssystems der Bundesregierung', in *Bulletin der Bundesregierung*, No. 97, 16.7.1970, 954; and 'Planung im staatlichen Bereich', in *Bulletin der Bundesregierung*, No. 113, 23.7.1971, 1237.

35. Cf. also H. Bebermeyer, 'Das Politische Planungssystem der Bundesregierung', in: R. Jochimsen und U. E. Simonis (eds) *Theorie und Praxis der Infrastrukturpolitik* (Berlin: 1970), 724 f.

36. The following arguments are based on an as yet unpublished manuscript by H. J. Dahms, on *Das Informationssystem zur Vorhabenplanung der Bundesregierung* (Bonn: 6.11.1974).

37. Parteivorstand der SPD, *Entwicklung eines ökonomisch-politischen Orientierungs-rahmens für die Jahre 1973 bis 1985* (Bonn: June 1972).

38. Cf. on this M. Crozier, 'Der bürokratische Circulus vitiosus und das Problem des Wandels', in: R. Mayntz (eds) *Bürokratische Organisation* (Cologne/Berlin: 1968), 277 ff.

39. Submission of the Federal Home Affairs Ministry of 21st October 1968 to the constitutive meeting of the previously mentioned Cabinet committee.

40. 'Projektgruppe Regierungs- und Verwaltungsreform' (at the Federal Home Affairs Ministry), First Report on the *Reform der Struktur von Bundesregierung und Bundesver-waltung* (Bonn: 1969).

41. Thus the text of the resolution by the Federal Cabinet of 23 October 1969.

42. This applies particularly to the investigations of medium-term finance planning by F. Naschold and his colleagues, cf. the summary of which is to be found in: F. Naschold, D. Seuster, W. Väth and O. Zipfel, *Thesen zur mehrjährigen Finanzplanung des Bundes* in: R. Mayntz and F. W. Scharpf (eds) (Munich: 1973), 146 ff.

43. Projektgruppe Regierungs- und Verwaltungsreform at the Federal Home Affairs Ministry, Third 'Report on the *"Reform der Struktur von Bundesregierung und Bundesver-waltung",*' (Bonn: 1972).

44. Among the reform commissions belonging to the Department Ministries themselves, the following deserve particular mention: the 'Organisationskommission des Bundesverteidigungs-ministeriums zur Neuordnung des Rüstungsbereichs' and the 'Kommission für die Reform des Auswärtigen Dienstes', 'Organisation Commission of the Federal Defence Ministry for the Reorganisation of the Armaments Sector', which was similarly active until 1971. Cf. Federal Defence Ministry, *Neuordnung des Rüstungsbereichs* (Bonn: 1971) and the Bulletin der Bundesregierung, No. 40, 421 ff.

45. Studienkommission für die Reform des öffentlichen Dienstrechts, *Bericht der Kom-mission*, (Baden-Baden: 1973), with 11 Supplementary volumes.

46. Independent of this, a project for the development of a personnel planning system is

currently getting under way as a cooperative undertaking by the Federal Labour Ministry and the Federal Ministry for Research and Technology.

47. Interministerielle Arbeitsgruppe Informationsbankensystem beim Bundesminister des Inneren, *Das Informationsbankensystem,* (Bonn: 1971).

48. Cf. also the *Bericht der Sachverständigenkommission für die Neugliederung des Bundesgebietes,* (Bonn: 1972).

49. Cf. on this Dt. Bundestag (chamber of the Federal Parliament) ed., *Fragen der Verfassungsreform, Zwischenbericht der Enquêtekommission des Deutschen Bundestages,* No. 1/73 of the series *Zur Sache.*

Theory of the State

Special Features of the Discussion in the FRG

Heide Gerstenberger

BOURGEOIS STABILIZATION THEORY OF THE STATE

AS HAS BEEN THE CASE IN SO MANY FIELDS, the fascist period has had a lasting impact on theoretical discussion about the state. It was typical of the post-war era to treat fascism as a kind of historical accident for which malicious dictators were to blame. This made it appear unnecessary to discuss critically the basic structures of bourgeois society and its state. All that seemed to be needed was the revival of the liberal principles to which the Western anti-fascist alliance programmatically adhered. Therefore, the discussion about the bourgeois state and its fascist aberration pursued didactic goals rather than theoretical ones. It is no coincidence that the main theme of the early discussion in the field of political science conceived the possibilities of political education. This tendency got forceful support from aggressive anti-communism, the corollary to the restoration of bourgeois-capitalist structures in West Germany.

This didactic tendency in political science was shaped by two assumptions that were never really explained: first, that the basic structures of bourgeois social organization guarantee liberty and common welfare and — secondly — that citizens have only to comply with the appropriate procedures.[1] West German political science reactivated, in this way, the basic substance of the dominant Anglo-American political theory at a time when this theory had already lost its influence in its countries of origin.

It was not only due to the expulsion, emmigration and death of German scholars that in the post-war era the social sciences adopted models of thinking that were then current in the USA. At first, this tendency was reinforced by a certain unease on the part of the German political scientists about their own values, an unease which had developed despite the systematic neglect of the fascist past which had been intended to work against this unease. However, the growing economic prosperity very soon restored this shaken self-assurance. This process is reflected in the attempt to reintegrate traditional German conceptions of the state. The successful functionalization of obsolete forms of political organization that was needed in Prussia-Germany for the success of the bourgeois form of production has produced a kind of mercantile conception of the state even for the liberal epoch. In this respect, it differs from the dominant Anglo-American tradition with its concept of 'government by law'. In Germany, the actions of the state have rarely been understood as the result of social struggles (not until the adoption of pluralism theories after the Second World War could this line of bourgeois theory gain influence here), but rather, the state apparatus itself is considered to be the source of the economic as well as the ethical welfare of the nation. In the fifties and early sixties, German social scientists tried to pick up this traditional concept of the state that had first been developed by the cameralists (cameralism is the German variant of mercantilism) and has since found its theoretical foundation in the philosophy of Hegel.[2] These scholars, however, either failed to notice or to mention that this tradition had also been integrated into the theory of fascist dictatorship. In their criticism of the purely positivistic methods of the contemporary, empirically-oriented political science, they formulated the program of a pragmatic theory that evokes the old unity of ethics and politics and tries to restore the state as the guardian of the ethical greatness and unity of the people. The government should not be conceived as a mere agent of the people's will, founded empirically in opinion polls and elections. Instead, the government is said to have a responsibility for the common welfare that goes beyond the manifestations of the people's will. In concrete terms, this means the formation of a strong executive that uses to the full its constitutional powers for an active policy. It further means the search for advice from experts who stand outside and above all parties.

Leftists critics have pointed out the ontological and anthropological foundations of this theory which serve as a specious foundation for it. Above all, it has been noted critically that this pragmatic political theory demands the government's responsibility for its actions, but does not advise policies and rather leaves those up to the politicians. While these critics of bourgeois ideology have concentrated on the foundations of the theories in discussion, they have nevertheless neglected the fact that — in spite of its faulty theoretical foundations — bourgeois theorizing may constitute the actual guiding line of political behaviour. The more adequate understanding of the functions of the bourgeois state for bourgeois society in the middle of the twentieth century — which did not gain prevalence in West Germany until the economic crisis of 1966-67 and the participation of the Social Democrats in the government — had been preconceived by these theoreticians of authoritarian forms of organization under the guise of a Hegel and Aristotle renaissance. By borrowing from the authoritarian German traditions, the appraisal of 'pragmatic science of government' helped a great deal to integrate ideologically the new forms of politics characterized by deliberate state-planning and Keynesian economic policies into the restoration of capitalism in West Germany.

The victory of Keynesian theory has proved in a striking manner that the faulty and inconsistent structure of a theory does not prevent it from guiding bourgeois crisis management. Every systematic discussion of the bourgeois theory of the state must have Keynesianism as one of its central topics, as Keynesianism defines the new understanding of the state as executant of the popular will. Now, systematic planning, prevention and management of crises are declared to be the main functions of the state. The reliance on the self-correcting laissez-faire in society has definitely been abandoned. Here, however, we do not discuss the general but rather a national development of bourgeois society's theoretical identity. Even after the Second World War, this national development has still been influenced by the fact that the bourgeois revolution in Prussia-Germany managed to establish only the bourgeois mode of production, but not its corollary, that is, bourgeois political rule. Therefore, the authoritarian ideology could survive almost untouched, and, on the other hand, a concept of the state could develop that accepted in a positivistic way the existing power structures.

How far the autocratic trait of bourgeois organizational concepts continued to exist in West Germany can be shown best by the later writings of the influential law professor, Ernst Forsthoff, especially in his book *Der Staat der Industriegesellschaft (The State of Industrial Society)*. His former glorification of Nazi Germany, which many critics have pointed out to unmask him, only constitutes part of the factual relevance of this book.[3] Since Forsthoff is able to restrain from using exultant words, he gains a far greater insight into the conditions for the stability of bourgeois society than Hegel's reactionary successors ever did.

'State', in the actual sense of the word, no longer exists for Forsthoff. For him, the concept of state is linked to ideas where practical realization is best achieved through constitutional monarchy (the change from the propagation of the form of fascist dictatorship to that of constitutional monarchy marks the concessions to the more democratic climate of today). This means a governing person who embodies the absolute sovereignty and the ethical ideal of the people, as well as a parliament with restricted functions of control (!).[4] But not only did 'state' in that sense perish, also the classical methods of ideological stabilization have now become obsolete. The latter had been achieved in two ways: On the one hand, the actual inequality of members of the bourgeois society could be veiled effectively by the legal equality of the citizens; on the other, the state was able to demand their obedience just because the authorities represented the ethical ideal of the nation. (The mixing of ideological structures of distinctly different conceptions about society not only characterizes Forsthoff's contradictory method of argumentation but also reflects the real contradictions in the Prussian-German ideological tradition. Disagreeing with the political theoreticians mentioned above, he sees no chance of reviving traditional ideological modes of stablization. Since the state of the industrial society is unable to give intellectual impulses,[5] moreover, social stability is no longer guaranteed by the recognition of the state as a moral authority. Stability rather results from a stable social development itself. The state's contribution to a stable order, above all, consists in 'Daseinsvorsorge' (a word brought into the German discussion by Forsthoff already in 1938, meaning a generalized conception of social security).[6] The further extension of social security is not considered to be necessary by Forsthoff.[7]

The abandonment of the traditional ideals of the authoritarian state (not of the state itself) is one aspect of Forsthoff's theory of the state; the justification of the new state activity is the other. Since, according to Forsthoff's view, stability cannot be achieved solely through the maintenance of ideas about social order, but rather through effective welfare policies, he is able to discard the theory (essential for ideological stability) of a clear distinction between state and society.[8] Already, during the Weimar Republic, he claims this distinction did not really exist; state and private economic activity tended to overlap increasingly and there occurred an enormous extension of the state's administrative functions. However the state's effective power did not increase as a result. This he sees much more clearly than leftist social-democratic theoreticians. Since the administration needs more and more qualified advice, the recruitment of experts from the private sector becomes as inevitable as the diminution of parliamentary influence. But, according to Forsthoff, governmental planning, as the new element in the state's activity, consists of nothing else than the coordination of particular interests through the state.[9] The remarkable resemblance of Forsthoff's theses to parts of approaches maintained by the theory of state monopoly capitalism is not only apparent in the positions mentioned, but is also particularly evident in his technological approach: to him, technology is not a process determined by the modes of production, but rather an autonomous process.[10] In the meantime, this process has yielded results that have to be taken care of by the state or by multinational institutions; otherwise, self-destruction of human life will become more and more likely. The problems of pollution have shown the limits of democracy,[11] as it became evident there that a need shared by all does not automatically secure representation through the state. This is because the state does not assert the needs of the majority, but only those of powerful organizations. The same position is put forward – partially with the same reasoning – by adherents of the theory of state monopoly capitalism. They hold that the conditions of capital reproduction, resulting from the development of productive powers as well as the conditions of social reproduction, which are partially not in accordance with those of capital reproduction, create the growing necessity of social organization and regulation through the state. This would necessarily transcend the typical forms of bourgeois organization. As far as the effective governmental intervention is concerned, Ernst Forsthoff is much less optimistic than left-wing Social Democrats, on the one hand, and communist theoreticians, on the other. The only result of the objective necessity of increasing state functions is the definitive abandonment of the ideal of pure government by law. Consequently, autocratic forms of government are on the agenda. This is a conclusion that cannot be ignored by simply pointing to the inconsistencies of Forsthoff's arguments.

If Forsthoff is to be considered as one of the few bourgeois theoreticians who try to analyse the political and economical aspects of stabilization, Niklas Luhmann has effectively proved that such an analytical approach is not indispensable for the development of a doctrine that aims at stability. In the sociology of the legal and judicial system, Luhmann has initiated a new stage of theorizing in West Germany.

Taking up the critique of Parsons's structural functionalism, Luhmann tries to derive the functions, not from the structural context, but to understand, in reverse, the structure as the result of the functions. By this functional structuralism, he can dispose of the central problems of the earlier structuralism: first, he does not need to discuss the factual necessity of systems and second, he derives all functions from the system's characteristic elements. For him, systems are devised by one function, the function of selection out of an environment of infinite multitude. The members of a system conceive this selectional achievement as a sensible entity, and through it they experience the legitimation of the system's existence. Applied to a distinct society, however, this conception implies that the individual experiences this sensible entity of the system because it has been born and socialized into it: not the experience of reduced complexity generates the generic identity, but rather, the concrete confrontation with different possibilities. The importance of the boundary, considered by Luhmann as one of the shortcomings of Parsons's concept, remains obvious, also in the explication of Luhmann's construction. There is no actual progress beyond Parsons. Picking up Max Weber's category of meaning (Sinn) only facilitates giving reasons for theoretical system stability.

The selective achievement not only generates the system as such, but also the differentiations within the system. It is not only the central, but almost the exclusive constitutive principle of social organization. This is a position that, in the meantime, has been criticized, even by proponents of systems analysis.[13] Luhmann himself answers the demand for a concrete outline of the functions (for instance of the political system of society) by this theorem of equivalent functionalism. Faced with the infinite multitude of possibilities that are offered by the system's environment, the reduction of complexity within the system can happen in many ways that are equivalent to each other. If the complexity of the system grows, it relies more and more on the lack of specification of single complexity-reducing decisions. Luhmann deduces these arguments from his theoretical concept of systems analysis. Occasionally, he gives empirical illustrations. But neither the presuppositions nor the conclusions have ever been tested, nor would their formulation allow empirical proof.

The empirical illustrations of the above theses can be found in Luhmann's sociology of law. If specified functions are not decisive for the system's existence, if its existence depends, instead, solely on the process of reducing complexity, one is tempted to deduce the high relevance of norm-guided procedures. And, as a matter of fact, the legal formality of the procedure is the eminent instrument of stability. In a remarkable essay (written in 1973), Niklas Luhmann's doctrine of political power reached its provisional end and climax.[14] Just as Georg Jellinek proposed a constitutional theory at the end of the 19th century that allowed the adaptation of the emancipatory theory of 'government by law' to the dominational requirements of monarchic but structurally bourgeois Germany, so Luhmann managed to remove even those impediments to domination that, in legal positivism, were still inherent in the obligation towards the actual constitution.

In his essay about political constitutions in the context of the social system, Luhmann remarks that the usual way of discussing constitutions by confronting norm and reality could not open the path to a constitutional doctrine that is adequate to modern society. In those approaches, one implicitly would insinuate that norms are still (!) capable of producing certain behavioral expectations. This way of thinking still clings to the classical constructive principles of bougeois constitutions, that is, the abuse of power. But today's constitutional reality does not pose the problem of an abundance of power, but rather, of a lack of it. The older discussions are bound to miss this point. Leaving constitutional exegesis, Luhmann is in search of a theory that allows him 'to omit' exegesis and to find a more relative point of view towards the constitution, without questioning its validity.

In an earlier essay, Luhmann had called the state a concept that remained obscure.[15] But in the meantime he grasps the theory of the separation of state and society as the proof for the incompleteness of the classical bourgeois conception of society. Differing from the feudal identity of political and economic organisation, the bourgeois society arose as an economically determined system that is forced to ascertain functional profiency from outside itself. 'The state maintained its unity as opposite to and as a compensation of the society'.[16] Therefore, it could not be conceived as part of the social system's differentiation. Accordingly, one is mistaken to talk of the end of that separation. Instead, one has to develop a more adequate theory that conceives the state – better called political system – as a differentiated part within the society. As a result of this differentiation, the political system has been assigned the function of making binding decisions for the whole system. In this context, Luhmann does not mention monetary, fiscal, employment, or foreign policy. For him, the guarantees of stability are the reductions of complexity, on the one hand, and the maintenance of a certain amount of complexity, on the other.

By developing a certain constitution, a society not only determines which areas are turned over to the realm of the political system, but also, which ones are to be kept out of the political sphere. This exclusion secures the capability of the political system to make decisions, but it does not secure the rationality or controlability of the conditions the system generates. According to Luhmann, the selectional achievement is, in itself, an absolute value. Its usefulness for society is not dependent on its positive consequences.[17] The legal formality of the procedures 'absorb the immediate motivational pressure on the political system, transform it into work-incentives of the system and into mechanisms of the absorbtion of discontent, which are compatible with more than one decision. Now, the structural conditions of the *feasibility* of decisions can be separated from the structural conditions of the *appropriateness* of decisions.'[18] The relevance of constitutions is not considered to be found in their ability to decide what is right or wrong. Instead a constitution decrees legal formality as the universal principle. This means that all decisions are to be submitted to a procedure which is excluded from the discussion about rationality and social expediency by institutional premise. For, as Luhmann properly concludes, the recognition of the principle of legal formality as a universal one needs a positivistic conception of law as its corollary: 'The law of ꞥ society is positive if the legitimacy of pure legality is acknowledged.'[19]

At this point, Luhmann's specific contribution to an administrative doctrine becomes evident. He laid the foundations for and strengthened the West German civil servants' and state officials' self-assurance,[20] which, in turn, immunized them against experts' disagreement and citizens' protest. He was able to achieve this because the administration's actual task is not the determination of the decisions' factual content, but rather, the formal procedure of their implementation. Here, he also points out the preeminence of the officials' status. In order to fulfill its decision-making function, the political system, according to Luhmann, requires a relative autonomy. Only then can the society become 'its object for policies and administration'.[21] This autonomy is achieved through the indifference of the members of the political system towards the roles every other member of the political system fulfills outside that system. The roles of civil servant, judge and politician, dominant as they are in relation to other roles, enable the political system to gain its relative autonomy.[22] The particular structure of the political role as opposed to other roles is, in Luhmann's view, determined by the fact that the agents within the political system (who make up the system in their roles as agents in other spheres) have no relevance for the interactions in the context of the political system. In Luhmann's administrative theory, officials can find their identity as role-agents which, in any case, they are inclined to have. Aloof from all social conflicts, they are called to their work. The regression to the bare principle of legality, that has been outlined theoretically, strengthens the conservative tendencies of officials.

Confronted with the actual problems of governmental administration and with daily discussions of the advantages and disadvantages of certain economic strategies, such theory might appear anachronistic. However, Luhmann does not ignore the development of certain administrative and planning techniques in daily politics. He points out that these have a deficit of legitimacy.[23] But, just as the law-abiding formality of procedures reduces acute and lasting conflicts, and, therefore, institutionally restricts the influence of public discussions, in practice, it allows the development of those practical administrative techniques, which, characterized by a lack of legitimacy, are indispensable for the preservation of bourgeois society.

Legal formality extends the scope of the state apparatus actions and, in this way, emancipatory bourgeois legal theory has been converted — even beyond classical legal positivism — to its overtly manipulative opposite.

CRITICAL THEORY OF THE STATE*

At the same time as Luhmann tried to make use of systems analysis for the explicit purpose of stabilization theory, such approaches were taken up with subjectively quite different intentions. Already in 1963, one could notice that rigid economic liberalism was slowly going to be abandoned in West Germany, entailing a different conception of the state. This development corresponded to the change in

---

* Under this heading, reformist as well as revisionist (meaning a revision of the Marxian critique of political economy) theories will be discussed.

the economic situation. While during the post-war era, due to a high reserve of qualified and cheap labor, an enormous capital accumulation could take place without requiring innovative investment, at the beginning of the sixties, the exhaustion of the national labor reserve and the increasing competition in the world market exacerbated the economic situation of West German industry. Infrastructural planning and deliberate educational measures were then called for as the indispensable prerequisites for the now necessary introduction of technological innovations. In this situation, the scientific advisory board for economic matters called for the development of long-term fiscal planning.

The Social Democrats, in particular, demanded the introduction of fiscal policy and a certain degree of state planning when they joined the government of the Great Coalition during the crisis of 1966-67; this caused a flood of writings euphorically appraising state planning.[24] All Western states have — with varying degrees of enthusiasm — passed through this stage of wild hopefulness about state planning. Therefore, this does not need to be outlined further here. It was accompanied by the introduction of the so-called 'Concerted Action', which assumed the working population's participation in the development of policy.[25] This makes it obvious that in West Germany the conceptualization of state planning has always been very closely related to the tradition of revisionist (or reformist) conceptions of the state. These are characterized by the hope that the state apparatus could achieve a transformation of capitalist society into democratic socialism. The active planning of the state is considered the precondition for an emancipatory policy. This hope, still widespread among Social Democrats at the end of the sixties (in the meantime the Social-Democratic party in West Germany has reduced its reformist perspective), was reflected in the writings of Dieter Senghaas.[26] Senghaas starts out from cybernetic systems analysis, in the way that it was developed for the political system by Karl Deutsch. This means that he considers the political subsystem, as well as society as a whole, as regulated systems, whose controlling mechanisms must be provided. He takes up and extends Deutsch's thesis that the solution of control problems requires a certain capacity in the social system to learn. He sees no possibility of increasing this capacity other than through social and individual emancipation.[27]

Already in 1969, Frieder Naschold criticized the aloofness from reality of such approaches in a text-book which he wrote together with Wolf-Dieter Narr, in which, for the first time, systems analysis was presented to an interested public in West Germany.[28] At this time, he still conceived systems analysis to be a material theory, that is, an approach that allows the adequate formulation of social structural relationships and developments. Together with various colleagues, he tried to validate these models of social control and regulation where they are most easily apprehended: in the conscious efforts of social planning. As an adviser to the federal government, he was taking part in the initiation of long-term fiscal planning in West Germany while, at the same time, he was becoming increasingly aware of the limitations of state planning. As a result of these empirical studies, Naschold now concludes that systems analysis cannot claim any material content, but that instead it is to be understood as a 'form of complex conceptualization'.[29] His criticism, which was previously aimed at the ahistoricity and pretended social neutrality of systems analysis, now merges with the critical analysis of the historical relevance of planning systems. The significance of their emergence for the process of economic concentration is clearly recognized: today's planning techniques are considered the most advanced problem-solving strategies to have been developed by capitalist societies. Comparisons with existing systems of planning, as well as the criticism of the predominant technocratic planning models, prevented Naschold from claiming the convergence of capitalist and socialist development.[30] As he explained in a programmatic lecture: 'The planning theories that follow the paradigm of action-theory lack the systematic analysis of the environment, which encompasses the political systems' planning apparatus. Central problem areas, such as economic development and the conflicts built into the social structure, are, as a rule, left out in this theory.'[31] Due to his research experience, he deems political-economic approaches to have a greater explanatory capacity. However, he criticizes their provisional status. In his view, Marxist theory is inclined to conceive the state's activity as being overdetermined by economics.[32] His investigation of the reality of political planning systems has convinced him that approaches guided by political economy are indispensable, but he has not yet himself presented such an analysis. This seems to be the reason for the fact that he is still able to present a planning theory which is partially founded on hope and belief. After pointing out that planning cannot achieve a change of the system or a basic reform of it, Naschold and Werner Väth express in their recent book the vague hope that social reforms can be realized, provided the circumstances are favorable. This could happen 'if, during acute problems of social reproduction, alliances and social coalitions are possible which take advantage of the progressive element in state planning, that is, the strategic planning of goals and the tendencies towards decentralization. These coalitions require a partial identity of goals, even if substantial differences of interest concerning specific sectoral reforms would continue to exist.'[33] This hope was presented less vaguely in 1972: Naschold assumes that the growing necessity of planning requires increasing participation. For him, this development does not include only the danger of atomization which is, itself, difficult to control. Instead, the growing need for participation might open the path to further democratic development.[34] One can expect that Naschold will not refrain from testing this thesis empirically. He would then have to deal with that broad movement for participation which, in West Germany, emerged at the end of the sixties in the form of voters' and citizens' groups. This movement has not remained untouched by the scholarly discussion just mentioned. Some scholars have actually dealt with concrete complexes of participation, particularly in the area of city planning. The practical results of these experiences show how drastically limited the citizens' influence has to remain. The 'symbolic uses of politics' are still the central substance of participation. A different direction and content for participation, however, does not automatically result from the growing necessity of state-planning. Only political struggles could secure this. It is, however, quite doubtful whether, as Naschold assumes,[35] the formation of a counter-force which would be able to take up such struggles could still be considered as being in accord with the existing social system.

The writings of Jürgen Habermas deal less intensively with the social reality of West Germany than do Naschold's. Nevertheless, they are a characteristic product of this reality. They reflect that historical development which, in the fifties, caused the impression that capitalist crises had been managed and that the working class had been successfully integrated into bourgeois society. Due to the empirical aloofness of his approach, Habermas did not notice that even the outer appearance of the political-economic system has changed in the meantime.

While the first generation of the Frankfurt School had been moved mainly by the fear of totalitarianism (the difference between bolshevik and fascist dictatorship never having been sufficiently analysed by these scholars) and has used historical materialism as a theory for cultural criticism, the second generation, represented primarily by Jürgen Habermas and Claus Offe, asserted that the central theses of the Marxian critique of political economy have been rendered obsolete by actual historical development. Already in his earlier writings, Habermas rejected Marx's value theory as inconclusive.[36] Instead, he adopted Offe's thesis 'that, in state regulated capitalism, the global conflict between classes is no longer the dynamic center of social change; increasingly, the latter is overlapped by "horizontal" systems of inequality, by a disparity of social possibilities.'[37] In the context of this disparity thesis, underprivileged conditions are no longer conceived as the outcome of the social mode of production in the bourgeois society. This makes it obvious that the analysis of the capitalist mode of production and its developmental conditions are not considered to be the necessary starting point for the analysis of society. The critical theory devises its critique of the bourgeois society outside the context of the critique of political economy. Starting from such a premise, it is amazing that in his latest book, Habermas[38] resorts even to very controversial topics of Marxist theory, when he uses the theory of the tendency of the profit-rate to fall[39] or when he tries to describe a problem 'in terms of value theory'.[40] This confusing procedure does not signify a revision of Habermas's revision of Marx. On the contrary it only manifests the deficiency of theoretical reflection which leads to the eclecticism of Habermas's theoretical conception of society. Habermas has made up his own conceptual image of a society, which he calls 'late capitalism' (Spätkapitalismus). This imaginative conception is then illustrated by highly heterogenous research results which he has recently published.

One can summarize his conception of the bourgeois society and its development as follows: just like the theoreticians of state monopoly capitalism, he adopts the phase model of capitalist development as it has been constructed by bourgeois ideology. According to this model, competitive capitalism does not represent merely a theoretical conception, but rather, a real historical phase.[41] According to Habermas, it is distinguished by the unpolitical nature of the relationship of the classes, as well as by a restriction of the state to functions which guarantee only the general – mostly legal – preconditions for the productive process. It was only during this period that explicit economic crises were occurring. Later, these class relations reassumed their political character, which in turn, caused a shift of crises from the economic into the political sphere. The 'power of the liberal-capitalist commodity-fetish' was broken,[42] which ended the anarchy of capitalist development. Now, such anarchy is unleashed, at the most, in a secondary way by administrative mismanagement.

The assessment of the new functions of the state which are supposed to have emerged through the political class relations remains vague and contradictory. Although we are occasionally reminded of the merely reactive character of state activity, the opinion seems to prevail that economic crises can be prevented by state intervention. According to Habermas, the class compromise has enabled the administrative system to develop a constricted capacity for planning.[43] It has now become capable of changing the determinants of the production of surplus value. Hereby, a different kind of crisis is likely to be produced. We no longer have economic crises; now, their place has been taken up by the need to justify the distribution of structurally scarce public budgetary resources. Not only do we have to register an increase in the need for legitimacy, there occurs, as well, an extension of the areas in which legitimacy is necessary. Through their establishment of the political nature of the class conflict, an increasing number of social conflicts are acquiring a political character. At the same time, the privatist mentality is undermined, which, due to successful socialization, had been one of the pillars of bourgeois stability. The destruction of the basic traditional modes of upbringing and socialization exposes even those areas to the need for legitimacy, which, like the cultural tradition and certain educational ideas, could be carried on unquestioned as before.[44]

For Habermas, the change in the typical forms of crises — the shift from economic to legitimatory crises — opens the path to social reform. Any kind of legitimation is dependent on conviction, and Habermas hopes that such conditions will be possible only when true reasons are provided. One could conclude that, according to Habermas, the scholar has the task of promulgating the basic insight that practical questions about norms can be decided by universally accepted reasoning, and that, in a free discourse, those convictions turn out to be sensible and true that are based on universal human interests. In this theoretical context, therefore, social reform consists primarily in creating the conditions for a free discourse.[45] From the assumption that only a policy based on reason can find legitimacy, it follows that only universalized human interests will be asserted. Jürgen Habermas's critical theory aims strategically at social reform. Habermas has gained great merit in explicating the relationship between knowledge and human interest. A whole generation of students, following his intentions, began to ask about the practical relevance of science. What blunts his strategy is not the deficit of political motivation, but rather, the lack of analysis. The whole reformist approach of Habermas's theory is encompassed by a conception of society that omits concrete historical analysis. It is therefore in danger of reflecting very strikingly the views of an institutionalized intellectual.

The strategy is based on the assumption of a growing need for legitimacy. It is claimed that the relationship of classes had previously been unpolitical and that the state's functions were restricted to creating the general conditions of production. (Habermas would only have had to deal with the German example to find out very easily that the state has always been part of the conditions of accumulation and that sometimes it has tried quite systematically to influence them.) The model of competitive capitalism with the corresponding state functions such as it has been conceived by some theories of bourgeois society, did not, even in Great Britain, have much historical reality. It had even less in those nations where systematic state intervention was required as a precondition for the competitive struggle with Great Britain in the world market. It is only by putting the model of a historical phase in the place of real history that one can speak of unpolitical (i.e. exclusively economic) class relations in the liberal capitalist age. The workers probably did not regard it as unpolitical when their strikes and assemblies were threatened and shattered by the police and the military. Surely the stability of bourgeois society rests also on the fictious consciousness of the free work contract and of the neutrality of the state, but more importantly on the brutal compulsion which condemns workers to lose their means of subsistence if they rebel against the existing order. The problem of legitimacy always arises on top of the dominational structure.

According to Habermas, such compulsion has apparently been abolished in the course of capitalist development. It is only thus that the argument that the maintenance of the capitalist system has become dependent on the successful legitimation of governmental policies seems possible. Since this theory fails to take account of the real living conditions of the majority of the people in a way that penetrates the outer appearance of Volkswagen owners, it proves to be the result of a limited academic point of view. According to Habermas, the class compromise is not only the possible result of the economic development and as such is actually pursued in labor union strategies – but it is understood to be its inevitable outcome. It is the essence of what Habermas calls late capitalism (Spätkapitalismus). The tendencies towards concentration did not entail only a monopolist price structure but also a monopolist wage structure. Therefore, the class struggle – at least in the monopolized sector (he does not consider the others) has reached a deadlock.[46] Taking no account of real living conditions of workers, Habermas claims that, in the meantime, 'a level of social wealth has been reached in which the protection against a few fundamental existential risks and the satisfaction of basic needs has no priority anymore.'[47] Evidently, there is no idea of what it means to worry about a job and how difficult the reproduction of a worker's family can be, even under contemporary conditions. Only this social theory's disregard for the analysis of the actual social reality allows the conclusion that the orientation to career attitudes and the great significance ascribed to the wage level have been undermined by the growth of use-value oriented production (especially in the public sector), whereas Habermas could easily have found out that exactly the use-value oriented educational sector proves the contrary. Against the assumption that the stability of the bourgeois social system will depend increasingly on its rational justification, the same could be said of Forsthoff, who maintains that stability can be attained only if the fulfillment of the people's basic needs can be guaranteed.

Habermas has decided beforehand that the management of economical crises *is* possible and that, therefore, the crucial point of stability is the need for legitimacy.

To illustrate his opinion, he adopts the research results of various authors, but, despite the flood of references and notes, he does not discuss the state's real possibilities for intervention in the economic process. Such analysis is not done by pointing to central planning and its problems or by reinterpreting the crisis cycle as a problem of regulation. These questions are not solved by the simple contention that there exists no logical incompatibility between the need for central economic planning and individual economic liberty.[49] Bourgeois research on economic policies as well as Marxist investigation into the concrete problems of state interventionism have shown signs of increasing cautiousness in judging the possibilities of state activity. Habermas does not take account of such findings. This aloofness from a thorough analysis of social reality, however, is apt to blunt enlightened reformist strategy. This is exactly what Habermas intends: with all the force that has ever been part of the European enlightenment, he hopes for the victory of reason. However, he can foster this hope only by giving up analysis and conceiving a fictitious development of society in which the victory of reason is programmed out of necessity. While in the age of bourgeois emancipation, the thinkers of the Enlightenment were still permitted to judge bourgeois society from the partial point of view of their hopes, nowadays only a – possibly painful – scientific investigation into bourgeois society is permitted. Analytical voluntarism does not further the final victory of reason, but rather it destroys the Enlightenment's heritage.

It has already been mentioned that Habermas took over the disparity thesis from Claus Offe. In their fundamental structure, that is, a revision of Marxian theory and the development of a theory of legitimation-crises of late capitalism, their approaches do not differ. A closer look at their works does, however, reveal noteworthy differences. While Habermas is a revisionist by intention who defines emancipation in the scope of the liberal revolutionary tradition, Offe and his co-authors[50] are trying to develop Marxism through connecting it with systems analysis, since, in their opinion, Marxist theory is not capable of analysing the special features of late capitalism.[51] For Offe, Marxism gives the frame for an analysis of society, which takes the inevitable contradictions of capitalist society as its basis.[52] Offe derives those contradictions, as well as the crisis-ridden development of bourgeois society, from the critique of political economy. But, after merging these elements with conceptual elements of systems analysis and sociology of organization, his argument deviates from the context of the critique of political economy. Against his own intentions, Offe is tempted by systems analysis to simulate various possibilities of crises. Despite his much more careful procedure, Offe's thesis of the increasing need for legitimation and of the shift of crises to the periphery of the social system is as much devoid of a thorough historical and a sound theoretical basis as the corresponding theses which Habermas has presented. Instead, these theses seem to be the result of the subordination of some empirical facts under the – critically conceptualized – scheme of systems analysis.

As Volker Ronge has pointed out,[53] this has to be said, as well, about Offe's analysis of state activity. He was one of the leading scholars to develop a theoretical approach which took the conditions of capital accumulation as the frame of state activity while, at the same time, stressing the relevance of an analysis of the organizational structure of the state apparatus.[54] But, after he had stated this approach, Offe does not adhere to it in his work; instead, he focuses almost exclusively on the state apparatus and loosens the connection with the analysis of capitalist development. This holds true despite Offe's attempt to deduce the growing thread of legitimacy crises in late capitalism as having its origins particularly in the change in the employment structure. The fact that a decreasing number of people are employed in the productive sector (and, so, directly in surplus-value production) is misinterpreted in such a way that employees' subjection to capital is diminished and, at the same time, an erosion of the social dominance of the principle of equal exchange is taking place. (The result of the negation of the relevance of value theory for the analysis of late capitalism seems to be its totally distorted application.)

Offe has pointed out the necessity of analysing not only the conditions for state activity but also the concrete origins of state actions. This research strategy implies for him, however, that the capitalist nature of state activity can be found out only ex-post facto.[55] Though criticizing the political science approach, Offe clearly contradicts the basic Marxist assumption that the class character of the bourgeois state is not constituted by its special actions, but rather is embedded in its basic structures: by granting formal equality to all citizens the fundamental inequality, consisting of the coercion of the majority to work for others, is sanctioned by the state's power.

APPROACHES TOWARD THE DEVELOPMENT OF A
HISTORICAL-MATERIALISTIC THEORY OF THE STATE

The development of a critique of bourgeois society going beyond the Frankfurt School coincides with the slowing down of the economic progress that had characterized the twenty years after the end of the Second World War. Since economic progress was no longer a foregone conclusion, economic analysis was again accepted as relevant. As the prevailing social integrationist assumptions lost ground, the theory of the crisis-ridden character of capitalist development no longer seemed as obsolete as it had previously appeared to be. These economic changes have found formal expression in, for example, the Emergency Legislation. The changes of the constitution (Grundgesetz) which were necessary to pass this legislation have initiated a broad disillusionment about the perspectives of a liberal political development in West Germany. Accordingly, the discussion pivoted mainly on the structures of the bourgeois legal and constitutional system.[56]

The decisive impact for the reconstruction and further development of a historical materialistic theory of the state has been created by the development of the theory of state monopoly-capitalism (so-called 'Stamokap'). This official theory of communist parties for the explanation of structures and developmental conditions of the present age was first introduced in West Germany through the works of scholars of the German Democratic Republic[57] and through the so-called Richta

Report.[58] Due to the particular political situation in West Germany, the Communist Party has remained not only politically, but also theoretically dependent on developments in the East. However, discussion about state monopoly capitalism has not been restricted to writings in those countries; on the contrary, it was later much influenced by the theoretical discussion in the French Communist Party.[59]

The approaches to a theory of state monopoly capitalism differ greatly from each other and have undergone considerable changes, due to the partial consideration of critical objections as well as changes in political perspective.[60] Since, in West Germany, this theory has been elaborated only in a very restricted way,[61] we will not deal with it extensively in this paper. Instead, its presentation will be limited to those basic assumptions from which in West Germany the Marxist discussion about state theory has originated.

The theory of state monopoly capitalism starts out by claiming that Marx's analysis contains the basic structures of capitalism, but that, because of the growing process of concentration during the imperialistic phase of capitalism, conditions arose which required that a specific theory be developed to make possible the analysis of this epoch. Following Lenin, the specific nature of the monopolistic phase of capitalism is elaborated and its transformation to state monopoly capitalism is investigated. Two characteristics of this transformation are stressed: increasing state activity, which chiefly pursues the monopolies' interests, and the increasing antagonism between monopolies and small capital. The latter has the effect that the monopolies (as an alliance of big industrial and financial capital together with the state) appear more and more clearly as the actual enemies of 'the people'. The political strategies which have been pursued in the last fifteen years by communist parties rest on this conception of 'the people' as the alliance of all anti-monopolistic forces.

The outline of the early explication of 'Stamokap' is not complete without mentioning two more elements: the theory of the scientific-technological revolution and a refined understanding of the Marxist theory of history. While the theory of historical materialism analyses those conditions which dertermine the historical effectiveness of the possibilities of human behaviour, doctrinal interpretation views historical processes as determined by some kind of 'natural law' of history. The necessity of revolution is deducted from the thesis that the contradictions between the mode of production and the development of productive forces bear the crisis-ridden preconditions for social change. For adherents of the theory of state monopoly capitalism, the acceleration of technological progress in the phase of state monopoly capitalism indicates the growth of the contradictions between the capitalist mode of production and the development of productive forces. Not only does this development further the need for social organization, but also, it brings about the need for a better qualified labor force and, thus, also strengthens revolutionary tendencies. Both aspects are interpreted as signs of the historical transition towards socialism. The communists are to support this transition by pushing the activities of the bourgeois state more and more towards the organization and regulation of the economic progress and by pointing out the evils of monopolies to the anti-monopolistic forces. The conceptions of the inevitable effects of the so-called scientific-technological revolution are sustained by a theory of the state which holds Marx's 'law of the tendential fall of profit rate' to be empirically valid and which conceived state activity as indispensable for the maintenance of capitalist production for profit. In addition, the competition with already existing socialist societies is said to be exacerbating all existing contradictions in capitalist societies

'Stamokap', as the only consistent theory of the historical development of capitalism, influenced left-wing discussion in the sixties to a greater extent than one is often aware. Particularly the discussions about the economies of the education sector received a very strong impulse from the theory of the scientific-technological revolution. (It seemed to sustain the optimism about reforms in the educational sector.)[62] The critical discussion of parts of this theory,[63] as well as of its theoretical foundations, emerged only very slowly.[64]

Though it is not denied that the theory of state monopoly capitalism succeeded in describing certain phenomena of the historical development, its capability to analyse the developmental conditions of historical capitalist formation has been basically questioned. It is argued that Lenin did not comprehend Marx's theory as the abstract analysis of the capitalist formation, but rather, misunderstood it as the analysis of a certain historical phase of capitalism. Lenin's successors are said to have almost completely lost the analytical approach to political economy. This explains how the category of monopoly (comprising economical as well as political factors) could have gained central importance in the theory of state monopoly capitalism. To the critics, it seems impossible to give a satisfactory definition of 'monopoly' which includes more than 'big capital'.

In contrast to the theory of state monopoly capitalism, it is held that the capitalist form of production does not change its nature, and that, thus, the phase theory of capitalism, as put forward by the theory of state monopoly capitalism, remains without theoretical foundation. Consequently, the category of 'the people', comprising all anti-monopolistic forces regardless of class boundaries, loses analytical value. Also, the hopes which were invested in the assumedly transitional character of the phase of state monopoly capitalism are criticized. They are confronted with Marx's concept of formal determination (Formbestimmtheit) which implies that, during the formation of a historical society, all developments are shaped (though not strictly determined) by the way (form) in which production is organized. Far from being the result of a 'natural' historical development[65] necessarily transcending capitalism, technological development can still be conditioned to the particularites of profit-oriented production. The same holds true for the possibilities of state activity. The development towards systematic and planned organization is as overrated[66] as the chance of achieving a revolutionary transformation of society by increasing the influence on the state apparatus. For a factual analysis, it is not enough to point to the alliance or amalgamation of monopolies with the state apparatus. In spite of the theory of monopoly state capitalism, the Marxist theory of the state is said to be still waiting for its elaboration.

Since the critics thought that the greatest mistake of the theory of state monopoly capitalism was to be found in its adherence to the outer appearance of capitalist development, they found it necessary to develop a basic theoretical approach to the analysis of the state before trying to interpret historical changes.

As Marx had not been able to accomplish during his lifetime a developed theory of the bourgeois state, attempts had to be undertaken to reconstruct his theoretical approach from the scattered statements he left and, then, to elaborate his approach. Here, the *explanation* of the bourgeois state plays the crucial role, that is, the proof of the necessity of its existence as an institution set apart from bourgeois society. The discussions of these last years have yielded different ways of explaining the bourgeois state.[67]

One of them tries to develop the necessity of the state out of an analysis of commodity production. Even as regards simple commodity production (but more so in its developed — capitalist-form), it is argued that the social connections between isolated individuals cannot be established without the state. An institutionalized power has to guarantee the modes of exchange, as well as their medium. Law and money are therefore conceived as the starting point for a theory of the state.[68] Blanke Jürgens and Kastendiek, who have most clearly developed this approach, deduce from it a systematic restriction of state activity in bourgeois society. Because of the danger of trespassing the boundaries of this historical social foundation, the state is declared to be restricted to those actions — here regulations of law and money — by which it can influence the accummulation process only through its role as a mediator.[69] The relevance of this approach is due especially to the fact that, while its authors do formulate a basic explanation of the bourgeois state, they do not think it possible to analyse its concrete functions without first analysing the historical development of class struggles and of the accumulation process. With this conception, they set themselves in opposition to another theoretical approach which has become quite influential.

Because of objections to the unhistorical character of certain approaches and to the cutting short, in others, of the relation between state and society, new approaches have recently emerged. These can be characterized briefly as follows: the overall structure of the bourgeois state is to be deduced from the most general theoretical analysis of bourgeois society (in the context of the theory of historical materialism this is called the level of general logic of bourgeois social formation). The state in bourgeois society cannot be explained through its general or specific functions. There has always been some form of dominational organization in society (called 'state' in everyday language) which has exercised certain functions for the existing society. What differentiates the bourgeois state from all previous organizations of social power is the fact that its dominational character is not obvious. The central organization of society is no longer the instrument of openly exercised power for one social group over the other. Instead, it takes on the *form* of a neutral state, of the representative of the whole society. This change in the form of domination is possible because of the reproduction of bourgeois social structures through those structures themselves. The basic causal factor for the possibility — and the necessity — of the neutral appearance of the bourgeois state is created through the capitalist wage system itself. The wage payed to the laborer determines the fact that the buyer of a commodity called the 'capacity to work' can get more out of this commodity than he has to pay for it. (The capacity to work can produce more value than it is worth itself; this makes profit possible in the capitalistic mode of production.) Therefore, the surface (Oberfläche) of bourgeois society can appear to be that of equal commodity exchange. To safeguard the existing system, the state has only to guarantee the (formal) equality of rights for all the members of society. If, however, the state openly appeared as the instrument of domination of one class over the other, the social reproduction of the class structures might not be possible.

The general structure of bourgeois society explains the general form of the bourgeois state as an institution which is set apart from society. In the history of bourgeois societies, this form of the state has always been potentially and actually contradicted through the functions of the state, which arise out of the class struggle and out of the crisis-ridden development of capitalism. Again and again, state actions have been called forth which could not be classified as neutral towards the class struggle, or which were directed to influence the accumulative process in more than merely a general way.

The basically contradictory character of the capitalist mode of production has been analysed by Marx in his law of the tendency of the profit rate to fall. This law states that the profit rate will fall through the growing of the organic composition of capital (i.e. an increase in dead, objectivated, labor – machines, etc. – in relation to living labor – the source of surplus value production). There are, however, countervailing tendencies which can be brought forth in the accumulation process. Most of the Marxist authors cited here are of the opinion that these countervailing tendencies will, in the long run, be unable to counteract the tendency of the profit rate to fall. However, even those who do not share this opinion take the law as the explanation of the basically contradictory character of capitalism and of the fact that the capitalistic mode of production is always anew producing its own barriers. Concrete state action is then explained as being one of the instruments of overcoming such barriers. In this context, much research work is being done in order to analyse the precise connection between crisis and state action.[75] Here, this approach will be illustrated with the thesis put forward by Joachim Hirsch, in which the technological progress itself calls forth growing state interventionism. In the cyclical development of capitalism (which, in its monopolistic phase, can also take on the form of long-term stagnation), there always occurs a time when new possibilities of profit-production can be achieved only through new, more productive forms of production. The process of developing productive resources (brought about through the competitive structure of capitalism and progressing in accordance with the crisis-cycle of capitalism) is said, itself, to produce conditions which, more and more, call forth state action. Private capital does not secure sufficient technological know-how or new research results. Instead, it is increasingly necessary to guide and to further technological progress financially through deliberate state activity. If the tendency of the profit rate to fall is to be counteracted, state intervention must be extended. The basically contradictory character of capitalism is, therefore, more and more openly established in the social production of the preconditions for private capital accumulation.

While such tendencies explain the general development of state action in accordance with the development of capitalism, they do not at the same time give methodological clues for the analysis of specific state actions. In the discussion about the analysis of the state, it has always been stated that state activity – in its general as well as in its specific form – must be seen as the result of those strategies which arise in a certain situation of accumulation (such situations are not to be interpreted in a limited economistic sense). However, only recently this statement of class struggle has gained methodological relevance. In the 'functional' approach, the basic assumption has been that the form and result of class struggle must necessarily be an exact reflection of the economic situation. Implicitly, it had also been assumed that the state is the 'ideal capitalist' in so far as it always takes those actions that, in any given situation, are the best possible for the entire capitalist class (whatever that might be in the monopolistic phase of capitalism). If, however, we conceive state activity as the outcome of specific economic and political strategies, that is, especially those of competition between capitalists and of capital against labor, then we must also admit the possibility that actual state activity does not always totally reflect the objective situation of the accumulation process.[77]

Flatow-Huisken and the so-called AK Group of Munich[70] maintain that the state has to be explained as resulting from the surface, and not the substance of bourgeois society. The individuals in bourgeois society do not deal with each other exclusively as the representatives of economic interests, but rather they come in contact with each other as citizens. The owners of capital and of the commodity of labor pursue opposing interests, although they all receive revenue and therefore – identically – strive for an increase of their revenue. As opposed to the many particular interests that make up the contradictory nature of bourgeois society, the state represents the general interest (of increasing revenue) in bourgeois society. And this representation is set forth not only in the ideology of the bourgeois society, but is also inherent in reality, insofar as the state keeps creating and stabilizing those conditions which maintain the typical bourgeois way of pursuing interests. The state, therefore, must be established as the representative of legitimate power for all citizens, so that an outbreak of violence is prevented and the bourgeois order is secured. The authors of this interpret Marxist analysis as a way in which all developments of bourgeois society can be deduced. They have eliminated the relevance of history from the theory of historical materialism.[71] It may well be supposed that because of this 'logical' understanding of Marxism, they are trapped by historical appearances. The development towards the welfare-state seems to set the background for a theory which makes the hopes which workers as well as the owners of capital set in the state, a constituent element of a Marxist explanation of the state.

Quite another approach has been set forth by Elmar Altvater, Dieter Läpple and others.[72] They set out from an analysis of capitalist production and point to the fact that the competition between single capital does not secure all preconditions for capitalist production. The necessity of the state, therefore, is explained through the function the state fulfills for the accumulation process. These functions will always be shaped by the special conditions that prevail in a certain country at a certain time, but they can be classed according to a few basic functions:

- the implementation of the general prerequisites of production (for instance, infrastructure);
- the creation and guarantee of the bourgeois legal order;
- the regulation of the conflict between wage-labor and capital and, if necessary, the political suppression of the working class by violent repression;
- the guarantee of a nation's ability to compete in world markets.

Objections have been made to this approach, maintaining that it does not explain why an institution which fulfills these functions is set apart from society, nor why the capitalist class does not itself organize the fulfillment of those functions. While most critics specify that such an explanation would be possible only as an outcome of the 'logical' analysis of the bourgeois mode of production, there have lately been attempts to explain the particular form of the bourgeois state as the result of the revolutionary process which established bourgeois society.[73] However, there is another objection which has become increasingly important.

While rightly stressing the relevance of an analysis of the historical development of the relation between the process of accumulation and the functions of the state, the functional approach does not sufficiently take into account that the state actually is an institution set apart from bourgeois society. Though — in the long run — there is always a correlation between the process of accumulation and the development of state activity, the latter cannot be conceived theoretically as a simple correlate of the accumulation process; if it were, the relation between 'base and superstructure' would be unduly simplified. More and more, it is pointed out that the relationship between politics and economics has not yet been clearly worked out[74] either theoretically or empirically.

Along with the subjective factor in history, the administrative system must be taken into account, since public administration constitutes one of the most important intermediaries through which specific economic and political strategies can be pursued in a given society. The administrative system should not be conceived as determining the general content of state actions, but rather, their specific content. Those scholars who have worked to produce a concrete analysis[78] have stressed the relevance of analysing the specific structures of the administrative system. More and more, it is not only the functional connection of state activity with the accumulation process that is pointed out, but also the structural irrationality of public administration. The theoretical relevance of this structural irrationality is still be to analysed. Perhaps this problem will constitute the starting point for the next stage in the development of a historical-materialistic theory of the state.

NOTES

1. Thomas Ellwein, Politische Verhaltenslehre (Stuttgart; 2, 1964).

2. They are known under the name of 'Freiburg-School' since most of them have either taught or studied at Freiburg. The following authors especially are to be noted in this context: Wilhelm Hennis; Politik als Praktische Wissenschaft. Aufsätze zur politischen Theorie und Regierungslehre, (Munich: 1960); Hans Maier, Politische Wissenschaft in Deutschland. Aufsätze zur Lehrtradition und Bildungspraxis (Munich: 1969); Arnold Bergstraesser; Politik in Wissenschaft und Bildung, (Freiburg: 1961); E. Voegelin, Die neue Wissenschaft von der Politik, (Munich: 1959); idem, Wissenschaft, Politik and Gnosis (Munich: 1959); Dieter Oberndörfer, (ed.), Wissenschaftliche Politik (Freiburg: 1962); Kurt Sontheimer, Politische Wissenschaft und Staatsrechtslehre (Freiburg: 1964).

3. Hans-Dieter Bamberg, 'Zu Ernst Forsthoffs Staat der Industriegesellschaft'; in Demokratie und Recht, 1973, 65 ff.; Peter Römer, Vom totalen Staat zur totalen bürgerlichen Gesellschaft in Das Argument, 1970, 322 ff.

4. Ernst Forsthoff, Der Staat der Industriegesellschaft. Dargestellt am Beispiel der Bundesrepublik Deutschland, (Munich: 1971), 105.

5. Op. cit. 58.

6. The category of 'Daseinsvorsorge' was first developed in: Ernst Forsthoff, Verwaltung als Leistungsträger (1938).

7. Ernst Forsthoff, Der Staat der Industriegesellschaft, op. cit., 32.

8. That the state is actually set apart from society and that this separation is not claimed only in bourgeois ideology will be discussed later. Here we deal only with the relevance of the statement in the context of bourgeois ideology.

9. Ernst Forsthoff, Der Staat der Industriegesellschaft, op. cit. 118.

10. Op. cit. 35.

11. ,Op. cit. 121.

12. Niklas Luhmann, 'Moderne Systemtheorie als Form gesamtgesellschaftlicher Analyse'; in: Jürgen Habermas, Niklas Luhmann, Theorie der Gesellschaft oder Sozialtechnologie (Frankfurt: 1971), 9 ff.

13. Otto Hondrich, 'Systemtheorie als Instrument der Gesellschaftsanalyse'; in Soziale Welt, 1972, 3; In this context, Günter Schmid has stressed the analogy to the anthropological theory of Arnold Gehlen: Günter Schmid, Niklas Luhmanns, funktionalstrukturelle Systemtheorie: eine wissenschaftliche Revolution? ; in PVS, 1970, 280 ff.

14. Niklas Luhmann, Politische Verfassungen im Kontext des Gesellschaftssystems, Part I; in: Der Staat, 1973, No. 1, Part II; in: Der Staat, 1973, No. 2.

15. Niklas Luhmann, Soziologische Aufklärung, Aufsätze zur Theorie sozialer Systeme (Cologne Opladen: 1970), 154.

16. Niklas Luhmann, Politische Verfassungen, op. cit., 53.

17. Op. cit., 169.

18. Op. cit., 175.

19. Niklas Luhmann, Soziologische Aufklärung, op. cit., 167.

20. This is elaborated in: Niklas Luhmann: Theorie der Verwaltungswissenschaft (Cologne Berlin: 1966).

21. Niklas Luhmann: Politische Verfassungen, op. cit., 155.

22. Op. cit., 155 f.

23. Op. cit., 176.

24. The writings of Jochimsen, who later became director of the government's planning staff, were particularly widely known: R. Jochimsen, 'Zum Aufbau und Ausbau eines integrierten Aufgabenplanungssystems und Koordinierungssystems der Bundesregierung; in: Bulletin des Presse- und Informationsamtes der Bundesregierung, 16.7.1970, op. cit. The way in which the

general opinion about planning gradually changed is described in: Hans-Joachim Arndt, *Der Plan als Organisationsfigur und die strategische Planung,* PVS, 1968, 177 ff.; about the same problem see also: K. Lompe, *Gesellschaftspolitik und Planung* (Freiburg: 1971).

25. The 'Konzertierte Aktion' is a gremium which was institutionalized in 1967, when the law for economic stability ('Stabilitätsgesetz') was passed. In this gremium, representatives of the federal government, states governments, national bank, labor unions and industrialists' unions meet to work out a concerted economic policy. However, in fact, this gremium has reduced its planning activities to the execution of influence on the labor unions' wage policy. Members of the labor unions, therefore, have developed an increasingly critical attitude towards their unions' cooperation in the 'Konzertierte Aktion'.

26. Dieter Senghaas, *Sozialkybernetik und Herrschaft,* Atomzeitalter, 1967, No. 7/8, 386 ff.

27. Op. cit., 395.

28. Wolf-Dieter Narr/Frieder Naschold, *Einführung in die moderne politische Theorie,* Vol. II: Naschold, *Systemsteuerung* (Stuttgart: 1969), 165 ff.

29. Frieder Naschold, *Zur Politik und Ökonomie von Planungssystemen;* in: Gesellschaftlicher Wandel und politische Innovation. Special issue of: PVS, 1972, 31.

30. Josef Esser, Frieder Naschold, Werner Väth (eds.), *Gesellschaftsplanung in kapitalistischen und sozialistischen Systemen* (Gütersloh: 1972), Editors' Introduction.

31. Frieder Naschold, *Zur Politik und Ökonomie . . .,* op. cit., 32.

32. Op. cit., 38.

33. Frieder Naschold, Werner Väth (eds.) *Politische Planungssysteme* (Opladen: 1973), Editors' Introduction, 61.

34. Frieder Naschold, *Zur Politik und Ökonomie . . .,* op. cit., 43.

35. Op. cit., 39.

36. The actual focus of Habermas's writings is epistemology and general social theory. In the sixties, his works strongly influenced academic youth, who later vehemently criticized his positions and his theoretical approach. A broad discussion of both developments is impossible here.

37. See: Claus Offe, *Politische Herrschaft und Klassenstrukturen. Zur Analyse spätkapitalistischer Gesellschaftssysteme;* in: Gisela Kress, Dieter Senghaas, (eds.) *Politikwissenschaft,* 2 ed., (Frankfurt: 1973), 160; For the general context of Offe's theory, see also: Claus Offe 'Krisen des Krisenmanagements-Elemente einer politischen Krisentheorie; in Martin Jänicke (ed.) *Herrschaft und Krise.* (Opladen: 1973), 197 ff.

38. Jürgen Habermas, *Legitimationsprobleme im Spätkapitalismus,* (Frankfurt: 1973).

39. Op. cit., 49.

40. Op. cit., 80.

41. At one point, he calls it 'a model that expresses the vertex of a very complex historical process' (op. cit., 37). The concept 'vertex' could mean anything from Max Weber's ideal type to a systematic abstraction. In his presentation, Habermas deals with his model as if it were a description of reality.

42. Habermas adds, 'meanwhile, everybody involved practises more or less the theory of value'. Here, the utter confusion of Habermas's arguments becomes obvious. If his statement were right, he could not, at another point, resort to the theory of the tendency of the profit rate to fall or to presuppositions of surplus value production. The central content of value theory is the analysis of those structures which are effective in capitalism without the awareness of the agents involved (they are established 'behind the backs' of the economic agents and even against their explicit intentions). What can be consciously practised in capitalism is the struggle for higher wages and higher profits, but not value theory.

43. Op. cit., 87.

44. As an example: Habermas presents the need to legitimize curricula in the educational system. One wonders if he does not succumb to the views of the ideology of participation. Who presents this demand for legitimacy and who articulates? What is endangered, if the legitimation fails? At the most, according to West German experience, a governing party's re-election is

influenced.

45. Some years ago, ideas for political action to establish such a situation were presented, and gained considerable influence among Social Democrats. Habermas confronts the so-called decisionist model of expert advice in politics (which leaves the decision and the responsibility to the experts). The latter is a model of public advice which develops strategic recommendations in the context of a public discussion. The movement for greater participation in politics has frequently and with good reasons resorted to Habermas's writings as its theoretical foundation.

46. Habermas takes this argument – as do quite a few others – from O'Connor. However, he forgets to mention that O'Connor formulates his argument much more cautiously and is talking only about the USA; James O'Connor, *The Fiscal Crisis of the State* (New York: 1973).

47. The general course of Habermas's revision of Marx cannot be discussed here. The book used here gives quite a few examples of the fact that Habermas always criticizes what he thinks is Marx's position, although that which he takes to be Marx's position cannot be found in the writings of Marx. (For instance, when he claims that Marx did not take into account the relevance of science for the development of productive powers.) Op. cit., 87.

48. Op. cit., 116.

49. Op. cit., 92.

50. R. Funke and C. Offe and V. Ronge, *Formwandel der Politikformulierung und delegitimatorische Prozesse*, Manuscript (Starnberg: 1973).

51. Claus Offe, *Strukturprobleme des kapitalistischen Staates. Aufsätze zur politischen Soziologie* (Frankfurt: 1972), 8.

52. Op. cit., 21.

53. Volker Ronge, 'Der "politökonomische Ansatz" in der Verwaltungsforschung; in Peter Grottian and Axel Murswieck (eds.), *Handlungsspielräume der Staatsadministration* (Hamburg: 1974), 90; Ronge, however, can save the political-economic analysis of the administrative system only by reducing Marxism to the 'type of an interpretative theory'. If historical materialism were not capable of analysis, but only of interpretation, it really should be given up.

54. In the meantime, this approach has been worked out by quite a few scholars. (References follow later in this paper.)

55. Claus Offe, *Strukturprobleme*, Op. cit., 90.

56. This phase is especially represented in the following works: Otto Kirchheimer, *Politische Herrschaft* (Frankfurt: 1967); Franz Neumann, *Demokratischer und autoritärer Staat* (Frankfurt: 1967), (this is the translation of the 1957 New York edition and is mentioned here because of its noteworthy influence on the discussion in West Germany); Wolfgang Abendroth, *Antagonistische Gesellschaft und politische Demokratie,* (Neuwied Berlin: 1967); Jürgen Seifert, *Der Notstandsausschuß* (Frankfurt: 1968); Johannes Agnoli and Peter Brückner, *Die Transformation der Demokratie* (Berlin: 1967).

57. *Imperialismus heute. Der staatsmonopolistische Kapitalismus in Westdeutschland.* Institut für Gesellschaftswissenschaften beim ZK der SED (Berlin (East): 1965).

58. R. Richta et al, *Politische Ökonomie des 20. Jahrhunderts* (Prague: 1968).

59. *Le Capitalisme Monopoliste d'état* (Paris: 1971).

60. A first sketch of the connection between theoretical development and political strategy in 'Stamokap' is found in: Werner Petrowsky, *Zur Entwicklung der Theorie des staatsmonopolistischen Kapitalismus;* Prokla, 1, 1971, 129 ff.; see also: Rolf Ebbighausen and Peter Kirschhoff, 'Zum Historisch-politischen Hintergrund der Theorie des staatsmonopolistischen Kapitalismus: Kommunistische Einheitsfront- und Bündnispolitik vor und nach dem zweiten Weltkrieg'; in: Rolf Ebbighausen, (ed.), *Monopol und Staat* (Frankfurt: 1974), 293 ff.

61. As exemption to this rule can be mentioned: Robert Katzenstein *Zur Theorie des staatsmonopolistischen Kapitalismus:* Prokla, No. 8/9, 1973, 1 ff.; Jörg Huffschmid, *Begründung und Bedeutung des Monopolbegriffs in der marxistischen Ökonomie,* manuscript (Bremen: 1974).

62. This has been expressed to some extent in: E. Altvater, F. Huisken, *Materialien zur*

politischen Ökonomie des Ausbildungssektors, (Erlangen: 1971); Joachim Hirsch, *Wissenschaftlich-technischer Fortschritt und politisches System,* (Frankfurt: 1970).

63. Martin Baethge, *Abschied von den Bildungsillusionen;* Betrifft Erziehung, No. 11, 1972, 19 ff.

64. In this context, the following writings were especially influential: Margareth Wirth, *Kapitalismustheorie in der DDR,* (Frankfurt: 1972); eadem, Zur Kritik der Theorie des staatsmonopolistischen Kapitalismus, Prokla, No. 8/9, 1973, 25 ff; Christel Neusüß, *Imperialismus und Weltmarktbewegung des Kapitals* (Erlangen: 1972); Projekt Klassenanalyse *Leninismus – neue Stufe des wissenschaftliche Sozialismus?* (Berlin (West): 1972); Rolf Ebbighausen, (ed.) *Monopol und Staat* (Frankfurt: 1974).

65. Here, the exactly identical conception of Habermas should be called to mind.

66. See: Volker Ronge and Günter Schmieg, *Restriktionen politischer Planung* (Frankfurt: 1973). These authors have worked out the structural restrictions of the state apparatus to planning. They have stressed particularly the point that the state apparatus is not capable of gaining an exact knowledge of the accumulative situation.

67. The first to have tried this were: Wolfgang Müller and Christel Neusüss; Die Sozialstaatsillusion und der Widerspruch von Lohnarbeit und Kapital. Prokla. Special Issue No 1, (Berlin: 1972), 59.

68. B. Blanke and U. Jürgens and H. Kastendiek, *Zur neueren marxistischen Diskussion über die Analyse von Form und Funktion des bürgerlichen Staates. Überlegungen zum Verhältnis von Politik und Ökonomie;* Prokla., No. 14/15, 1974, 51 ff.

69. Op. cit., 81.

70. Resultate der Arbeitskonferenz, No. 1, 1974, 47 ff.; Sybille von Flatow and Freerk Huisken, *Zum Problem der Ableitung des bürgerlichen Staates;* Prokla, No. 7, 1973, 83 ff.; Projekt Klassenanalyse, *Oberfläche und Staat* (Berlin: 1974).

71. For a critical statement see: Helmut Reichelt, Einige Anmerkungen zu Sybille von Flatows und Freerk Huiskens Aufsatz zum Problem der Ableitung des bürgerlichen Staates; in: *Gesellschaft. Beiträge zur Marxschen Theorie.* I, (Frankfurt: 1974), 12 ff.

72. Elmar Altvater, *Thesen zum Staatsinterventionismus,* Prokla, No. 3, 1973, 1 ff.; Dieter Läpple, *Staat und allgemeine Produktionsbedingungen. Grundlage zur Kritik der Infrastrukturtheorien,* (Berlin: 1973).

73. Ulrich K. Preuß, *Legalität und Pluralismus* (Frankfurt: 1973); Hunno Hochberger, 'Probleme einer materialistischen Bestimmung des Staates', in: *Gesellschaft. Beiträge zur Marxschen Theorie.* II (Frankfurt: 1974), 155 ff.

74. Heide Gerstenberger, 'Klassenantagonismus, Konkurrenz und Staatsfunktionen'; in *Gesellschaft. Beiträge zur Marxschen Theorie,* III (Frankfurt: 1975), 5 ff.

75. See especially: Joachim Hirsch, *Staatsapparat und Reproduktion des Kapitals* (Frankfurt: 1974), 252 ff. (since this work sums up the endeavours Hirsch has made in state-analysis, his previous writings are not cited here).

76. See, for example: Elmar Altvater, op. cit., part IV (crisis-regulation), Gudrun Lindner, *Die Krise als Steuerungsmittel;* Lev., No. 3, 1973, 342 ff.

77. This has been pointed out by the AK, op. cit., Joachim Hirsch, op. cit., Heide Gerstenberger, op. cit.

78. Hirsch, op. cit.; Peter Grottian and Axel Murswieck, (eds), *Handlungsspielräume der Staatsadministration* (all the essays in this book deal with the problem of determining the possible range of state activities).

Development and Present Situation of GDR Research in the Federal Republic of Germany

Clemens Burrichter and Eckart Förtsch

THE SCIENTIFIC INTEREST IN THE POLITICAL and social system of the GDR is governed by the same conditions as science and research in general: it has its roots in a constantly changing social and political environment from which the interest directing the research (*Worterkenntnisleitendes Interesse*) is stimulated. We have structured the following analysis in historical sequence because the present state of this research becomes apparent only when seen in the perspective of its development. A retrospective of this type shows the special complexity of GDR research with regard to society and policy, and certainly does not involve a loss of scientific autonomy. On the contrary, the interdependence of science and history reaches a balance in the momentary historical situation. This proportion, which applies to the relation of science and society in general, has to be even more differentiated in view of the specific type of this research. It is only then that our judgement on its development as well as our conclusions regarding the present situation and its perspectives become intelligible. That is why we want to examine GDR research under four separate but interdependent perspectives.

a. Our reflections on the basis of the theory of cognition begin at a point where science is understood, although still very abstractly, as an activity (in the sense of producing innovation) which has as its purpose the solution of specific problems. (This functional definition of science is accepted even by representatives of the most controversial positions on the theory of cognition.) We proceed on the assumption that problems have emerged from the division of Germany into two parts and two different social systems; these provoked scientific attention, although it was expected that any problems would be solved mainly by political decisions. Hence, the relationship of GDR research to policy — especially the 'Deutschlands-politik' — has to be analysed starting with these aspects.

b. Despite the distinct affinity of GDR research towards the actual 'Deutschland-politik', the analysis cannot be restricted to this field of external factors of influence. After all, the problematic nature of the division of Germany existed and exists not only in the political field. The society, or, as present developments indicate will be the case in the future, the two German societies, should be seen served as the potential focus of the results of this research, irrespective of whether individual members are concerned either consciously or unconsciously. This means that the relationship of GDR research to the society of the FRG must also be taken into consideration.

c. Furthermore, GDR research is confronted with an object of cognition whose actual situation and political and social change influences the process of cognition indirectly and directly. (Besides this, the GDR's reaction toward the research which deals with its own system is both sensitive and delicate; this as well might have its influence on the process of cognition.) Therefore, the relations of GDR research to its analytical object have to be included in the analysis. It has to be taken into account that this concerns a politically founded and structured object, with which scientists in the FRG are confronted politically and ideologically as well as scientifically.

d. Finally, it should not be neglected that GDR research as a part of the scientific system relates in a general way to the development of science as a whole, as well as being concerned with itself as a single discipline. Therefore it receives impulses and restrictions from very different sources.

Through the examination of these questions, our presentation of the development of GDR research is structured in a very general and not always systematic manner. These aspects are employed especially when it is necessary to analyse the present situation and the perspectives of development (In Section V). This way of proceeding is helpful since those aspects which we have mentioned in way of an introduction have only from time to time been consciously and systematically used and reflected in GDR research itself. Generally in the GDR, research objects have been chosen and judgements formed in an unreflected and undirected manner, especially in works concerning relations between GDR research and policy; with a certain naiveté, GDR researchers have sometimes also ignored and denied these perspectives.

We want to distinguish between three stages of development in GDR research. Especially 'deutschlandpolitische' [domestic German political] actions, or, as the case may be, GDR internal actions of relevance to Deutschlandpolitik — actions which have to be seen in light of their effect throughout the world — serve us as criteria for classification. (We ourselves can show the momentary strategic marginal conditions only to a very limited degree.) Although we classify with respect to external criteria only, we do not want to deny the existence and significance of a change of paradigm which is inherent in research. The stages are the following:

1. From the foundation of the two German states in 1949 to the beginning of the stage of consolidation of the GDR in 1961/62, and, simultaneously, to the termination of the third and last stage of the "cold war" after the Cuba-crisis in 1962;[1]
2. From the beginning of the stage of stabilization in the GDR to the beginning of the enforcement of the new East and German politics (Ost- und Deutschland-

politik) in the FRG with the formation of the social-liberal coalition in 1969;
3. The phase of 'German coexistence' (Egon Bahr) since 1969/70.

During these phases, the image that GDR research had of itself changed, especially with regard to its functions, the interest directing its course of research and its methodological instruments. Therefore it is hard to distinguish whether and when there are impulses from outside or from inside, i.e. from individual scientists. It need not be stressed that our presentation aims only at a general outline.

II

The first phase is characterized by the establishment and formation of the two different social systems in Germany. The West Germans have been confronted in the GDR with a system which manifested and realized a completely different understanding of property, political democracy, human rights, social relations, etc. This system has increasingly been perceived and classified as strange; this alienation has been intensified since the massive class warfare in the GDR aggravated the antagonism and since their repressive policy forced the number of refugees to new records.

Additionally, there was a contrast in economic and living standards; the economic advancement in the FRG showed up the gap between the GDR and the FRG very clearly. Moreover, this advancement was accompanied by an almost general acknowledgement of the parliamentary-democratic system. Their own prosperous system was not called into question politically or economically by most scientists in the FRG. The stronger the GDR presented itself, experimenting, being at the stage of class warfare, and having its existence as a political system denied by the population in the East and West, the more the GDR functioned as a negative object toward integration attempts. The dominating political understanding of government and opposition led as well to the shattering of such attempts since most Germans in the FRG considered the GDR a transitory state, a passing episode. Preconditions for an early 'reunification in peace and freedom' (understood as a union of the GDR with the FRG and her system) were to be created by integration of the FRG into the West and by a 'policy of strength' towards the Soviet block and the USSR. For the Federal Government, which considered itself the agent of the interests of the GDR population on the national and international scene, the USSR, as a victorious occupying force, was the natural aim for material on the policy of reunification. The GDR was ignored as a state, isolated in the international scene and condemned politically and morally; it was looked upon as a 'Western Province of Moscow', shaken by crises, one of which, it was supposed, would put an end to the system. The social, economic and political system as it developed in the GDR seemed singular and unstable at the same time. This double approach influenced the early GDR research, which had in part been sponsored by FRG policy. The research concerned fundamentals of the new sovereignty and social system, although – as for instance in the acitivities of the Research Advisory Board (Forschungsbeirat)[2] – it inquired first of all into the spheres of life of the GDR which were aiming at a change in GDR relations towards the system of the FRG. The singularity of the observed developments and structures was analytically integrated as simply totalitarianism – theory and a specific anti-communism which affirmed the conditions in the FRG.

The theory of totalitarianism, taken from American communism research,[3] presented a plausible model of interpretation for the GDR system, which was understood as being a system of an entirely different kind. However, as early as the fifties, this theory was put into question: while many researchers – and, to a certain degree, also political lecturers and journalists – still held on to C. J. Friedrich's theory of totalitarianism (concerning the political superstructure), M. Drath started his theory of totalitarianism from the system of standards in the society and thus widened the possibilities for its utilization.[4] Likewise, anti-communism gradually came to appear as a stable framework for judging the system in the GDR. This was first confirmed by the events in the GDR and the development in the FRG. However, anti-communism included also solidarity with the people afflicted by the social revolution in the GDR – and those were not only members of the "exploiting class" .– which meant a dominating attitude of resistance in the GDR. This attitude in the FRG had not in the least been confirmed by the refugees; meanwhile, increasingly differentiated reports became known, which contributed, although only step by step, towards a more exact judgement about the GDR. It should not be overlooked that scientific research, as well as the interested public, was dependent on reports based on experience of all kinds, because a direct way to the object of research was blocked. Reports[5] which had authenticity thus supplied material for explanation and filled information gaps. In this situation, the scientific analysis of the GDR was dependent particularly on those who knew this social system through their own experience. The other scientists in the FRG and West Berlin used these reports from inside, as well as information from refugees and specific kinds of 'participant observation'. All of these were acknowledged over a long period of time as important sources of information, and they had the function of forming the opinion of the general public and of serving as an empirical basis for analysis during the early GDR research.

The most important center of scientific research about the GDR during this stage was the Institut für Politische Wissenschaft at the Free University of Berlin, which was headed by Prof. Otto Stammer, who himself made remarkable contributions to the totalitarianism model and GDR research. Already in the 1950s, studies concerning the political and social system which effectively influenced GDR research were being made in this institute. These were mainly analyses of the emergence of a new intelligentsia,[6] the system of science and education,[7] the Sozialistische Einheitspartei Deutschlands [SED],[8] agitation and propaganda[9] and the proportion of party and state apparatus in the GDR.[10] These works made use of the theory of totalitarianism in a differentiated way and, mostly, without emotional overtones. They remain impressive today because of the wealth of sources, the outstanding treatment, and the attempt to understand the fundamentals of the GDR system per se – which was seen as an ideologically and politically motivated revolutionary system – as an adoption of Soviet models.

These works and others[11] took note of specific aspects of the control and socialization system, which they presented historically and systematically. Thus they made an important contribution to the analysis of Marxism-Leninism as a control ideology long before a specialized discussion about the communist theory or concepts of society took place in the FRG.

A second field of GDR research at this stage was the investigation of the economic system and economic policy. For this purpose, the 'theory of the central administrative economy' (Theorie der Zentralverwaltungs wirtschaft) had been developed[12] and was applied to the economic system and economic policy of the GDR (revolution of the conditions of property, change to long-term planning, structures of planning, problems of reparation, new foreign-trade relations). Also, special investigations of single economic branches were published.[13] Using the theory of the central administrative economy, it was possible to comprehend the new structures and methods of controlling the economy; mistakes, misproportions, imperfections in planning etc., could be reduced to causes which were immanent to the system. In this way, real problems of industrial growth were indeed pushed to the periphery of interest and judgement.[14]

A great number of surveys, chronicles, and reference-books were distributed during the first (and second) stage by the 'Bundesministerium für gesamtdeutsche Fragen'.[15] Besides scientific circles, a wide public (journalism, schools, adult political education) made use of those materials and of current Fachberichte [professional reports] and press digests. With the *SBZ Archiv*[16] GDR research received a special journal for articles, comments, reviews, documentations and continuous chronicles which was, to begin with, predominantly journalistic and later increasingly scientific. The first surveys about the GDR, as well as the first analyses of the development of the German problem, were published[18] in the *SBZ Archiv*.

Later, this first stage of GDR research was viewed critically by Peter Ludz:

Although without reflecting ill intentions, the presence of a tendency towards black and white painting is undeniable. Often, the political and social conditions in the FRG and the liberal system of society and law in the West were juxtaposed with the totalitarian system of terror, the ordered and controlled economy, the state of injustice. Combined with this type of comparison, there was, indeed, also the tendency to describe the control technique of the SED towards party, state and economy, but at the same time to neglect to take into consideration the dynamic nature of the society and the effect of the society on the control system. Very often, the structure of the control system and the axioms and principles of Marxist-Leninist ideology were compared and, thus, devalued uncritically with the "West" or with the conditions in the FRG. This thinking corresponded not only to a preference to idealize the conditions in the FRG, but also to the intention of propagating a definite political-ideological idea of the reunification: the political and social system in the GDR was to be integrated into the FRG at 'X-Hour'.[19]

This judgement on GDR research during the first stage is, on the whole, appropriate, all the more so as Ludz reduces the described methods of proceeding and the judgements on the research to the oppressive character of numerous actions by the GDR leadership as well as to the official hopes of reunification in the FRG.

Today, after a longer time interval, it is possible to offer another attempt at explanation. It must be taken into consideration that there was then a deep-ranging process of insecurity which, in the consciousness of the population, was due to the establishment of such a radically different model of society and to its rigid methods of establishment. Confronted with something new which developed under pressure and whose outline was not yet visible, bourgeois intellectuals in the West as well as in the GDR — and not only they — reacted with a lack of understanding and with rejection.

Additionally, the official policy of the FRG aimed at the abolition of the GDR. Further, the GDR research work did not want to attribute to its object more stability than it had at this time. Thus, in the relationship between Deutschland-politik and GDR research, the affirmative function of this research dominated; a critical function towards German political thinking and acting was not yet apparent. Latent and cyclic crises in the Eastern block (for instance, 1952 or 1956) seemed to support the opinion of those who thought of the socialist system as being unable to survive, especially on account of its undemocratic character. GDR research, at that time without this name and mostly without a reflected interest of cognition, performed its analysis in order "to judge, and sometimes also to condemn".[20] Whatever one may think about it, GDR research during this stage did not remain in an ivory tower of scientific autonomy; on the contrary, it was connected to the political and social systems and developments in the FRG as well as in the GDR. One can only make the reproach that it paid more attention to programmatic concepts of the GDR and specific political actions than to the beginnings of social change in GDR society.

III

In the second phase, a quantitative and qualitative progress of research and output was recorded. In building the Wall, the GDR showed — to the Germans of the FRG and foreign countries — that this state was preparing itself for a long term; one could no longer consider the GDR as a short term transitional stage. After the total collectivization of the agriculture (Vollkollektivierung der Landwirtschaft) in 1960 and the building of the Wall, the 'victory of the socialist way of production' [Sieg der sozialistischen Produktionsverhältnisse] was announced; this was the precondition for the introduction of economic and social reforms. These reforms — the 'new economic system' — were observed with interest in Western Germany, as, parallel with the introduction of this new system, the international position of the GDR improved. Under these conditions, the official and semi-official hopes for reunification were gradually replaced by an acceptance of the status quo; at this time, signs of an international policy of detente became apparent in the FRG. Moreover, recession, student revolts and other events in the 1960s allowed the importance of questions of the reunification to recede into the background, especially after the SED-leadership withdrew its attempt for a dialogue with the SPD in 1966 and started a policy of delimitation [Abgrenzungspolitik]. The increasing politization of the general public in the FRG brought about the consequence that their own social and political system was called into question. Thus this system could no longer be the obvious stable framework for a judgement about the GDR. And finally, with the foundation of the Great Coalition (1966), the Ostpolitik of the FRG started to change; recognition of the GDR has, since then, been discussed more and more. Against the background of political change, a gradual change of paradigm in GDR research took place. It was initiated especially by Peter Christian Ludz, who — in the discussion of the theory of totalitarianism — developed new theoretical concepts of the analysis and introduced them into the scientific debate. Ludz designated the social change, the deviation in the execution of sanctions, the dynamics of social development, the social and political conflicts and similar processes in the GDR with his theory of a 'consultative authoritarianism' [konsultativer Autoritarismus]. At the same time, he presented general uses of empirical methods of research for the GDR and the SED; through his work, interest in methodological questions of GDR research was stimulated.

Nevertheless, during this stage theoretical and social science oriented research existed side by side with descriptive phenomenological studies as well as with research which still used the theory of totalitarianism. Very often, all directions of research laid claim to the same methodological demand, that is, the comprehension of the GDR system based on its own image of itself, its own conditions. This demand was a main element in progress towards the first stage: it made possible seeing the GDR as a self-reliant model of society, and not so much as a radical deviation from an idealized model of democracy. More and more, sections of the social and political system of the GDR became objects of the analysis. A central part of analysis was still the economic system. Besides comprehensive works about the structures of the economic system and economic-political processes,[22] analyses were published which dealt with specific economic and social problems,[23] as well as numerous further reports edited by the 'Gesamtdeutsches Ministerium' and a very great number of articles in periodicals. In GDR research dealing with political science and jurisprudence, standard works have been published, especially about constitutional and economic law.[24] Concerning the SED, analyses on individual and on joint aspects[25] were published; some scientists researched the bourgeois parties and the 'mass organizations' in the GDR.[26] There were investigations of policy towards science, universities, education and culture,[27] among them the first attempt at a comparative analysis of science and research in the two German states.[28] Studies on the whole of the GDR's-development[29] as well as reports based on experience by individual politicians[30] rounded off the heterogenous literature. The wealth of German political analyses cannot be covered even in summary; in addition to this, there exist numerous, mostly unpublished dissertations and masters' theses.

The discussion about aims and methods of GDR research — a discussion which has been held between the scientists as well as with individual politicians — proceeded in relation to the quantitative increase and the qualitative progress of the research. The result of these discussions were some structural changes: the *SBZ-Archiv* was remodelled into a representative specialist periodical and its name changed to *Deutschland Archiv*, in 1968.[31] Since then annual informative conferences have been held where GDR researchers, journalists and also some politicians meet. More important was the establishment of structures for communication and reflection about the self-awareness of GDR research. It seemed that GDR research, which had begun spontaneously through the initiative of individual researchers, had developed without a direct political programme and without having a directed choice of object, or framework of evaluation. Now, the necessity of coordinating the individual centres of research has been recognized, but before this could happen, functions and structures had to be clarified generally. The first meeting of GDR researchers in Tutzing in September 1967[32] was representative of this discussion: it was a meeting initiated by Ernst Richert, who was at that time the most important of the GDR researchers. The actual political situation after the foundation of the great coalition in the Federal Republic dominated the discussions which, since then, have been carried on in the *Deutschland Archiv.*

The 'long-range objective of reestablishment of a united Germany' in the 'Deutschlandpolitik' of the Federal Government had been supplemented by the medium-term aim of a 'Well-conducted "Nebeneinander" [co-existence] and, if possible, by a "Miteinander" [co-operation] of both parts of Germany'. This concept requires 'objective information and scientific research about conditions in the other part of Germany' – a way of thinking which implies that the Federal Government still speaks for the population of the GDR.[33] Whereas some GDR researchers interpreted this policy as giving support to the need for change in the GDR – for instance enabling the SED to communicate within the German area[34] or 'offering proposals for a solution, addressed to the GDR' (under the premise that, in both states, 'it is possible to learn from each other')[35] – others wanted a strict abstinence in matters of politics.[36] Ludz, however, (who had stated that 'aims formulated by policy are to be given to the research in advance') – formulated the following as tasks for GDR research: 1. *Information* for science itself, for policy and for the general public; 2. *Presentation* of forecasts and of analyses 'which consider closely the dynamic of power, economy and society in the other part of Germany'; 3. *Comparative research* (East-West comparison and East-East comparison); 4. *Contribution* to the relaxation of taboos and to political decisions being non-ideological and rational.[37]

It was in such definitions of function and position[38] – the criteria of which had to be sought in theory as well as in the postulated relationship to policy – that the spectrum of approaches during the second stage was to be found. The different reactions to the change in object and in conditions of the researchers which, in any case, had been imposed essentially by the parent disciplines were a result – a reflex of the 'inter-social conflict and competition situation' between the German states,[39] which, however, had not been carried through to effect the reflection and disclosure of the single knowledge-guiding interest. However, a minimum agreement was seen as one aim: 'Presentation and careful consideration of social experiments in the GDR which could be of interest for the society and, thus, for the policy of the FRG'.[40] Such a demand was to be fulfilled in the field of social studies and by scientific discussion rather than in the field of politics, in which (in practice) information relevant and helpful for decision-making was almost never sought.

The products and discussions of GDR research had, of course, an echo in the GDR itself. There, the analyses and criticisms of GDR research in the FRG are, in general, specialized and professionally managed. Definite differences can be noticed: for instance, in regard to the proportions (the 'imperialism research' in the GDR which concentrates on the FRG is much better provided with staff and more concentrated than West German GDR research), in regard to theory (the research on 'imperialism' is provided with uniform theories and methods), in the area of policy (its function is to help in decision-making), in the system of classification (the research on 'imperialism' approaches its object more critically than does the GDR research its object), and in regard to certain other aspects. Having taken the relationship between science and policy which is used in the GDR as a basis for transfering to the FRG and GDR research, the judgements during the second stage followed definite basic patterns.[41] One easily recognizes in these basic patterns and in the concrete judgements the model of a political and social system which is completely different from our conception. GDR analysts of GDR research saw as the most important and general tasks of the West German GDR research the following:

1. to give the Federal Government help in decision-making for a policy of 'Transition from open to clandestine counterrevolution'[42]
2. to contribute to an 'ideological infiltration' of the GDR[43]
3. To help isolate the GDR from her alliance partners and to divide the Soviet block[44]
4. to manipulate the GDR image held by the West-German general public and to prevent propagation of a 'positive-realistic GDR image'.[45]

Almost all GDR researchers and all research results were seen quite summarily and undifferentiated in regard to these tasks. They were reproached with 'fighting against' the GDR, with searching for ways and methods to influence the GDR population in the context of psychological warfare.[47] Further, the GDR researchers were accused of trying to divide party and population, GDR and Soviet Union, economic rationality and socialist economy, basis and superstructure. These examples are representative of the judgements about GDR research published in the GDR at the end of the second stage. At present, there is a tendency to make more differentiated judgements. However, during all stages, there predominated in the GDR (and still predominates) a critical view of the GDR research, which ranged (and still ranges) from political principles and categories to the classification of scientific intentions and contributions. Thus the differentiations are dependent less on the submitted scientific analysis itself, less on its scientific stringency and quality than on the political strategy of the GDR leadership.

IV

The present stage of GDR research is politically defined by the situation which has been created by the SPD and FDP Governments — established in 1969 and 1972 — in regard to the Eastern and German Policy agreements with the USSR, Poland and Czechoslovakia, the Transit Agreement with the GDR on the basis of the Berlin Agreement, the 'Grundvertrag' with the GDR as well as successive agreements, and the admission of the two Germanies to the UN. The policy proceeds on the assumption of a long-term co-existence of the two German states; for the general public of the FRG also, this premise obviously is dominant. In the GDR, where the policy of delimitation is being continued in regard to contacts with the population, the change of leadership from Ulbricht to Honecker (1971) demonstrated the stability of the political leadership. In addition, there is a continuity of the 'Deutschlandpolitik' of the SED. In fulfilment of the Grundvertrag, journalists of the FRG have been accredited in East Berlin. Visits of FRG citizens to the GDR are on the increase; thus, there are additional possibilities of information. Moreover, works by social scientists of the GDR during the last years give more well-grounded information concerning GDR society than did those of several years ago.

GDR research during this stage is discussing the problem of its functions. These discussions, individual works, and the dissolution of the 'Forschungsbeirat für Fragen der Wiedervereinigung Deutschlands' in 1974 — which was replaced by an 'Arbeitskreis für vergleichende Deutschlandforschung'[48] established by the Bundesminister für innerdeutsche Beziehungen (Federal Minister for Domestic Relations) — meet with public interest. However, this is still insufficiently outlined and, therefore, without much influence on the discussion in GDR research.

During the present stage, the following internal developments in the science are characteristic for GDR research which is compelled to work with changed political conditions:

1. *The interest directing the research* of most analysts of the GDR is concentrated on the relationship between social change and stabilization of the government in the GDR. 'The western scientist nowadays does not in his daily analysis call into question the whole political and economic system of the GDR. He supplies information about the situation, perhaps gives advice which fits into the system, but he does not abolish it with his proposals'.[49]

2. *A stronger, although sometimes still quite diffused, public interest* about the GDR — which is stimulated just as much by the German political actions and discussions as it is by socio-political discussions at the universities, schools and in the mass-media of the FRG — corresponds to a further quantitative increase of the output of GDR research. Many of these studies go more and more beyond a pure description, guided by different theoretical and political extensions. This is true of surveys[50] as well as of analyses of single fields of life.

3. *New fields are made accessible* through the analysis of GDR society. A great number of analyses are published on the following fields:

science policy, system of science[51] and the development of single sciences.[52] With this focus, the new role that science and technique have acquired in the

GDR during the 'scientific-technical revolution' is taken into consideration.

comparison of single areas of life in the two German States[53] (political system, law, economy, social system, educational system, social groups and organizations, etc.). In some of these studies — even without a methodology of comparison — the two German industrial societies are analysed and confronted with each other in regard to common or analogous areas of problems and their specific solutions.

the attitude of single social groups, empirical analyses of workers, or young people, for instance, as much as literary analyses of problems of conscience;[54]

culture, art and literature; these include anthologies, surveys, individual analyses and documentations, which deal particularly with literature and investigate its development against the background of the cultural policy of the SED.[55]

4. As in the preceding stage and *corresponding with the structure of the object of cognition* — the GDR — analyses of the economy,[56] the system of constitution, law,[57] and forms of government[58] are furthermore a central field of the research, including special analyses of education (including adult education, military education, political education) and family.[59]

5. Alongside the 'established' GDR research, which we have been preoccupied with up to now, there appeared a *special branch of research*. This is directed by scientists who consider themselves Marxists or socialists and who analyse the GDR, especially the economic system, in this light.

They use Marxian categories and methods without having to adopt the interpretation and utilization of Marxism-Leninism in the GDR or that of the SED (and the 'Deutsche Kommunistische Partei' in the FRG).[60]

V

An analysis of the present situation of GDR research is confronted with two fundamental difficulties: the changing self-conception of GDR-research is still recognizable only in outline and a clarifying process in the discussion is still going on. On the other hand, an analysis at this time — so close to the event — will be subject to all imperfections and doubts which characterize such works generally and remind the reader of the necessity of reading critically. Nevertheless, we also consider such an attempt necessary and legitimate, if justice is to be done in an inventory of GDR research.

In the middle of 1973, the editorial staff of the periodical *'Deutschland Archiv'* initiated a discussion about GDR-research with the following introductory argument:

The new situation in the relations between the two German states after the signing of the Grundvertrag allowed the question of tasks, aims and organization to become again a point of immediate interest for GDR-research.[61]

During the following months, about 20 scientists, politicians and specialized journalists took part in this discussion, which stressed the necessity of defining the problem. The definition of the function of GDR research is nowhere near being settled under the changing conditions of the German political scene.[62]

First of all, it seems necessary to investigate the motives of discussions about GDR research in regard to new problems which have come up. It is obvious that there is a causal connexion between the signing of the 'Grundvertrag' and the status of uncertainty, which, of course, may be positive in the functional self-understanding of GDR research. Beyond that, it should be pointed out that, through this set of agreements, a new stage has been established for the competition between systems in the German area. Against the background and in consequence of the world political changes, the Grundvertrag has to be understood as the adaptation to the general process of détente between East and West — in consideration of the specific situation in Germany. Certainly, the competition between systems will not be removed by the enforced effort for détente, but it takes on a new quality.

Transferred to the German situation, this means: the relations between the different systems of society can no longer be developed only from positions of conflict.[63] An objectivization of each other and idealization of their own position as a criterion of the 'Cold War', together with the competition between systems directed exclusively towards conflict form no basis for strategic political thinking because of world-wide interdependencies in the scientific-technical struggle for existence in and between highly developed industrial countries. The hostile brothers in Germany have also learned to take this into account.

Today, the competition between systems is characterized by the fact that the aspects of conflict are more and more overlapped by the search for possibilities of co-operation and by the enforced consideration of social-political competition. We perceive a quality of the contest between systems since there are still, of course, aspects of conflict but, at the same time, also competition and co-operation. Competition or contest — in contrast to conflict — results in the fact that the different societies must cope increasingly with analogous problems in the framework of the 'scientific-technical revolution'. One of the decisive questions which, because of the violence and urgency of the problems, cannot be answered with the ideological formula of world-wide class-warfare, is that about the potentiality for problem-solving in the different systems.[64] This is evident in discussions held in the FRG about, for instance, education policy, in which corresponding experiments and experiences of the GDR are more often taken into consideration. This co-operation is being enforced by the fact that the limited capacities of every highly developed industrial country can be magnified by international co-operation in economics, science, technique and other fields.

From our point of view, the present definition of function has to be formed against this background. For that reason, we want finally to turn to the conditions for GDR research which we outlined briefly, including the statements about the competition and contest between systems.

It is characteristic of the discussion of GDR research that most contributions — implicitly or explicitly — respond to and call into question the relationship of this research to policy.[65] The meta-theoretical plurality is expressed as well as the principal difficulties of GDR research. They show a basic problem with which the sciences have to cope with.

The central question here is: Does political motivation of GDR research exclude from this research a scientific character?[66] Three things have to be considered to answer this question. Firstly, this is not a problem which can be tackled only from the perspective of the sciences in a shortcut theoretical way. Therefore, secondly, a learning process is called for within the political system. This is necessary as long as it is still believed that "the benefit which policy gets out of science is the greatest possible, if science is wholly itself", as long as the relationship between policy and science is understood by a conception of science which is today practically everywhere reduced to absurdity on grounds of the principle of autonomy idealized in it. The problem of structuring anew the relationship between GDR research and the German political decision-making bodies of the Federal Government must be tackled from both sides. Therefore, thirdly it is necessary to clear up the problems which are of common interest to both sides, which consist of the competition and contest in Germany today. Only if this question has been answered is it possible to define in regard to the different aspects of the function of solving problems by policy and science. The novel competition of systems has an actual and long-term dimension for political decision. Ideally, actual decisions have to be derived consistently from long-term conceptions. If those preconditions are missing in preparing a decision, it only remains to resort to dates and information provided by science and research. It is doubtful whether policy made use of those possibilities continuously and whether, in view of the increasing complexity and differentiation, it is sufficient to use scientific results, especially to enforce subsequently taken decisions. In this connection, the obligation of policy to develop long-term conceptions seems to be more important. Especially here, we consider that the co-operation with the sciences is a necessary condition.

When we say that the new quality of the competition and contest between systems produces special difficulties in realizing the new concept, it must be asked whether these are to be solved only through the creative potential of policy. We think that the reservoir of political solutions is not sufficient, in view of the changed constellation of competition and contest, and that it is a function of science to be innovative in this direction. The traditional strategies of conflict solving do not deal with the novel problem of co-operation between different systems of society. A strategy using only models and experiences, which – primarily pragmatic – have 'functioned well' in some fields during the last years abandons the chance for an optimal utilization. It is enough to consider only the various fields of co-operation such as economies, culture and science, which are provided by the 'Grundvertrag'. When we look at such relations being firstly not expected under the aspect of conflict – although the situation still remains virulent – and when we, on the contrary, take the competition between different systems of society as point of reference, policy must, in practice, include new possibilities and variants in decision-making. It is doubtful whether a 'brain-storming' of a ministerial bureaucracy is sufficient.

Under those conditions, GDR research and policy have to recognize that the traditional forms of cooperation do not adapt to the new or to the anticipated situation. Without dismissing policy obligation to make the final decision, it can be expected that policy members will accept the critical, creative function of science as an unalterable precondition. To reduce GDR research to being merely a supplier of possibly even 'pure' dates and information would mean, on a long-term basis, evaluating the actual and future relationship between the two social systems in Germany in terms of the categories of the 1950s.[68]

The relationship of GDR research to the general public is, in regard to the object, closely connected with the relationship to policy. If policy does not pave the way between science and the general public, the contact between the two will often remain rudimentary. After all, it is still one of the anachronisms of today's science that it presents its results first to the scientific community and then perhaps, formulates them into policy. It is rarely tried, however, because of science's definition of itself, to reach directly with its results and findings the sections of society which are afflicted by the problems. This often resulted in interposition of the popular media, the quality of whose mediation is debatable.

This was true also for GDR research. As far as policy is concerned up to now, it has not been included in the process of preparing decisions, but rather, it was used to supply dates and information for 'German political education'. This might have been sufficient under the political conditions in former times, but during the process of realization of the 'Grundvertrag', for the most different social groups in the FRG, the actual and future situation is characterized increasingly by the incorporation of the individual citizen into system-competition.

When in the future, sporting, cultural and scientific relations are established with the corresponding partners in the GDR, the competition between systems will be carried out directly by the members of society who so far have derived their knowledge and approach to the other social system from not always serious sources. We admit that it is true that, since the construction of the Berlin Wall, the Deutschlandpolitik was restricted to the narrow field of official policy and that the citizen only passively took notice of it. Direct concern was reduced largely to still existing familiar contacts. In the same measure as the Grundvertrag is realized, the competition between systems is transferred to the society and its members. The leadership of the GDR has recognized this fact clearly; their reserve shows that they draw conclusions from the popular judgement on their actions.

From the point of view of the FRG, it should be taken into account that especially the social-political situation of contest should be seen together with the insecurity which frequently has its source in disorientation. The untroubled self-confidence of former times has been considerably eroded by the development of our conflict-ridden society.

In compiling its catalogue of functions under the changing conditions, GDR research also has to consider this constellation. It has to be taken into account 'that its own scientific work is a constituent part of the comprehensive competition between systems in the East and the West . . .'[69] From this point of view, a supply of information with scientific accuracy is no longer sufficient; the problems and conflicts of society have to be offered against the background of social-theoretical discussions. For the citizen of the FRG, who is included in the competition systems, GDR-research has the possibility of becoming an institution which makes its critically creative function available for him. (Departing from these considerations, the comparative analysis evidently gets also, a field of assignment of GDR research.) Not only policy, but also all possible social groups and individuals are to be recognized in future as direct actors and affected parties in the competition between systems. It is an essential of a new catalogue of functions for future GDR research that they are forced to accustom themselves to the potentials of conflict, that the conflict situation becomes clear to them, and that they develop their field of possibilities and their willingness to co-operate.

In our introductory comments, we mentioned that the actual self-criticism of GDR research has to take into consideration its relation to the object of cognition, to the GDR society. From our point of view, two aspects are in the foreground: the results of GDR research have an echo in the GDR. The response to and discussion with analyses of GDR-research, carried on chiefly by GDR 'imperialism' research, effect more people than the limited circle of researchers. We would not underrate this active element if we state that, during recent times, a more objective judgement and a differentiated dealing with the activities of the GDR research is apparent. GDR research which receives an objective reciprocation due to its own impartiality and fundamentally critical-creative attitude is able to make a contribution to reducing the 'Feindbild' (image of the enemy) in the GDR. At present, this thinking might not fit into the calculations of the political leadership in the GDR. However, if it is no longer possible for the GDR to ignore that, today, competition between systems means not merely conflict, but rather competition and co-operation, then the image of the FRG in the GDR must be revised gradually. The side which meets his counterpart with a dogmatic alienated picture-puzzle is necessarily at a disadvantage in dealing with the reality of co-operation and competition.

Especially these analyses may stimulate a process of learning in the GDR, which may elaborate the analogous problems in both systems in a critical and self-critical way and bring them in relation to the system-specified attempts of solution. In this lies a function of comparative works in regard to GDR society. However, the comparative analyses require an improved access to sources and information in the GDR. It looks as if, for the present, the very unsatisfactory actual situation cannot be redressed, although it may be supposed that, in this regard, the GDR may feel compelled to react. If the GDR leadership is basically interested — as we suppose — that the GDR research contribute to a realistic image of the GDR also in the FRG, this leadership must act to alleviate the problem of sources and information for this research. Neither scientists who sympathize with the SED or with the KPD in the FRG nor an intensified journalistic influence of the 'imperialism' research on the FRG are able to form the GDR image in this country. On the other hand, scientific GDR research has the possibility of achieving this and of making an objective presentation, if and when scientific contacts and scientific competition have started.

Our remarks on the interdependence of GDR research and politics in the FRG, to society in the FRG and the GDR as object of cognition do not mean that we assume a total determination for this research by political and social — meaning external — factors. Indeed, we believe that, at the present time, GDR research is compelled to pose and to answer 'questions regarding the relativity and the possibility of utilization of its results' (Zimmermann). But, this cannot mean the use of such research as an instrument. In each case, the degree of political and social determination has to be considered in relation to the relative autonomy of the research.[70] The demand for the autonomy of science — deduced from its specific character — affects GDR research as a field of research in the social sciences through its receptive and productive relation to the other social sciences. To formulate it negatively: GDR research which has lost the contact to the parent discipline — whether economics or sociology or historiography — will lose its necessary scientific substance. This substance enables it to resist the pressure of external demands and preoccupations in case its scientific character is being questioned. Stated positively, this means: the increasing complexity of the problems which are elements of today's competition of systems will lead to many expectations centered around GDR-research. The limited capacity of this research alone requires decisions on priorities. In the discussions about these decisions, GDR research has to bring in not only external political and social argument but also scientific internal arguments. In consideration of the momentary situation of theoretical and methodological discussion in the social sciences, GDR research has to refer to the priority of research on the theoretical fundamentals of social sciences. Furthermore, being informed about the development of empirical methods and, on grounds of its specific methodological problems — a definite independence is an unalterable precondition for GDR research to develop its own instruments. Thus, it has the task of formulating also that research — based on the immanent scientific situation — which seemingly has no practical political relevance. It is only in this case that we consider the autonomy of science to be justified — when it produces a dialogue oriented towards the problems, in relation to politics as well as to the members of society who are afflicted by the novel type of competition between systems.

APPENDIX

Institutions of GDR Research in the FRG

Institute	*Area of Interest*
Forschungsstelle für gesamtdeutsche wirtschaftliche und soziale Fragen, Berlin:	Economic system of the GDR (structure, Comecom-integration, foreign and inner-german trade, processes of production, agricultural research etc.)
Deutsches Institut für Wirtschaftsforschung, Berlin, Abt. DDR und östliche Industrieländer:	Constant observation and analysis of the economic development, calculation concerning political economics, studies on population, occupation and income, foreign and inner-german trade; system of planning and management
Osteuropa-Institut der Freien Universität Berlin, Abt. Bildungswesen Abt. Wirtschaftswissenschaften Abt. Recht Abt. Medizin	GDR research within the scope of fields which are represented by the Dept. embedded in the "Ostforschung"
Zentralinstitut für sozialwissenschaftliche Forschung der Freien Universität Berlin, Arbeitsbereich DDR-Forschung und − Archiv:	Political and sociological analysis of the political structures in the GDR
Institut für Sozialökonomie der Landschaftsentwicklung der Technischen Universität Berlin:	Agricultural research
Fachbereich Rechtswissenschaften der Universität Konstanz:	Analysis and comparison of the industrial law-system in the GDR and the FRG
Institut für Sozialwissenschaften der Universität Mannheim:	History of the GDR, SED, Party-system, history of German communism
Institut für Gesellschaft und Wissenschaft an der Universität Erlangen-Nürnberg	Science research within the scope of a comparative German research
Institut für politische Wissenschaft an der Universität München	Scientific-sociological studies, political system, Foreign politics, problems of comparison of systems
Lehrstuhl für Strafrecht, Strafprozeß- und Ostrecht der Universität Regensburg:	Development of law in the GDR, standardization of the law in the Comecon

Institut für politische Wissenschaft der Universität Würzburg:	System of power and law
Universität Bremen:	Economic policy and -theory
HW- Institut für Wirtschaftsforschung Hamburg:	Economic system, foreign economic policy
Seminar für osteuropäische Geschichte der Universität Frankfurt:	History of the Nationale Volksarmee, German problem in the schoolbooks of the GDR
Zentrum für kontinentale Agrar- und Wirtschaftsforschung der Universität Gießen:	Agricultural research
Fachbereich Soziologie der Universität Gießen:	Sociology of industry, family, sports, youth, medicine
Forschungsstelle für vergleichende Erziehungswissenschaft der Universität Marburg:	Comparative studies on the educational theory
Forschungsstelle zum Vergleich wirtschaftlicher Lenkungssysteme der Universität Marburg:	Comparison of the economic systems and economic theory
Forschungsstelle für Jugendfragen Hannover:	Interdepartmental youth-research
Ostakademie Lüneburg:	Constitution, cultural policy, ideology, foreign policy
Institut für Pädagogik der Universität Bochum:	Education and pedagogics in the GDR
Forschungsinstitut der Deutschen Gesellschaft für auswärtige Politik Bonn:	Foreign policy of the GDR
Forschungsinstitut der Friedrich-Ebert-Stiftung Bonn:	Foreign policy, developing policy, history of the GDR
Forschungsstelle für vergleichende Erziehungswissenschaft der PH Dortmund:	Preparatory school, school education and learning in the GDR
Institut für Bankwirtschaft und Bankrecht der Universität Köln:	Civil-, economic and industrial law
Institut für Ostrecht der Universität Köln:	International law, question of law concerning the whole of Germany, civil and economic law in the GDR

Bundesinstitut für ostwissenschaft-
liche und internationale Studien
Köln:

Home politics of the GDR, SED,
Deutschlanpolitik

NOTES

1. We keep to the classification and definition as used H. Lades and J. Pfister and C. D. Kernig in the article *'Kalter Krieg'*, in: Sowjetsystem und demokratische Gesellschaft. Eine vergleichende Enzyklopädie, Freiburg 1969, Vol. 3, column 497: The cold war came to an end at last at that time, "when the pressure to avoid a great war-like conflict between the world powers was acknowledged as unalterable and inevitable". (Outcome of the Cuba crisis and the learning process of the Soviet-leadership resulted from this acknowledgement.)

2. The 'Forschungsbeirat für Fragen der Wiedervereinigung Deutschlands beim Bundesminister für gesamtdeutsche Fragen' which was installed in 1952 had as its function to inform about economic and social questions of the GDR, to give a stock-taking, and to submit proposals for the transformation of the nationalized GDR-industry – all within the context of the concrete expectations for re-unification of Germany which the administration had at that time. The *Forschungsbeirat* had "to prepare intellectually the re-unification in the economic and social fields". In its concrete activity, the scientific analysis was granted more importance than the scientific preparation of the re-unification; in its fifth and last report, the Forschungsbeirat avoided giving recommendations for the practice of re-unification.

3. Roger E. Kanet, *Neue Tendenzen in der amerikanischen Kommunismüsforschung*, Osteuropa 4/1973, p. 24 f.

4. Martin Drath, *Totalitarismus in der Volksdemokratie*, in: Ernst Richert, *Macht ohne Mandat. Der Staatsapparat in der Sowjetischen Besatzungszone Deutschlands*, (Cologne: 1959).

5. The most important reports: Wolfgang Leonhard, *Die Revolution entläßt ihre Kinder*, (Cologne: 1955); Herbert Prauss, *Doch es war nicht die Wahrheit* (Berlin: 1960); Fritz Schenk, *Im Vorzimmer der Diktatur – 12 Jahre Pankow*, (Cologne: 1962).

6. Max Gustav Lange and Ernst Richert and Otto Stammer, *Das Problem der neuen Intelligenz in der sowjetischen Besatzungszone*, in: Veritas, Justitia, Libertas. Festschrift zur 200-Jahrfeier der Columbia-Universität (New York, Berlin: 1953).

7. Max Gustav Lange, *Wissenschaft im totalitären Staat. Die Wissenschaft der sowjetischen Besatzungszone auf dem Wege zum "Stalinismus"* (Stuttgart: 1955); idem, *Totalitäre Erziehung. Das Erziehungssystem der Sowjetzone Deutschlands*, (Frankfurt: 1954).

8. Joachim Schultz, *Der Funktionär in der Einheitspartei. Kaderpolitik und Bürokratisierung in der SED*, (Stuttgart: 1956); Carola Stern, *Portrait einer bolschewistischen Partei. Entwicklung, Funktion und Situation der SED*, (Cologne: 1957).

9. Ernst Richert and Carola Stern and Peter Dietrich, *Agitation und Propaganda. Das System der publizistischen Massenführung in der Sowjetzone*, (Berlin: 1958).

10. Ernst Richert (Note 4).

11. Martin Drath; *Verfassungsrecht und Verfassungwirklichkeit in der sowjetischen Besatzungszone Deutschlands* (Bonn: 1956); Gerhard Möbus, *Kommunistische Jugendarbeit. Zur Psychologie* und *Pädagogik der kommunistischen Erziehung im sowjetisch besetzten Deutschland* (Munich: 1957); Marianne Müller and Egon Erwin Müller, *"Stürmt die Festung Wissenschaft". Die Sowjetisierung der mitteldeutschen Universitäten seit 1945* (Berlin: 1953); Ek-

kehart Krippendorff, *Die Liberal-Demokratische Partei Deutschland in der SBZ 1945-48* , (Düsseldorf: 1959); Siegfried Mampel, *Die Verfassung der Sowjetischen Besatzungszone Deutschlands. Text und Kommentar,* (Frankfurt/Berlin: 1962); Gustav Leissner, *Verwaltung und öffentlicher Dienst in der sowjetischen Besatzungszone Deutschlands* (Stuttgart: 1961).

12. K. Paul Hensel, *Einführung in die Theorie der Zentralverwaltungswirtschaft,* (Stuttgart: 1954).

13. Besides the reports (Tätigkeitsberichte) of the Forschungsbeirat, especially the studies of Erich Klinkmüller, *Die gegenwärtige Außenhandelsverflechtung der Sowjetischen Besatzungszone Deutschlands* (Berlin: 1959); Klaus Dieter Arndt, *Wohnverhältnisse und Wohnbedarf in der sowjetischen Besatzungszone* (Berlin: 1960); Werner Bosch, *Marktwirtschaft-Befehlwirtschaft. Vergleich der Wirtschaftordnungen in West- und Mitteldeutschland,* (Heidelberg: 1960); Erich Klinkmüller and Maria E. Ruban, *Die wirtschaftliche Zusammenarbeit der Ostblockstaaten,* (Berlin: 1960); Fritz Schenk, *Magie der Planwirtschaft,* (Cologne: 1960).

14. Heinz Lippmann, *Der Grundvertrag und die DDR-Forschung,* Deutschland Archiv, 5/1973, p. 499 f.p.

15. *SBZ von 1945 bis 1954. Die Sowjetische Besatzungszone Deutschlands in den Jahren 1945 bis 1954,* (Bonn: 1956); further issues: *SBZ von 1955 – 1956* (1958), *SBZ von 1957 bis 1958* (1960), *SBZ von 1959 bis 1960* (1964), *Chronik 1961-1962* (1969); *SBZ-Biographie. Ein biographisches Nachschlagebuch über die Sowjetische Besatzungszone Deutschlands,* (Bonn: 1961) (³1965); *SBZ von A. bis Z. Ein Taschen- und Nachschlagebuch über die Sowjetische Besatzungszone Deutschlands,* (Bonn: 1953, ¹¹1969).

16. *SBZ-Archiv. Berichte und Kommentare zu gesamtdeutschen Fragen,* (Cologne 1950-1968).

17. Peter J. Nettl, *Die deutsche Sowjetzone bis heute – Politik, Wirtschaft, Gesellschaft* (Frankfurt, 1953); Horst Duhnke, *Stalinismus in Deutschland. Die Geschichte der sowjetischen Besatzungszone,* (Cologne: 1955).

18. Ernst Deuerlein, *Die Einheit Deutschlands. Ihre Erörterung und Behandlung auf den Kriegs- und Nachkriegskonferenzen 1941 – 1949. Darstellung und Dokumente,* (Frankfurt: 1957).

19. Peter Christian Ludz, *Situation, Möglichkeiten und Aufgaben der DDR-Forschung,* in: SBZ-Archiv 20/1967, p. 322.

20. Ludwig Auerbach, *DDR-Forschung im Spannungsfeld der Politik,* in: SBZ-Archiv 20/1967, p. 325.

21. Peter Christian Ludz, *Entwurf einer soziologischen Theorie totalitär verfasster Gesellschaft,* in: Studien und Materialien zur Soziologie der DDR. Sonderheft 8 der Kölner Zeitschrift für Soziologie und Sozialpsychologie, 1964; idem: *Parteielite im Wandel. Funktionsaufbau, Sozialstruktur und Ideologie der SED-Führung,* (Cologne/Opladen: 1968), (especially ch. I).

22. Bruno Gleitze, *Die Industrie der Sowjetzone unter dem gescheiterten Siebenjahrplan,* (Berlin: 1964); Karl C. Thalheim, *Die Wirtschaft der Sowjetzone in Krise und Umbau,* (Berlin: 1964); Joachim Nawrocki, *Das geplante Wunder. Leben und Wirtschaften im anderen Teil Deutschlands* (Hamburg: 1967); additionally the Tätigkeitsberichte IV (1961-65) and V (1965-69) of the Forschungsbeirat, Bonn 1965 resp. 1969.

23. Dietrich Storbeck, *Soziale Strukturen in Mitteldeutschland,* (Berlin: 1964); Karl V. Müller, *Die Manager in der Sowjetzone,* (Cologne/Opladen: 1962); Gernot Gutmann, *Theorie und Praxis der monetären Planung in der Zentralverwaltungswirtschaft,* (Stuttgart: 1965); Hannelore Hamel, *Das sowjetische Herrschaftsprinzip des demokratischen Zentralismus in der Wirtschaftsordnung Mitteldeutschlands,* (Berlin: 1966): Wolfgang Förster, *Rechnungswesen und Wirtschaftsordnung. Ein Beitrag zur Diagnose der Zentralverwaltungswirtschaft sowjetischen Typs und ihrer Reformen aus betriebswirtschaftlicher Sicht,* (Berlin: 1967); Peter Mitzscherling, *Soziale Sicherung in der DDR. Ziele, Methoden und Erfolge mitteldeutscher Sozialpolitik* (Berlin: 1968); Konstantin Pritzel, *Die Wirtschaftsintegration Mitteldeutschlands,* (Cologne: 1969); Hannsjörg Buck, *Technik der Wirtschaftslenkung in kommunistischen Staaten,* Coburg 1969, 2 vol.).

24. Siegfried Mampel, *Die Entwicklung der Verfassungsordnung in der sowjetisch besetzten*

Zone Deutschlands von 1945 bis 1963, (Tübingen: 1964); idem,; *Das Recht in Mitteldeutschland. Staats- und Rechtslehre – Verfassungsrecht,* (Cologne: 1966); idem; *Herrschaftssystem und Verfassungsstruktur in Mitteldeutschland. Die formelle und die materielle Rechtsverfassung der "DDR",* (Cologne: 1968); idem; *Beiträge zum Arbeitsrecht der sowjetischen Besatzungszone,* (Bonn: 1963); Klemens Pleyer, *Zentralplanwirtschaft und Zivilrecht. Juristische Untersuchungen zur Wirtschaftsordnung der SBZ,* (Stuttgart: 1965); Reinhold Krevet, *Das Vertragsrecht in der mitteldeutschen Industrie;* (Cologne: 1966); Dietrich Müller-Römer, *Die Grundrechte in Mitteldeutschland,* (Cologne: 1965); Hans Wiedemann, *Das sozialistische Eigentum in Mitteldeutschland,* (Cologne: 1964); Klemens Pleyer and Joachim Lieser, *Zentralplannung und Recht,* (Stuttgart: 1969).

25. Besides the studies of Ludz (note 21), especially: Martin Jänicke, *Der dritte Weg. Die antistalinistische Opposition gegen Ulbricht seit 1953,* (Cologne: 1964); Carola Stern, *Ulbricht. Eine politische Biographie,* (Cologne: 1964); Ernst Richert, *Die DDR-Elite oder Unsere Partner von morgen?* (Hamburg: 1968); Eckart Förtsch and Rüdiger Mann, *Die SED,* (Stuttgart: 1969).

26. Norbert Matthedi, *Gründung und Entwicklung der Parteien in der sowjetischen Besatzungszone Deutschlands,* (Bonn: 1966); Roderich Kulbach and Helmut Weber and Eckart Förtsch, *Parteien im Blocksystem der DDR. Aufbau und Funktion der LDPD und der NDPD,* (Cologne: 1969); Hans-Peter Herz, *Freie Deutsche Jugend,* (Munich: 1965); Hartmut Zimmermann, *Der FDGB als Massenorganisation und seine Aufgaben bei der Erfüllung der betrieblichen Wirtschaftspläne,* in: Studien und Materialien . . . (note 21).

27. Ernst Richert, *"Sozialistische Universität". Die Hochschulpolitik der SED,* (Berlin: 1967); Thomas Ammer, *Universität zwischen Demokratie und Diktatur. Ein Beitrag zur Nachkriegsgeschichte der Universität Rostock,* (Cologne: 1969); Wolfgang J. Görlich, *Geist und Macht in der DDR. Die Integration der kommunistischen Ideologie,* (Freiburg: 1968); Joachim H. Knoll and Horst Siebert, *Erwachsenenbildung – Erwachsenenqualifizierung. Darstellung und Dokumente der Erwachsenenbildung in der DDR* (Heidelberg: 1967); Gerhard Möbus, *Unterwerfung durch Erziehung. Zur politischen Pädagogik im sowjetisch besetzten Deutschland* (Mainz: 1965); Heinz K. Heil, *Das Fernsehen in der Sowjetischen Besatzungszone Deutschlands 1953 – 1963* (Bonn: 1967); E. M. Herrmann, *Zur Theorie und Praxis der Presse in der sowjetischen Besatzungszone Deutschlands,* (Berlin: 1963).

28. Report *"Wissenschaft und Forschung im geteilten Deutschland",* Deutscher Bundestag Drucksache V/4631, (Bonn: 1969).

29. Ernst Richert, *Das zweite Deutschland. Ein Staat, der nicht sein darf,* (Gütersloh: 1964); Hermann Weber, *Von der SBZ zur DDR. 1945 bis 1968* (Hannover: 1968); Ernst Deuerlein, *Die DDR. Geschichte und Bestandsaufnahme,* (Munich: 1966).

30. Erich Gniffke, *Jahre mit Ulbricht* (Cologne: 1966); Ernst Lemmer, *Manches war doch anders. Erinnerungen eines deutschen Demokraten,* (Frankfurt: 1968); Heinz Brandt, *Ein Traum, der nicht entführbar ist. Mein Weg zwischen Ost und West,* (Munich: 1967).

31. Besides the Deutschland Archiv, it is to be quoted as a journal with regular GDR-reporting: Deutsche Studien (ed. by the Ost-Akademie Lüneburg since 1963), furthermore, there exists since 1968 a journal with reviews of books and periodicals of the GDR: *Gesellschaftswissenschaftliche Informationen* (Ed. Werner Riese, Stuttgart). Scientific analyses concerning the GDR are also published in most special journals of single social sciences, also in journals of the Osteuropaforschung.

32. Contributions: Dieter Haack, Gesamtdeutsche Politik braucht die DDR-Forschung; Peter Christian Ludz, *Situation, Möglichkeiten und Aufgaben der DDR-Forschung;* Ludwig Auerbach, *DDR-Forschung im Spannungsfeld der Politik,* in: SBZ-Archiv 20/1967, pp. 319 f.

33. Dieter Haack (note 32), p. 320 and 319.

34. Hans Lades, in: Die Welt 29.7.1966.

35. Eckart Förtsch, *DDR-Forschung und gesamtdeutsche Politik,* in: Deutschland-Archiv 2/1968, p. 148 f.p.

36. Carola Stern, *Antwort an Eckart Förtsch,* in: Deutschland-Archiv 3/1968, p. 149.

37. Peter Christian Ludz (note 32).

38. Ernst Richert, *Möglichkeiten und Grenzen der DDR-Forschung,* in: Deutschland-

Archiv, 2/1968, p. 144 f.p.

39. Clemens Burrichter, *Fragen zu einer soziologischen Theorie der DDR-Gesellschaft,* in: Deutschland-Archiv 7/1969, p. 698 f.p.

40. Ibidem, p. 704.

41. Eckart Förtsch and Rudolf Schwarzenbach, *DDR-Forschung. Kritik aus der DDR,* in: Deutschland Archiv 11/1970, p. 1214 f.p.

42. Günter Benser and Manfred Teresiak, *Neue Tendenzen in der westdeutschen Geschichtsschreibung über die DDR,* in: Zeitschrift für Geschichtswissenschaft 8/1969, p. 1034 f.

43. Ibidem.

44. Heinz Heitzer, *Andere über uns,* (Berlin (East): 1969), p. 23.

45. R. Graf and H. G. Müller, *Westdeutsche DDR-Forschung – Instrument psychologischer Kriegsführung,* in: Dokumentation der Zeit 24/1969, p. 4.

46. Heinz Heitzer, *Das DDR-Bild in der westdeutschen Geschichtsschreibung,* in: Geschichtsunterricht und Staatsbürgerkunde 9/1969, p. 838.

47. Benser and Teresiak (note 42), p. 1055.

48. Peter Hort, *Ein Umriß für die DDR-Forschung,* in: Frankfurter Allgemeine Zeitung 18.9.1974.

49. Klaus-Dieter Arndt, in: *DDR-Wirtschaft. Eine Bestandsaufnahme* (Frankfurt: 1971), p. 23/4.

50. Rüdiger Thomas, *Modell DDR. Die kalkulierte Emanzipation,* (Munich: 1972); Kurt Sontheimer and Wilhelm Bleek, *Die DDR – Politik, Gesellschaft, Wirtschaft,* (Hamburg: 1972); Hermann Rudolph, *Die Gesellschaft der DDR-eine deutsche Möglichkeit?* (Munich: 1972); Heinz Rausch and Theo Stammen (eds), *DDR – Das politische, wirtschaftliche und soziale System,* (Munich: 1974); Wolfgang Pfeiler, *DDR-Lehrbuch,* (Bonn: 1974).

51. Hans Lades and Clemens Burrichter (eds.), *Produktivkraft Wissenschaft. Sozialistische Sozialwissenschaften in der DDR* (Hamburg: 1970); Peter Christian Ludz (ed.), *Wissenschaft und Gesellschaft in der DDR,* (Munich: 1971); Gert Glaessner and Herwig Haase and Ralf Rytlewski, *Student und Studium in der DDR* (Bonn: 1971); *Wissenschaft in der DDR. Beiträge zur Wissenschaftspolitik und Wissenschaftsentwicklung nach dem VIII. Parteitag* (ed. by the Institut für Gesellschaft und Wissenschaft Erlangen), (Cologne: 1973).

52. Günter Lauterbach, *Zur Theorie der sozialistischen Wirtschaftsführung in der DDR,* (Cologne: 1973); Emil Schmickl, *Soziologie und Sozialismustheorie in der DDR,* (Cologne: 1973); Frank Reuter, *Geschichtsbewußtsein in der DDR – Programm und Aktion,* (Cologne: 1973); Manfred Zuber, *Wissenschaftswissenschaft in der DDR,* (Cologne:1973); Hermann Weber, *Ansätze einer Politikwissenschaft in der DDR,* (Düsseldorf: 1971); Dieter Riesenberger, *Geschichte und Geschichtsunterricht in der DDR,* (Göttingen: 1973); Gudrun Traumann, *Journalistik in der DDR,* (Munich: 1971); Hans-Peter Schäfer, *Jugendforschung in der DDR,* (Munich: 1974).

53. Especially the three *"Bericht(e) der Bundesregierung und Materialien zur Lage der Nation"* 1971, 1972 and 1974 (ed. by the Bundesministerium für innerdeutsche Beziehungen); Horst Siebert, *Bildungspraxis in Deutschland: BRD und DDR im Vergleich,* (Düsseldorf: 1970); Peter Mitzscherling, *Sozialpolitik im geteilten Deutschland,* (Hannover: 1971); Edith Niehuis, *Analyse der Erwachsenenbildung in der BRD und DDR,* (Heidelberg: 1973); Armin Hegelheimer, *Berufsausbildung in Deutschland,* (Frankfurt: 1972); Dieter Schuster, *Die Gewerkschaften in der BRD und DDR,* (Stuttgart: 1972); Gisela Helwig, *Zwischen Familie und Beruf. Die Stellung der Frau in beiden deutschen Staaten,* (Cologne: 1974); Gebhardt Schweigler, *Nationalbewußtsein in der BRD und der DDR,* (Düsseldorf: 1973); Bernd Rüthers, *Arbeitsrecht und politisches System. BRD – DDR,* (Frankfurt: 1972); Georg Brunner, *Kontrolle in Deutschland. Eine Untersuchung zur Verfassungordnung in beiden Teilen Deutschlands* (Cologne: 1972).

54. Jürgen Miksch, *Jugend und Freizeit in der DDR* (Opladen: 1972); Dieter Voigt, *Montagearbeiter in der DDR. Eine empirische Untersuchung über Industrie-Bauarbeiter in den volkseigenen Großbetrieben,* (Darmstadt: 1973); Gebhard Schweigler (note 53); Dietmar Kreusel, *Nation und Vaterland in der Militärpresse der DDR,* (Stuttgart: 1971); Peter Jungermann,

Die Wehrideologie der SED und das Leitbild der Nationalen Volksarmee vom sozialistischen deutschen Soldaten, (Stuttgart: 1973); Frank Reuter (note 52).

55. Konrad Franke, *Die Literatur der Deutschen Demokratischen Republik,* (Munich: 1971); Hans Dietrich Sander, *Geschichte der schönen Literatur in der DDR,* (Freiburg: 1972); Elimar Schubbe, *Dokumente zur Kunst, Literatur und Kulturpolitik der SED,* (Stuttgart: 1972); Fritz J. Raddatz, *Traditionen und Tendenzen. Materialien zur Literatur der DDR,* (Frankfurt: 1972); Heinz Klunker, *Zeitstücke, Zeitgenossen, Gegenwartstheater in der DDR,* (Hannover: 1972); Manfred Jäger, *Sozialliteraten. Funktion und Selbstverständnis der Schriftsteller in der DDR,* (Düsseldorf: 1973); Bernhard Greiner, *Die Literatur der Arbeitswelt in der DDR,* (Heidelberg: 1974).

56. DDR-Wirtschaft (note 49), 1974[3]; Bruno 'Gleitze and Karl C. Thalheim and Hannsjörg Buck and Wolfgang Förster, *Das ökonomische System der DDR nach dem Anfang der siebziger Jahre,* (Berlin: 1971): Werner Bröll, *Die Wirtschaft der DDR. Lage und Aussichten,* (Munich: [2]1973); Hans Immler, *Agrarpolitik in der DDR,* (Cologne: 1971); Siegfried Kuppe, *Der innerdeutsche Handel,* (Cologne: 1972); Peter Scharpf, *Europäische Wirtschaftsgemeinschaft und Deutsche Demokratische Republik* (Tübingen, 1973).

57. Siegfried Mampel, *Die sozialistische Verfassung der DDR. Text und Kommentar,* (Frankfurt: 1972); Herwig Roggemann, *Die Gesetzgebung der DDR,* (Berlin: 1971); Klemens Pleyer and Joachim Lieser, *Das Zivil- und Wirtschaftsrecht der DDR im Ausklang eines Reformjahrzehnts,* (Stuttgart: 1973); Jörg Weck, *Wehrverfassung und Wehrrecht der DDR,* (Cologne: 1970); Jens Hacker, *Der Rechtsstatus Deutschlands aus der Sicht der DDR,* (Cologne: 1974).

58. Hermann Weber and Fred Oldenburg, *25 Jahre SED. Chronik einer Partei,* (Cologne: 1971); Heinz Lippmann, *Honecker, Porträt eines Nachfolgers,* (Cologne: 1971); Ursula Hoffmann, *Die Veränderungen in der Sozialstruktur des Ministerrats der DDR 1949 – 1969,* (Düsseldorf: 1971); Karl Wilhelm Fricke, *Warten auf Gerechtigkeit. Kommunistische Säuberungen und Rehabilitierungen,* (Cologne: 1971); Anita Dasbach-Mallinckroth, *Wer macht die Außenpolitik der DDR? Apparat, Methoden und Ziele,* (Düsseldorf: 1972); Peter Joachim Lapp, *Der Staatsrat im politischen System der DDR (1960-1971),* (Opladen: 1972); Herwig Roggemann, *Die Staatsordnung der DDR* (Berlin: 1973).

59. Horst Siebert (note 53); Hartmut Vogt, *Schule und Betrieb in der DDR,* (Cologne: 1970); Arnim Hegelheimer (note 53); Friedrich W. Busch, *Familienerziehung in der sozialistischen Pädagogik der DDR* (Düsseldorf: 1972); Heinz Martes, *GST – Vormilitärische Ausbildung in der DDR,* (Cologne: 1970); Hans-Joachim Winkler, *Sport und politische Bildung,* (Opladen: 1973).

60. For instance: Renate Damus, *Entscheidungsstrukturen und Funktionsprobleme in der DDR-Wirtschaft,* ·(Frankfurt: 1973); Peter Hennicke (ed.), *Probleme des Sozialismus und der Übergangsgesellschaften,* (Frankfurt: 1973); Philip Neumann, *Der "Sozialismus als eigenständige Gesellschaftsformation"* in: Kursbuch 23 (1971); Margaret Wirth, *Kapitalismustheorie in der DDR,* (Frankfurt: 1972); Willy Wyniger, *Demokratie und Plan in der DDR. Probleme der Bewältigung der wissenschaftlich-technischen Revolution,* (Cologne: 1971); U. Freier and P. Lieber, *Politische Ökonomie des Sozialismus in der DDR,* (Frankfurt: 1972). Further contributions in periodicals such as e.g. Das Argument, Sozialistische Politik.

61. Deutschland Archiv 5/1973, p. 485.

62. These discussions may enter into our presentation, but our reflections describe no status; the reflections are understood as a contribution to the discussion.

63. Cp. our explications and annotations about the first stage of GDR research. For this problem s.a. Wilfried von Bredow, *Abgrenzung und Entspannung,* in: Deutschland Archiv 3/1973, p. 252 f.

64. In addition to this s.a. Hartmut Zimmermann, *Zu einigen innenpolitischen Aspekten der DDR-Forschung,* in: Deutschland Archiv 7/1973, p. 716: "The in principle similar form of the technical production on comparable levels results often in fundamentally similar problem situations in both systems. To mention only some: Significance of almost all disciplines of science for the economic – social development and for the political decision-making process

increases, planning of education and education-economy becomes a necessity, the section of service increases . . ."

65. C.f. especially: Peter Christian Ludz, *Die Zukunft der DDR-Forschung,* in: Deutschland Archiv 5/1973, p. 492 f; Wolfgang Pfeiler, *Über den politischen Wert einer wissenschaftlichen DDR-Forschung,* in: Deutschland Archiv 5/1973, p. 497 f; Hermann Weber, *Die DDR-Forschung nach dem Grundvertrag,* in: Deutschland Archiv 6/1973, p. 588 f, Kurt Erdmann, *Kritische Analyse unerlässlich,* in: Deutschland Archiv 6/1973, p. 598 f.; Hartmut Zimmermann, *Zu einigen innenpolitischen Aspekten der DDR-Forschung,* in: Deutschland Archiv 7/1973, p. 713 f.; Ludwig Bress, *Hat die "DDR-Forschung" eine Zukunft?* in: Deutschland Archiv 7/1973, p. 718 f.; Wilfrid von Bredow, *Die DDR als Forschungsobjekt,* in: Deutschland Archiv 8/1973 f. 822 f.; Peter Mitzscherling, *Forschungsgebiet DDR-Wirtschaft. Anmerkungen aus der Sicht des DIW,* in: Deutschland Archiv 10/1973, p. 1034 f.; Gero Neugebauer, *DDR-Forschung nur Büttel der Politik?* in: Deutschland Archiv 10/1973, p. 1036 f.

66. Wolfgang Bergsdorf, *Eine dritte Phase der DDR-Forschung?* in: Deutschland Archiv 6/1973, p. 591 f.

67. Bundesminister Franke in his speech about GDR research, in: Deutschland Archiv 4/1974, p. 370 f.

68. We suppose that the "Arbeitskreis für vergleichende Deutschlandforschung", which has to take the place of the "Forschungsbeirat", will only act as an advisory institution. In this council representatives of science and politics come together although without a preliminary clarification of special tasks and functions.

69. Wilfried von Bredow, *Abgrenzung* (note 63), p. 255.

70. C.f. in addition to this, our remarks in: Deutschland Archiv 7/1969 (note 39), and in: *Analysen und Berichte aus Gesellschaft und Wissenschaft* (ed. by the Institut für Gesellschaft und Wissenschaft) 6/1974, pp. 42-58. S.a. Clemens Burrichter and Eckart Förtsch, *DDR-Forschung im System Wettstreit,* in: Deutschland Archiv 101/1975, p. 1035 f.

Multinational Banks, the State and International Integration

Gerd Junne

WHEREAS INDUSTRIAL MULTINATIONAL CORPORATIONS have roused the special interest of political scientists during the last decade, the internationalization of banking has, in contrast, been neglected. It seems far less impressive because it does not lead to large visible production facilities, does not create much employment, and is mostly of a more recent origin. If one looks, however, at the magnitude of capital involved (cf. Table 2, p. 123), at the speed with which this internationalization takes place, and at the global scope of this process (cf. *Steuber* 1974), it seems rather important, indeed, all the more so from a theoretical point of view because, in the banking sector, truly multinational entities have come into being whose capital stems from different countries, whereas almost all 'multinational' industrial corporations still have their home country from which the majority of their capital originates, where the bulk of their production facilities is concentrated, and where they usually have their most important market.

The banking sector becomes more important as industrial corporations are less able to finance their investment and their day-to-day operations from their own internal cash-flow because of the capital needs that result from violent structural change and inflation. This change is the consequence of rapid technological advances enforced by strong international competition as well as by the international shortages of energy and raw materials.

Since capital markets dry up in inflationary periods, the corporations cannot raise enough money by public issues in the bond market or in the stock markets. Therefore, everywhere in the Western world, companies become more dependent on bank finance (for a divergent point of view see *Juergens and Linder* 1974, 136-149). To ensure a proper use of their capital, however, banks participate in

Expanded version of a paper presented to the workshop on 'Multinational Corporations as Political Actors' at the Joint Session of Workshops of the European Consortium for Political Research at Strasbourg, April 1974.

117

many firms in one form or another. The productive capital owned by large banks has reached considerable proportions, not only in Germany where the universal banks are famous for their equity stakes in industry and commerce, but also in other countries as the *Metcalf/Muskie Report* has recently revealed in the case of the United States (see *Disclosure of Corporate Ownership*, 1974).

The banking system, consequently, becomes more important. This is not only at the national but also at the international level, since it is, first of all, via the private banking sector that the huge sums paid to the oil exporting countries are channelled back to the consumer countries in order to finance their balance of payments deficit. In this way, some of the power the Middle Eastern countries derive from their oil wealth is shared by the international banks that can decide which of the capital-thirsty consumer countries have reached their credit ceiling and which have not.

The present article *first* describes the various *causes* of the internationalization of banking, with reference to new trends in the international division of labour as a framework for interpretation. It then presents the different *forms* that this process takes, i.e. international branch networks, the creation of multinational consortia banks and the formation of international banking groups.

Secondly it will be asked what these different forms of international banking mean for the fulfilment of state functions. Some state functions will be described and direct and indirect mechanisms will be discussed which allow *international banks to contribute to limiting the effectiveness of state activities* intended to steer the economy as a whole.

The *third* part will deal with the question of how *relations between states* are affected by the internationalization of banking. It will be asked whether the newly formed multinational banks can be interpreted as system-stabilizing supporters of a common interest of the dominant classes in different capitalist states and to what degree international banking may further political integration.

CAUSES AND FORMS OF THE INTERNATIONALIZATION
OF BANKING

The Intensification of international credit relations as a result of trends towards a new international division of labour

International financial flows are no isolated phenomena that can be explained by themselves. They are closely linked to the international flow of goods, services and manpower that has been intensified during the past ten years, in which a trend towards new forms of international division of labour have appeared.

These new forms, organized primarily by multinational corporations, consist of

a. the intensification of an intra-branch 'horizontal' division of labour between industrial capitalist economies that are increasingly tied to each other through intensive cross-investments,

b. the extension of the traditional exchange of raw materials against manufactured products between developed and developing countries to include the exchange of labour-intensive products, produced in some 'growth islands' in the third world, against machinery and know-how from industrial countries.

c. the quickly advancing inclusion of socialist countries into the international division of labour (*Elsenhans* and *Junne* 1974). The socialist countries offer raw materials and relatively labour-intensive manufactured goods (whose production demands a degree of qualification of the workers that does not exist in most developing countries) for high technology capital goods (that seldom find a market in developing countries).

Trends towards such new forms of international division of labour are discussed elsewhere in detail (*Elsenhans* and *Junne* 1975). Stimulating world trade and foreign investment, these new forms lead in several ways to an intensification of international credit relations:

1. International mergers and acquisitions, cross-investment between industrial countries as well as the resulting intensification of international trade flows need considerable international financing.
2. Different interest rates in several countries cause international flows of capital. Differing interest rates used to be caused by differing business cycles in the past, but now, due to the internationalization process, business cycles are, in fact, becoming more and more similar. However, interest rate levels are now much less determined by the business cycle than they used to be. They are actually much more influenced by official monetary policy, which usually is different from country to country because of different economic structures and different instruments for state intervention.
3. The actual run on raw materials stimulated by the 'oil crisis', the rising of prices for most commodities as well as the fear that some countries may reserve their resources for their own use have led to large exploration and exploitation efforts during the last one or two years, together with a considerable intensification of the necessary infrastructure construction. These developments cause credit needs for at least five participating parties — for the developing country (specifically, its infrastructure), for the multinational corporation (or, eventually, the state corporation) that explores and exploits the resources, for the buyer of the raw materials, who needs larger credits to finance his orders, for the speculators that stockpile raw materials and buy up shares of raw material firms, and, lastly, for the governments of the consumer countries that have to finance the balance of payments deficit that result from higher prices for raw materials.
4. The partial industrialization of developing countries leads to an enormous demand for investment in machinery and infrastructure. International capital is especially willing to finance this investment through private credits, as long as it is of use for the subsidiaries of multinational corporations that stand for the economic 'soundness' of the undertaking.

5. The intensification of trade and industrial co-operation with socialist countries has quickly led to a large deficit in these countries and has brought with it large credit needs that are met, first of all, by large private Western banks.

With the always more sluggish development of the national economies in the western industrial countries, the big banks increasingly turn to all kinds of international business where large profits can still be made, although competition is there more intense than within the national economies.

Different forms of the internationalization of banking

Banking is one of those spheres in almost all economies that are most extensively regulated by government law or other official regulations. Although the banks of most industrial countries have always done a considerable international business, this has been managed — at least until the Second World War — mostly from the desk at their home office. Exceptions to this rule are the extensive branch networks of British and French banks in the colonies of their countries as well as those of US banks in their quasi-colonies in Latin America and other regions. International business was mostly effected with the help of *correspondence banks* — friendly banks which have accounts with each other so that they can draw checks on these accounts to effect international payments.

However, with the increasing internationalization of production, this system was no longer sufficient. Banks had to provide more information on the chances of business abroad, and they could only provide such information (cf. p. 128-129) if they themselves were represented abroad.

This has led to a considerable increase in the number of *representative offices* in foreign countries. These offices could collect the necessary information, they contact potential foreign investors that might become clients in the home market, and arrange for their bank to participate in international consortia of all kinds. These offices could not do any business themselves, however. If a client at home needed not only advice about foreign markets, but also foreign currency credit to finance an installation there, in most cases, he had to be referred to one of the correspondence banks.

This has not only obvious disadvantages for the bank, which has to renounce potential business, but also for the client, who has to prove his credit worthiness to another bank in a foreign environment in order to get his plans financed.

At the present time, therefore, the most important forms of the internationalization of banking are those dealt with below.

a. The extension of international branch networks: Representative offices often are only the first step to enter a market and to prepare the establishment of a full service branch (*Koszul* 1974, 460) or to look for candidates to become affiliates or subsidiaries. Foreign branches serve not only to attract foreign investors who want to invest in the home country of the bank, but also to help clients at home to invest abroad. If some banks have branches abroad, others are forced to follow, otherwise they would lose part of their *domestic* business: American banks with branches abroad flatly demand a share of the home business of those corporations which they finance abroad (*Fry* 1969, 618).

Another reason for extending the international branch network lies on the passive side of banking business: many banks have extended their branch network to the centres of the Euromoney market, to London first of all, in order to participate in this primarily inter-bank market, where banks may refinance their financial engagements whenever they need it. The establishment of an international branch network necessitates strong links to the Euromoney market, since, initially, new foreign branches have no deposit base of their own and can expand their credit business only if they can refinance their loans in the inter-bank market.

Only the biggest banks reach a business volume large enough to support an extensive international branch network. As can be seen from Table 1, very few branches or subsidiaries of banks from the original six member countries of the EEC are present in others of the original EEC countries. Close contacts among banks from the 'Six' have led to implicit standstill agreements that reserve each country's market to that country's banks. With the spread of American bank branches all over Europe, however, these contacts had to become institutionalized to meet the American competition (cf. *Falk-Bjerke* 1972, 108-111).

b. The foundation of international banking groups: The institutionalized close co-operation with banks in other countries as practised by EUROPARTNERS, European Banks International (EBIC) and the Associated Banks of Europe (ABECOR) is an alternative to extending the individual international branch network. In the case of these groups, a customer has to prove his standing only once to the bank in his home country and can then get financial support in all the countries where banks of the group are active.

Table 2 shows the participants of five international (mostly European) banking groups about which Table 3 provides some more detailed information. It can be seen that, out of the four biggest banks in each EEC country (with the exception of Denmark and Ireland and taking into account that only three big banks exist in Belgium as well as in the Netherlands), *all* are members of one of these banking groups or are at least associated with one of these groups. How important these groups are can be estimated if one knows that, out of the first 30 of the 'Top 300' list published annually by 'The Banker', 19 banks belong to these groups as members or as (formal or informal) associates.

The international banking groups, however, could not be a sufficient defence against the fast growing network of branches of mainly US-based banks if their structure were not strengthened by specialized institutions.

c. The installation of international consortia banks: Consequently, most international banking groups, as well as many other banks, have founded international consortia banks to serve a certain area, a certain type of business (e.g. medium-term loans) or even a certain type of industry (e.g. energy, shipping).

That these banks are by no means merely 'the poor man's solution for inter-

TABLE 1

Number of banks with foreign subsidiaries (S), branches (B), agencies (A), and representative offices (R)

In → / from ↓	Belgium S	Belgium B	Belgium R	Luxembourg S	Luxembourg B	Luxembourg R	Netherlands S	Netherlands B	Netherlands R	France S	France B	France R	Germany (FRG) S	Germany (FRG) B	Germany (FRG) R	Italy S	Italy B	Italy R	Great Britain S	Great Britain B	Great Britain R	Switzerland S	Switzerland B	Switzerland R	USA S	USA A/B	USA R	Japan S	Japan B	Japan R
Belgium				5	–	–	–	–	–	–	1	–	1	1	–	–	–	–	1	1	–	3	–	–	–	–	3	–	–	1
Netherlands	1	–	–	5	3	–				–	–	1	1	1	2	–	–	–	–	1	–	2	–	–	–	1	3	–	1	–
France	2	3	–	5	3	–	2	–	–				1	4	17	–	1	3	4	5	3	4	5	2	2	2	8	–	3	6
Germany (FRG)	–	–	–	17	–	–	1	–	–	–	–	2				–	–	–	1	5	3	5	1	–	–	2	4	–	2	4
Italy	1	–	5	–	–	–	–	–	–	2	–	7	–	–	14				1	3	10	13	–	6	–	5	4	–	1	1
Great Britain	1	2	–	1	3	–	2	3	–	6	4	4	2	6	2	–	–	1				12	4	3	3	6	4	–	5	9
Switzerland	1	–	–	1	3	–	–	1	–	–	–	1	–	1	1	–	–	2	2	10	4				1	2	6	–	2	3
Canada	–	1	2	–	–	–	–	1	1	2	–	1	–	4	1	–	1	1	–	5	–	–	1	1	4	5	5	–	–	5
USA	3	6	4	8	7	–	–	6	–	12	7	5	5	14	8	2	5	6	14	40	13	16	8	4				–	15	15
Japan	–	4	–	1	1	–	–	–	1	2	2	1	1	7	7	–	1	–	2	16	6	2	–	1	6	14	8			
Other countries	6	–	7	5	1	–	–	–	5	29		17	6	10	37	–	–	6	30	53	26	18	1	10	8	25	40	–	12	21

Sources: For banks in Belgium: *Muellander* 1974; in Luxembourg: *Memorial* – Amtsblatt des Grossherzogtums Luxembourg, No. 61, November 29, 1973; in France: *Koszul* 1974; in Great Britain: *The Banker*, November 1973; in Switzerland: *Schuster* 1973; in Japan: *Drumwright* 1974. Figures for Italy, the Netherlands, and the United States have been compiled from *Who owns what in World Banking 1973-4*, published by The Bankers Research Unit, London, and *The Bankers' Almanac and Yearbook*, 1973-74 edition. These two reference books have also been used to complete the information given on foreign banks in other countries.

TABLE 2

Member Banks of International banking groups

Group	EBIC European Banks International Company	ORION	ABECOR Associated Banks of Europe Çorporation	EUROPARTNERS	INTER-ALPHA
Year of foundation	(1963) 1970	1970	1971 (1974)	1971	1972
Member Banks and Associated banks from	(Assets as at the end of 1973 indicated in parentheses)				
Austria	Creditanstalt-Bankverein (3.1 billion $)		(Österreichische Länderbank) (2.2 billion $)		
Belgium	Société Générale de Banque (9.1 billion $)		Banque de Bruxelles[d] (7.7 billion $)		Kredietbank[a] (6.2 billion $)
Canada		Royal Bank of Canada[b] (18.4 billion $)			
France	Société Générale (24.2 billion $)		Banque Nationale de Paris (30.8 billion $)	Crédit Lyonnais (24.0 billion $)	Crédit Commercial de France (4.4 billion $)
Germany	Deutsche Bank (24.6 billion $)	Westdeutsche Landesbank (19.5 billion $)	Dresdner Bank (20.9 billion $) Bayerische Hypotheken- und Wechselbank (9.5 billion $)	Commerzbank (14.5 billion $)	Berliner Handelsgesell-schaft – Frankfurter Bank (4.4 billion $)
Great Britain	Midland Bank (19.1 billion $)	National Westminster Bank (27.6 billion $)	Barclays Bank (30.9 billion $)	(Lloyds Bank[c]) (17.6 billion $)	Williams & Glyn's Bank[d] (3.1 billion $)
Italy	Banco Commerciale Italiana (38.4 billion $)	Credito Italiano (29.2 billion $)	Banco Nacionale de Lavoro (41.1 billion $)	Banco di Roma (24.7 billion $)	Banco Ambrosiano (6.0 billion $)
Japan		Mitsubishi[d] Bank (26.2 billion $)	(Sumitomo[cd] Bank (27.3 billion $)	(Mitsui Bank[cd]) (19.6 billion $)	
Netherlands	Amsterdam-Rotterdam Bank (9.7 billion $)		Algemene Bank Nederland (10.2 billion $)		Nederlandsche Middenstandsbank (4.3 billion $)
Spain				Banco Hispano-Americano (11.9 billion $)	
United States		Chase Manhattan Bank (36.8 billion $)	(Bank of America[c]) (49.4 billion $)		
Total assets of member banks	128.2 billion $	157.7 billion $	151.1 billion $	75.1 billion $	28.4 billion $
Total assets of members and associated[e] banks			230 billion $	112.3 billion $	

a Assets at the end of March 1974
b Assets at the end of October 1973
c Not formally associated
d Assets at the end of September 1973
e Names of (formally or informally) associated banks in parentheses
The assets are total assets (including contra accounts) as taken from the Annual Review 'The Top 300 in World Banking', The Banker, June 1974, 643-85.

nationalization of banking' is proven by the fact that 35 out of the 50 largest banks of the world are shareholders of one or more multinational consortia banks ('Financial Times', 10 April, 1973).

TABLE 3

Group	EBIC	ORION	ABECOR	EUROPARTNERS[b]	INTER-ALPHA
Total assets[a] (in US-$ million)	107 399	138 628	133 500	58 276	25 253
Capital and reserves (in US-$ million)	2 850	5 555	3 819	1 111	920
Total deposits (in US-$ million)	98 880	113 438	111 100	48 559	19 661
Offices in Europe	9 469 (worldwide)	n.a.	8 740	ca. 4 000	1 900
Number of countries in which group is represented	15 (group represent-ation only)	n.a.	ca. 100	more than 55	40
Joint representation offices	Toronto Johannesburg		Johannesburg Mexico Sydney Teheran	Johannesburg Mexico Singapour Sydney Tokyo	Sao Paulo Singapour Tokyo
Joint ventures	Banque Européenne de Crédit (Bruxelles), European-American Banking Corp./ European-American Bank & Trust Co. (New York), Europäisch-Asiatische Bank (Hamburg) European Banking Co. (London), Franklin National Bank (USA)	Orion Bank Ltd. (London), Orion Term Bank (London), Orion Pacific Ltd. (Hongkong)	A.B.D. (New York)	Europartners Bank (Nederland) (Amsterdam), Commerz-Credit-Bank AG Europartner (Saarbrücken), Europartners Leasing S.A. (Paris), Institutional Research and Investment Services S.A. (Geneva)	Inter-Alpha Asia S.A. (Luxembourg)
Joint participations	Euro-Pacific Finance Corp. (Melbourne), European-Arab Holding (Luxembourg)	Libra Bank (London)	Société Finan-cière Européenne (Paris), IBIN, (Bad Homburg)	ADIG (München, Düsseldorf), Euro-Partners Securities Corp. (New York), International Commercial Bank (London), Mithal Europartners Finance and Investment Ltd., (Bangkok), Nippon Europartners Consulting Co. (Tokyo), Sligest (Beirut)	Brown, Harriman and International Banks Ltd., (London)
International credit facility	Ebicredit Ebiclease		Telecredit	Transcredit	Alpha-Credit

All figures as at the end of 1973.
Source: Information kindly provided by the German member banks of the groups.
a Figures on assets differ from Table 2 because contra accounts are not included in this table.
b Banco Hispano-Americano does not yet participate in most of the ventures of EUROPARTNERS.

Actually, there are about 60 multinational consortia banks. Almost half of them are installed in London (cf. the table on participation in and location of multi-national banks in *Junne* 1973, 80), where they participate in medium- and long-term Euromoney business.

These international banks are truly 'multinational' as far as the origin of their capital is concerned.[1] They demonstrate the existence of a highly integrated system of international finance capital that can be supposed to work quite independently of the interests of the dominant capital groups in single countries. So far, their relations to national governments have been rather harmonious however, partly because national governments have recently become the most important borrowers of international consortia banks in their efforts to equilibrate their balances of payments, which show a deficit because of rising prices for crude oil and other raw materials.

THE DISTURBANCE OF THE FULFILMENT OF STATE FUNCTIONS BY INTERNATIONAL BANKING

In spite of these harmonious relations, the main argument of this article is that the above described process of internationalization of banking hinders the implementation of some functions that the state apparatus has acquired in the historical development of modern capitalist societies.

This statement does not include any moral judgement. It does not intend to contrast the 'democratic' state with private hierarchic business structures. It does not mean that the state is a neutral authority that implements certain functions in order to further the general welfare, and that any disturbance arising out of the internationalization of banking thus is 'bad' and should be controlled or stopped. Perhaps it should be but that depends largely on the specific context.

This article is a rather descriptive one. It sees the internationalization of banking (as well as of production) as a necessary development at a certain stage of the national economic development of capitalist societies. The case is the same with certain state functions or tasks that come about as a by-product of a process of crises that are produced by the same development (cf. *Altvater* 1972).

A disturbance of the fulfilment of state functions by the internationalization of banking (both being products of exactly the same process) is thus only as 'bad' as the system that provokes them both. On the other hand, it may be 'good' insofar as it contributes to make the contradictions of the system more manifest in order to overcome this system.

State functions in capitalist societies

It is not necessary to mention all modern state functions here (a good list is contained in *Murray* 1971). Only two functions have to be stressed in the context of this article:

a. The state apparatus in present industrial capitalist societies must provide economic coordination and *orchestration* to prevent an overheating or a stagnation of the economy. The state apparatus tries to implement this, first of all, by
   - an indicative or prescriptive economic planning.
   - its influence on the framework of economic activity through legislation, taxation, and central bank policy, and
   - the direct state demand for goods and services.

b. The state apparatus must manage part of the *external relations* of the national economy, – that means the defence against negative influences from foreign countries and the support of economic operations of national capital abroad. One of the preconditions for both is, in most countries, a rather equilibrated balance of payments and a movement of the exchange rate of the national currency that corresponds to the dominant interests in the national economy.

These two functions are quite fundamental, as regards the other functions of the state apparatus, – e.g. guaranteeing property rights, disciplining the labour force, providing the general conditions of production (economic infrastructure, particularly energy and communication, educated labour . . .), etc.

The less the function of economic orchestration is fulfilled, the more difficult it may be in times of inflationary crisis to discipline the labour force, and the less the state budget may be able to provide the necessary infrastructure for the economy.

The less the external relations are controlled, the less the function of economic orchestration may work, with all the consequences this may have.

It cannot be stressed too much that *this point of view does not imply that the state functions of economic orchestration and management of external relations can be fulfilled without any frictions.* At 'best', the state's activity in this field may be successful temporarily or more successful than in neighbour states.

It is the capitalist structure of the economy itself that requires these functions to be fulfilled and prevents, in the long run, measures being taken with any degree of success to implement these functions. When it is stated in this article that this or that factor limits the effectiveness of state actions, it is meant only that even the temporary or gradual success that might have been possible does not come about at all or, at least, is less feasible than it might have been otherwise.

Direct disturbances

Multinational banking may hinder the fulfilment of state functions directly and indirectly. Direct disturbance of the fulfilment of state functions works in various ways:

1. The internationalization of banking provides banks with *more and better information about lending and borrowing opportunities* abroad, and it makes the *international money transfer easier,* in order that more money will cross the exchanges. The international monetary flow will become even more interest-sensitive. That means that smaller interest differences than formerly are sufficient cause to provoke considerable international monetary transfers. This has the consequence that *governments and central banks have even more difficulties than before in isolating their economies against negative economic trends in other countries.*

2. The growth of the international network of branches and subsidiaries of big banks has the consequence that these banks will have larger accounts in foreign currencies, which may be mobilized in case of probable changes in currency parities. The larger international activities of banks thus lead to a *greater potential for international currency speculation* (and a greater incentive to use this potential,

too). Even if home and host countries introduce exchange controls, an extensive international network gives a bank the opportunity to *circumvent the countries' exchange controls* because it may manipulate the international monetary flow at its own convenience.

3. As the internationalization of the banking sector gives it the chance to circumvent measures taken by the state, which is endeavouring to fulfill its function of protecting the economy against negative outside influences and of helping its expansion abroad, it may *disturb, as well, the function of implementing a certain economic orchestration of the economy:* The larger international activities lead to manifold possibilities of circumventing the official credit policy and evading the consequences of official measures taken to influence the business cycle.

4. Finally, the internationalization of banks leads to a higher degree of concentration in the banking sector itself, since smaller banks are forced to unite with others to be able to go abroad or to hold their ground against competition by foreign banks. A higher degree of concentration, however, makes it more difficult for the government or the central bank to implement its credit policy,[2] at least in countries where the authorities try to implement their policy by influencing monetary aggregates (money supply, liquid assets . . .). Although they do not have direct control over interest rates and credit allocation, larger banks have more possibilities for internal compensation for the consequences of official measures influencing monetary aggregates; thus, in order to be effective, the official measures have to be more rigid; this in turn, will probably have unwanted side effects. The more polarized the banking structure is, however, the less rigid the official measures will be allowed to be, since a really tight monetary policy would harm mostly the small banks that depend to a larger degree for their liquidity on the rediscount facilities of the central bank.

The failure of a large private German bank, the Bankhaus Herstatt, in June 1974, due to large-scale foreign exchange speculation, precipitated a further polarization between the larger banks that are internationally active and the smaller banks active almost only within the national borders, because the smaller banks face more intensive difficulties now if they try to enter the international scene.

The more polarized the banking structure is, the less effective a global money and credit policy will be: if it allows the smaller banks to work with a profit, the central bank measures will not succeed in restricting the activity of the larger banks effectively. If it is tight enough to prevent any circumvention by the larger banks, the smaller banks will not have enough liquidity left to continue their business. Since government and central bank officials, as well as private banks, are interested in avoiding any bank failures, (because the international credit standing of all banks of the country is affected by such failures, the saving habits of the population are negatively influenced, and banks lose the interbank loans granted to the bankrupt institutions) the second alternative is almost out of question. Consequently, money and credit policy can less and less be a very conclusive one.

Indirect disturbances

More important than the direct disturbance, however, seems to be the indirect disturbance of the fulfilment of state functions. It is taken for granted in this article that the *internationalization of production* leads to a reduced effectiveness of the fulfilment of state functions. The indirect disturbance of the fulfilment of state functions by multinational banks is seen *in their promotion of the internationalization of production.* It is not the concern of this article to explain in detail how the internationalization of production, itself, hinders the effective implementation of state functions; the following catalogue, however, may serve to remind one of the relevant points in this context (for bibliographical notes on most of these points, see *Parry* 1973):

The effectiveness of state interventions may be limited by

1. neglect for, or circumvention of, central economic orchestration of the economy by multinational corporations (MNCs),
2. negative balance of payments effects by direct capital transfer, effects of foreign ownership of international subsidiaries on their export and import behaviour, and evasion of exchange controls,
3. tax revenue losses and circumvention of price control via transfer prices for the exchange between subsidiaries of MNCs,
4. effects on the technology balance of a country, imports of foreign technology, restrictions on the use of imported technology, discouragement of national research and development efforts,
5. negative influences on the structure and performance of the industries in which international firms operate (e.g. more concentration),
6. dependence of employment on the location decisions of MNCs,
7. intra-national and international brain-drain via MNCs,
8. extra-territorial law application by foreign governments in host countries of subsidiaries of MNCs,
9. difficulties in obtaining information needed to steer the economy as a whole and to control multinational enterprises.

It was said at the beginning that the internationalization of banking is largely the consequence of the internationalization of production. This does not exclude, however, that the internationalization of banking, in return, strengthens the spread of multinational industrial enterprises and the transition of formerly national corporations to multinational dimensions. This happens in different ways:

1. The international banks, probably the most informed actors on the international scene (although certainly not omniscient, as is shown by the huge losses from foreign exchange speculation that even some very large banks had to endure), use their international network, first of all, to *provide information* for all those that may be inclined to enter foreign markets with exports as well as with foreign production facilities. The banks provide information on general market conditions, the performance of comparable enterprises, the standing of potential customers, on

potential competitors, suppliers, on official market regulations, custom duties, taxes, exchange controls, credit conditions, currency risks, government incentives, company law, wages, social responsibilities, trade union policies, prices, rents, environmental regulations, regional differences, overall political climate, etc.

2. The banks *arrange contacts* with agents, consultants, lawyers, brokers, government officials, customers, suppliers, potential partners for joint-ventures, industrial associations, managers, firms that might be bought partly or totally, etc.

3. The banks continually help to *organize the international business* of multinational corporations, they provide international cash management facilities, and they help to evade credit controls and exchange regulations, to minimize tax payments and to optimize interest earnings on liquid funds. The banks even invite firms through large advertisements in business newspapers to 'hedge' in order to avoid losses from parity changes, i.e. to compensate their exposure to foreign exchange by adverse foreign exchange or international credit operations that have the same effect for official currency policy as ordinary currency speculation.

4. The banks *provide capital in foreign currencies* to finance the acquisition of foreign enterprises or participations in foreign enterprises as well as the *know-how* for drafting the contracts with foreign enterprises. International banks even *promote international mergers* without the initiative of non-bank firms consulting them. There would be numerous international mergers and acquisitions, of course, without the activity of international banks, because the international economic development makes them necessary. However, the international banks do more than just execute the inevitable. Business executives complain about a 'merger mania' increasingly brought about by international banks. The borrower from these banks, 'if he is not careful, may find that the control of his company has slipped into the hands of his "friendly banker" who may decide that a merger with his competitor in a cross border transaction represents an attractive goal' (*Saint-Phalle/Heptonstall* 1973, 9). International banks that are specialists in mergers become active in even foreign domestic business in order to facilitate take-overs.[3]

5. International banks thus further the process of international concentration and centralization at the national as well as at the international level. The resulting degree of concentration has twofold implications for the effectiveness and the character of state interventions.

Firstly, higher economic concentration leads to a more direct impact of the activity of big firms on government policy, whether there is a close communication and mutual understanding between both sides or not. Governments have to care more for the needs of these firms, because so much employment, so much investment and production, and so much foreign trade depends on the smooth running of these firms' business.

Secondly, the bigger and more internationalized the firms are, the easier it is for them to circumvent state interventions aimed at steering the economy as a whole. The merger movement thus fosters the polarization between a highly monopolized and internationalized sector and other parts of the economy that form the small business competitive sector (cf. *O'Connor* 1973). As in the case of the polarization of the banking structure (cf. p. 127), this division within the economy makes any kind of global steering of the economy very difficult, if not impossible, because any measure strong enough to reach the intended goal and to influence the business behaviour of the monopolized sector will endanger the survival of small business, whereas measures that do no harm to small business in the competitive sector are ineffective in influencing the big firms.

It is this split that *constitutes one of the fundamental reasons for the present 'stagflation'* in all capitalist industrial countries.

THE IMPACT OF INTERNATIONAL BANKING ON INTERNATIONAL RELATIONS

The reduced effectiveness of state interventions in the economy, partly due, as described, to the activity of internationally active banks, is of utmost relevance for international economic as well as political relations.

If those two of the basic state functions described above are insufficiently fulfilled in any one country, the government concerned will be forced to take drastic measures to restabilize economic development and the balance of payments. These measures consist of defensive and offensive actions. They almost inevitably include controls and impediments for international flows of goods, services and capital to protect the economy against negative influences from abroad and to prevent the escape from internal regulations. In many countries, 'stagflation' leads the governments to promote exports more strongly (by devaluation, export credits, subventions and political pressure on potential customers), giving rise to more intense international competition and, eventually, to international political conflict.

The activities of international banking thus tend to disturb the very basis of its own existence: an expanding international division of labour and a liberal international political climate.

The interest of international banks in conflict prevention

A development such as that just described does not lie in the interest of the international banks. One may ask, therefore, whether the international banks compensate for the loss of steering capacity that the national state apparatus endures. This they could do by contributing to an *international* economic and political coordination that counters the trend towards disruption of the international division of labour and political struggle.

Internationally active banks that look after the common interest of the competing parties on the international scene with the purpose of maintaining and enlarging their own profits have a long tradition. The relative stability during the last quarter of the nineteenth century and the first decade of the twentieth century may be explained, first of all, by the activity of 'high finance'. According to *Polanyi* (1945, p. 20), 'high finance' 'functioned as the main link between the political and the economic organization of the world. It supplied the instruments for an international peace system, which was worked out with the help of the Powers, but which the Powers themselves could have neither established nor maintained.' Although this is not a very elaborated view, it can be taken for granted that international finance was interested in avoiding a major confrontation between the great powers of that time, because its business would have been impaired if a general war had interfered with the monetary foundations of the system.

Today, no 'high finance' is necessary to prevent a major war between Western industrialized states. A war between these countries has become unthinkable, due to military integration (which did not prevent the Greek-Turkish clash over Cyprus, however), as well as to the external challenge by socialist countries and to the fact that there are almost no stakes imaginable that would justify the use of modern weapons against another Western industrial state. A major war between capitalist industrial states would certainly not only destroy more markets than it would open up for any segment of national capital, but would probably also destroy the capitalist system as such. What remains quite possible, however, is a major confrontation between Western states in the economic field.

One way in which the major international banks contribute to avoid such a situation is through acting to postpone an actual crisis in order to give governments more time to decide on coordinated measures. An example of this type of action is credits to finance balance of payments deficits that would otherwise force some governments into a more protectionist policy, which, in turn, might induce other governments to give way to the protectionist demands of different groups in their own countries.

A more permanent instrument to avoid such crises are possibly the multinational consortia banks, which have to reconcile within themselves the possibly diverging interests of their shareholders from different countries. This interpretation, however, goes too far. Whereas, before the First World War, international consortia were often formed with the purpose of overcoming excessive competition between different imperial powers, international consortia banks today are generally created to be active in fields where the shareholder banks do *not* compete (*von Clemm* 1971, 126).[4] Consortia banks are created to bolster the competitive position of their shareholders against outside banks. The advent of some 60 international consortia banks has thus *stiffened* international competition for profitable outlets of money, rather than reducing it.

However, this competition is no longer between national fractions of international finance capital, but rather between more or less loosely structured international banking groups. This means that the banks involved cannot, as a rule, fall back on their national government as an ally, because banks from one and the same country will probably be on both sides of the conflicting parties. This makes it less probable that economic competition will turn into political conflict.

Additionally, the frequent meetings of the shareholders' representatives (as well as the meetings of the representatives of international banking groups) have become permanent panels for the top executives of the world's most important banks. They regularly exchange ideas and views and, thus, become more aware of developments in other countries and of the problems of other economies.

This is probably even more the case with banks that command a wide international branch network. In mid-1972, at least ten of the big American banks held more than one-fourth of their total deposits as deposits at foreign offices — five of them held more than one-third at foreign offices, and two almost half their total deposits (*Brimmer* 1973, 40). It is evident that these banks become more aware of and interested in a smooth running of those economies where a large part of their business is located.

One of the big differences between the present period and the time before the First World War is that international finance is no longer the only segment of capital interested in avoiding a major international economic conflict between the capitalist states. Up to the time of the First World War, the international activities of most firms consisted almost exclusively of exports which had to be sold against the competition of exporters from other countries. Presently, international cross-investment has reached a scale that makes it more and more difficult to speak of a 'national capital'. Most big corporations have very strong stakes in other countries and are therefore interested in preserving the free international flow of goods and capital on which the successful internal international division of labour within the corporation depends. It has been shown above (p. 128) how the internationaliza-tion of banking — itself, in its present form, a by-product of the internationaliza-tion of production — strengthens the trend towards a further global spread of production facilities and trade of multinational corporations. This is a very im-portant indirect way in which international banking helps to foster common in-terests of dominant classes in different countries and, thus, to avoid international economic conflict.

It is a very ambiguous process, however, because, although economic inter-nationalization strengthens common international interest, it may have disruptive effects *within* single countries. As discussed above, the trend towards a polarization between an internationalized monopolized sector of the national economy, on the one hand, and the competitive small business sector, on the other, makes state intervention less effective, which leads, in the long run, to stronger compensating measures that have negative effects on the international division of labour and may, therefore, be conflict producing. In general, however, the economic internationali-zation process helps to *shift the major lines of conflict articulation from inter-national to intra-national conflict.*

The limited interest of international banking in regional political integration

International banks are interested not only in preventing economic conflict between states, but can best pursue their interest when a more cooperative position is reached. They are very interested in removing any barriers that may stand in the way of more intense international exchange of goods, services, and capital. This interest in the absence of barriers may be called the interest in 'negative inte-gration'. More intense international exchanges, however, limit the steering capacity of national governments, which must then be complemented by international co-ordination and supranational decision-making.[5] Common political decision-making in supranational institutions may be regarded as 'positive integration', while 'negative integration' implies nothing more than a common market without any political institutions.

In order to avoid the negative consequences of unfulfilled state functions, international banks should also be interested in 'positive integration'. Some doubts can be expressed, however, whether they really are.

Any kind of regional integration results not only in a closer co-operation within the region, but also in some differentiation between relations within the region and those with outside partners. If this differentiation is not made, no economic orchestration inside the region will be possible. Regional integration, therefore, necessarily goes along with a certain dissociation from the outside world. Since nobody is more cosmopolitan than capital and banking, some reservations can be made about banks in this regard.

a. The services of international banks constitute something resembling a substitute for international integration, because they help to realize the international transfer of goods, services and capital, as if there were almost no international barriers. This has twofold implications: on the one hand, the pressures of those interested in international integration are reduced because the activity of international banks grants them almost a 'functional equivalent' to international integration. On the other hand, a great deal of very lucrative business in international banking stems from the fact that there is no international political integration. Any such integration would thus take away some business from international banking.

b. Internationally active banks from inside as well as from outside the integrating region do not want any discrimination between banks from member countries and other banks, because such discrimination would hamper business expansion, both outside the member countries for banks from these countries, and inside the community for outside banks.

c. The big banks are not eager to see the different banking laws inside a community be assimilated, because such a compromise would necessarily strengthen state control in those places with the most permissive supervision where international banks have concentrated their international business, such as London or Luxembourg e.g. within the European Community.

d. Banks that belong to international banking groups generally do not expand in those countries where other member banks of the group are located (cf. Table 1). They are thus not really interested in a liberalization of legal norms that regulate the installation and activity of foreign banks, because it would not promote their own business (but possibly that of competitors).

e. Banks that do not expand into the countries of partner banks have to concentrate their expansion on third countries (mostly outside the community). This fosters the development of ties with third countries that lead to a preference for the enlargement of the community (in the case of the European Community, e.g. for including Spain and, perhaps, Greece), in opposition to an intensification of international integration.

f. Common currencies within a community would diminish the competitive advantage that the international banks have in comparison to those banks that are active only within one national market. It would thus reduce their predominant position in international banking.

g. Even if international banks were in favour of regional political integration (as they verbally are), the foreign exchange speculation of international banks would aggravate international currency crises provoking interventions from national governments and, thus, leading to a backlash in international integration.

The interest of internationally active banks in positive integration is therefore rather limited indeed. Besides, it can be questioned whether the centralization of state intervention by a supranational *regional* institution would be sufficient to compensate for the losses in steering capacity on the national level referred to above. Since the economic internationalization process is global in scope, any integrative effort restricted to a regional level and leaving out major economies will only shift the problem to another level and may aggravate it, instead of alleviating it. It is only consistent that actual world economic problems are handled by the Group of Ten (cf. *Braun* 1970), or, more recently, the governments of the Big Five, the United States, Great Britain, France, the Federal Republic of Germany, and Japan, and not (predominantly) on a regional basis such as that of the European Community.

CONCLUSION

The economic internationalization process, of which the internationalization of banking is only a part, is strong enough to lead to such close connections between the capitalist industrial economies that no individual state apparatus alone may be able to fulfill the state functions that have become more and more crucial for the economic process in actual capitalist societies.

However, the internationalization process does not lead, at the same time, to the creation of coordinating institutions that effectively compensate for these losses of steering capacity on an international level.

The internationalization process has led to an international synchronization of business cycles in different countries. For the first time since the Second World War, the capitalist Western countries face a common recession of their economies, in which economic problems in one country aggravate those in other countries, in contrast to earlier recessions contained within single countries and balanced and alleviated by better business conditions elsewhere. The 'oil crisis', which is now made responsible for the imminent world recession, only precipitated this development that had been foreseeable for a long time.[6]

The more grave the international recession becomes, the more it is probable that individual governments, under the pressure of interested groups, will fall back on protectionist measures (making the situation for foreign economies even worse).

The multiple forms of coordination that exist in international organizations, on the inter-governmental level and in the sphere of international private business, including international banking, may perhaps work to prevent a repetition of the

Great Depression of the Thirties, but they may not be sufficient to avoid a development that falls little short of that.

NOTES

1. It may be questioned, however, whether the term 'multinational banks' should not be reserved for banks with offices in several countries (which most consortia banks lack) in order to parallel the term 'multinational corporation', which designates a company with production facilities in different countries. – *Steuber* 1974, 22.

2. This proposition is a controversial one: *Hodgman,* 1973, 150 says just the opposite, but perhaps he is thinking more of countries with more direct credit controls, such as France, rather than of countries where officials try to influence monetary aggregates as they do in the Federal Republic of Germany or in the Netherlands.

3. Cf. e.g. the Annual Reports of the Bankers Trust International Ltd, London, a subsidiary of the Bankers Trust New York Corporation (the seventh largest U.S. bank), of 1970 (3), 1971 (4), 1972 (4), and 1973 (4).

4. That banks participating in consortia continue to pursue other international business separately, can be taken from the following: of those 27 banks listed by the Bank of England as consortium banks in March 1973 (see 'Bank of England Quarterly Bulletin' 1973, 329), 21 have shareholders from different countries. Of these 21 banks *all* non UK shareholders of at least 12 banks and many other shareholder banks keep their own London branches, some of which were established even *after* the foundation of the consortium bank in which the banks concerned hold a participation (with the exception of one shareholder that is not a bank, two out of 35 shareholders of the 12 banks that have only representative offices at London, but no branch, and one bank that has no branch or representative office but is itself a subsidiary of a bank that has a branch at London).

5. *Zellentin* (1973, p. 22/23) claims that coordinated national policies may correspond better to the actual degree of economic internationalization in Europe than would a supra-national authority. She does not give any reasons for this point of view, however, and does not tell why *national* governments can be supposed to make decisions that may lie in a hypothetical common interest of an international community but which are not backed by strong fractions of the dominant classes within the country or which are taken even against important interests of such fractions.

6. The 'oil crisis' may even contribute to overcoming a world recession, since it gives rise to vast investment in exploration, exploitation and transport equipment and stimulates the replacement of capital goods that have suddenly become obsolete with higher costs of energy, petrochemicals and other raw materials. This may stimulate demand in other fields, but at the price of still higher levels of inflation. It will do so very differently in different countries, however, provoking a further unequal development among industrial capitalist countries, with all the conflicts that this involves.

REFERENCES

Altvater, Elmar, 1972: 'Zu einigen Problemen des Staatsinterventionismus', in: *Probleme des Klassenkampfes,* No. 3, May, 1-53.

Braun, Frank, 1970: *Die Zehner-Gruppe, Stellung und Kooperation der Zehner-Gruppe im internationalen Währungssystem,* Würzburg: Physika-Verlag, Bankwirtschaftliche Studien, 2.

Brimmer, Andrew F., 1973: 'Changing fortunes of US branch banks in London', in: *International Currency Review,* vol. 5, No. 2, 37-41.

Clemm, Michael von, 1971: 'The rise of consortium banking', in: *Harvard Business Review,* vol. 49, No. 3, 125-142.

O'Connor, James, 1973: *The Fiscal Crisis of the State,* New York: St. Martin's Press

Disclosure of Corporate Ownership, 1974: Report prepared by the Subcommittee on Intergovernmental relations, and budgeting, management, and expenditures of the Committee on Government Operations, United States Senate, 93d Congress, 2d Session, Document No. 93-62, Washington: Government Printing Office.

Drumwright, J. R., 1974: 'Foreign banks grow despite funding problems', in: Japan survey, *Euromoney,* March 1974, 29-32.

Elsenhans, Hartmut and Junne, Gerd, 1975: 'Einige Aspekte des gegenwärtigen Wandels der internationalen Arbeitsteilung', paper submitted to a conference of the German Association for Political Science, published in: Klaus Jürgen Gantzel (ed.), 1975: *Herrschaft und Befreiung in der Weltgesellschaft,* Frankfurt: Campus.

Elsenhans, Hartmut und Junne, Gerd, 1974: Wirtschaftswachstum und Deformation. Die Auswirkungen der wirtschaftlichen Ost-West-Kooperation auf die osteuropäischen Länder, in: *Leviathan,* vol. 2, No. 4, December, 534-571.

Falk-Bjerke, Hans, 1972: *Die Veränderungen im Bankwesen der EWG unter besonderer Berücksichtigung der zunehmenden EWG-Integration,* Wien: Manzsche Verlags- und Universitätsbuchhandlung, Schriftenreihe der Osterreichischen Bankwissenschaftlichen Gesellschaft, 41.

Fry, Richard, 1969: 'The Heart of the Financial World', in: *The Banker,* vol. 119, No. 521, 617-624.

Hodgman, Donald R., 1973: 'The Effectiveness of Monetary Policy in the EEC', in: *The Bankers' Magazine,* October, 147-153.

Jüergens, Ulrich and Lindner, Gudrun, 1974: 'Zur Funktion und Macht der Banken', in: *Kursbuch,* No. 36, June, 121-160.

Junne, Gerd, 1973: 'Euromoney, Multinational Corporations and the Nation State', in: *Instant Research on Peace and Violence,* vol. 3, No. 2, 74-83.

Koszul, Julien, 1974: 'Les Banques étrangères en France', in: *Banque,* No. 329, May, 459-469.

Muellender, Hubert, 1974: 'Das Bankwesen in Belgien', in: *Kammerzeitschrift der Deutsch-Belgisch-Luxemburgischen Handelskammer,* July-August.

Murray, Robin, 1971: 'The Internationalization of Capital and the Nation State', in: *New Left Review,* No. 67, May/June, 84-109.

Niederlassungen ausländischer Banken in der Bundesrepublik, 1973, Frankfurt: Knapp.

Parry, Thomas G., 1973: 'The International Firm and National Economic Policy: A Survey of Some Issues', in: *The Economic Journal,* vol. 83, No. 332, December, 1201-1221.

Polanyi, Karl, 1945: *Origins of our time. The great Transformation,* (London: Gollancz).

Robinson, Stuart W. Jr., 1972: *Multinational Banking. A study of certain legal and financial aspects of the postwar operations of the U.S. branch banks in Western Europe,* Leiden: Sijthoff.

Saint-Phalle, Thibaut de and Heptonstall, John, 1973: 'International banking services in Europe – a user's view', in: *Euromoney,* February 1973, 4-9.

Schuster, Leo, 1973: *Bankstrukturen ausgewählter Länder,* St. Gallen, Bankwirtschaftliches Skriptum.

Steuber, Ursel, 1974: *Internationale Banken. Auslandsaktivitäten von Banken bedeutender Industrieländer,* Veröffentlichung des HWWA-Institut für Wirtschaftsforschung, Hamburg: Verlag Weltarchiv.

Takeuchi, Ichiro, 1973: 'Expansion of Japanese banking abroad', in: Japan survey, *Euromoney,* March 1973, 2-9.

Takeuchi, Ichiro, 1974: 'Japanese banks overseas in 1973', in: Japan survey, *Euromoney,* March 1974, 7-15.

Zellentin, Gerda, 1973: 'Übernationale Zusammenschlüsse als Bedingung der Globalsteuerung in Europa', paper delivered at the Annual Meeting of the 'Deutsche Vereinigung für Politische Wissenschaft' in Hamburg, October 1-4. An expanded version of this paper is the following article.

Supra-National Associations as Conditions for Global Guidance in Europe

Gerda Zellentin

BOURGEOIS RESEARCH ON REGIONALISM AND INTEGRATION has up to now taken little notice of the Marxist-Leninist theories on the merger of states and producers in capitalism. However, the more the process of European integration progresses and affects the interests of various national and trans-national producer-groups, the greater the need becomes to recognize the criteria and mechanisms for steering this process, i.e. the changes in the state apparatus and its functions, as well as in the relations between the state and supra-state bureaucracies and the private firms.

Marxist-Leninist writings on political economics contain a wealth of untested hypotheses on global guidance in capitalist systems under conditions of the disintegration of the state and of trans-national economic concentration. A critical reception and empirical analysis of these ideas could prove exceptionally fruitful in the field of integration research.

The aim of this article is to deal with some controversial questions: will the national activity of the state and the associations for crisis-avoidance, which seek to provide global guidance in concerted action, be replaced by corresponding supra-national actions and − provided this can be proven − will a supra-national guiding of economy and society lead to the removal or to the aggravation of capitalist contradiction, to the creation of a supra-state or to the disintegration of state associations?

In the first section the integration theses of the Marxist-Leninists are to be presented in historical order. In the second part a number of the theoretical assumptions will be confronted with events in the European Community; finally, the initial efforts at crisis-guidance under conditions of denationalizing state power will be discussed.

Translation: Susan Johnson

I MARXIST-LENINIST THESES ON REGIONAL
INTEGRATION. SUPRA-NATIONAL ORGANIZATIONS:
FORMS OF THE DECLINE OR GROWTH
OF CAPITALISM?

Since the turn of the century mainly two partially contradictory explanations of the international relations of capitalist systems have been offered by Marxist-Leninists: The first is based on the assumption that international capital is able to create for itself lasting forms of supra-state amalgamation in which conflicts are settled peacefully. The second proceeds from the idea that 'the bourgeoisie . . . [has] its special interests in each country and . . . [can] never go beyond its nationality';[1] if it does temporarily, regional capital and state associations reproduce the persisting, violent conflicts on the trans-national or global level. Communists vacillate between the two explanations according to the economic and political development of capitalism and the ideological demands it consequently imposes on their Parties. This suggests a degree of theoretical uncertainty vis-à-vis trans-national economic and political forms, which turns directly into political helplessness in mobilizing the social groupings which are the losers of capitalist integration. The contradictions between these two positions – represented by Hilferding, Lenin and Bucharin on the one hand, and Kautsky, Bernstein, Trotsky (Luxemburg) on the other – arose partly from the fact that their protagonists did not make a sufficiently clear distinction as to the level on which they were analyzing international relations (the global or the national), what period of development they had in mind, and what kind of foreign economic relations (e.g. foreign trade or international mergers) they were assuming to be characteristic of capitalism.

Hilferding and Lenin proceed from the assumption that imperialism represents a degenerate form of capitalism and that the conflicts between imperialists are bound to increase and become more intense. They consider foreign trade and capital export to be essential forms of the international activity and expansion of (national) capital and regard both as being conducted in keen competition and, finally, solved with the help of the foreign-power monopoly of the states, i.e. by threatening or using military force against other capitalists and their states. 'Political power thus becomes decisive in economic rivalry and finance-capital comes to have an immediate profit-interest in the state's power position'.[2]

To the same degree as the world market intensifies the contradictions between national capital oligarchies, the latter – according to Hilferding – seek protection from the state's monopoly on the use of force; armaments are increased. Inside the states growing concentration creates higher prices, a greater tax-burden, and solidarity of the middle-classes with the proletariat, which leads to a polarization of society. However, the monopolization of finance-capital also has a socializing function; in the external and internal conflicts mentioned above 'dictatorship of the capital magnates' can turn 'into the dictatorship of the proletariat'.[3] According to this theory the nationalistic and aggressive imperialists must consider any kind of 'harmony of capitalist interests' as 'sentimental humanitarianism'.[4]

Hilferding's basic theses were adopted by Lenin; however, Lenin's imperialism theory became considerably more complex and ambiguous as a result of his criticism of the exponents of 'ultra-imperialism'.[5] They assumed, in contrast to Hilferding and Lenin, that imperialism stabilized capitalism. On the basis of experience of war production, they maintained that the internationalization of capital could assume forms of action other than capital export and competition on the world market, namely economic *co-operation* emerging from competition and subsequent concentration.

Karl Marx had already seen the 'co-operative form of the working process on a continually growing scale' on which 'the *conscious* technical application of science, the *planned* exploitation of the earth' develop as an attendant phenomenon of the 'centralization or expropriation of a large number of capitalists by a few'[6] (the concentration of ownership as the necessary form of a process of capitalist expropriation).

Marx further postulated a connection between the progressive internationalization of capital and the corrosion of the national state, which would then lead to a reduction of international conflicts.[7]

Kautsky stuck closely to these Marxian theses in his evaluation of his empirical data. The 'increasing international interlacing of the various cliques of finance-capital'[8] to be observed was among the factors which led him:

> to consider whether it might not be possible that the present imperialist policy would be ousted by a new ultra-imperialist one, which would end the fight between national finance capitalists and lead to a joint exploitation of the world by an international league of finance-capital.[9]

The emergence of either an ultra-imperialism based on a compromise between finance-capitalists or an antagonism between them was, according to Kautsky, dependent upon the reactions of the finance-capitalists to the events of the First World War. If, full of national hatred, they would continue the arms race, he considered a second world-war inevitable. However, the participants in the War might take a different view:

> The longer the war lasts, the more it exhausts all those involved and makes them shrink from a repetition in the near future, the closer we move towards the latter solution (the replacement of imperialism by a 'Holy Alliance of Imperialists'), however unlikely this still seems at present'.[10] 'If it does come to such an era of ultra-imperialism, it is possible that at least the tendency towards the moral exhaustion of capitalism might temporarily be weakened ... for a time ultra-imperialism could bring an era of new hopes and expectations within capitalism.[11]

The question raised by Kautsky as to whether the calculation of the cost of wars does not finally lead to peaceful co-operation between the imperialists has up to now been answered in the affirmative at a regional level. On a global scale no answer has yet been given.

In this context Kautsky's idea that international capitalist mergers would create institutional forms which in turn would influence economic development is worth noting. To these 'international institutions for controlling or even deciding disputes between peoples and states' Kautsky attributed a dynamic effect on the economic basis.

> Once an economic emergency has paved the way to this association for the purposes of general disarmament and establishing international courts of arbitration — again as a result of economic needs — is soon bound to spread to further areas of political and economic life. As in the case of domestic politics, here too we are dealing with initial steps which lead farther and farther beyond themselves.[12]

According to Kautsky, (who quotes Engels in support), these international institutions, as the political form of the proletarian International, belong 'to the conditions for the final victory of the working class'.[13]

It is precisely this idea that is also taken up by Trotsky, Luxemburg and Bernstein, i.e. the introduction of proletarian Internationalism as an explosive force into the bourgeois forms of the supra-state.[14] An alternative explanation of the international forms of capitalism was put forward by Rosa Luxemburg in her book *The Accumulation of Capital.* (1913). Here she attempted to explain why capitalism did not collapse. She argued that a constant expansion of the capitalist system and a continual incorporation of new markets in the highly industrialized countries would not enhance proletarian revolution but rather raise the standard of living, thereby turning the proletariat gradually into a 'middle class'. It would not be until the colonial territories were transformed into capitalist systems that the final collapse of the capitalist world would come about.[15]

Lenin criticized these theories with the assertion that imperialism, as a decadent form of capitalism, did not delay the victory of the proletarian revolution but, on the contrary, directly prepared the way for it. 'In its imperialist stage capitalism leads close to the all-round socialization of production . . .' He contradicted the forecasts which expected the continuance of imperialism to bring about a stabilization of the capitalist system on the basis of a delimitation of the interests of finance-capital. In his opinion the economic antagonisms between the imperialists would, on the contrary, become more profound, the economic and political concessions to the masses (of which Luxemburg spoke) would be withdrawn, and thus the class struggle would inevitably come to a head. Despite his option for the eventual collapse of capitalism in the imperialist stage, he considered

> *temporary* agreements between capitalists and between powers to be possible. In this sense the United States of Europe are also possible as an agreement between *European* capitalists . . . on what? Purely and simply on how to jointly suppress Socialism in Europe and to jointly defend the colonies *against* Japan and America . . .[16]

With Lenin's endorsement of the temporary and regional nature of capitalist associations the difference between him and Kautsky can be reduced to consisting merely in the denial of the possibility of a global ultra-imperialism.

No doubt, the development is tending in the *direction of a single world trust swallowing up all the companies and all the states without exception.* But this development is taking place under such circumstances, at such a rate, amid such contradictions, conflicts and blows — by no means merely of an economic nature, but also political, national, etc., etc. — that *before* a single world trust, an 'ultra-imperialist' world union of national finance-capital is established, imperialism must of necessity explode, and capitalism will turn into its reverse.[17]

Whereas Lenin does not specify the economic activity which enables the capital to form coalitions (temporary, regional), Bucharin stipulates it unambiguously:

In only *one* case can we say with certainty that a solidarity of interests will come into being; that is, when we have an increase of partnership and joint financing in mind, i.e. when as a result of the joint stock-holding one and the same object is collectively owned by capitalists from various countries. Here a true 'Golden International' really does develop. Here is not merely a simple similarity, or . . . 'parallelism' of interests; here a unity of interests comes into being.[18]

Kautsky's vague anticipation of multi-national firms is thus defined precisely by Bucharin, who, however, adds the idea that a peaceful form of imperialism is impossible because an association of this kind would require comparable positions on the world market, whereas the actual unequal rate of development in the world economy leads to an intensification of capitalist conflicts.[19]

That completes the presentation of the main theses on the organizational ability of imperialism before the world economic crisis. It was not until after the Second World War that the Marxist-Leninists vis-à-vis growing state interventionism also gave thought to the trans-national conditions for economic guidance and planning.

Up to about 1963 the analysis of the West European unification movement was based on Lenin's ideas regarding the stagnation of capitalism and increasing capitalist contradictions. The application for membership of the EEC by the EFTA-states then promoted a reappraisal of the Common Market.[20] Despite its purported temporary nature and the persisting contradictions between the classes, interest-groups, and states, between the EEC and the USA, between supra-national institutions and governments, it was conceded to the Common Market that in it

a real technical and scientific revolution . . . together with an enormous renewal of the industrial structure of capitalism was to be observed. '. . . The EEC possesses a remarkable viability and has created objective situations which cannot be eliminated without serious consequences.'[21]

In the course of this reappraisal of capitalist integration there was also a discussion of the guidability of capitalist systems in the much discussed book published in the German Democratic Republic *Imperialismus heute*[22] and other writings specifically on the EEC.[23] In *Imperialismus heute* it is assumed that monopolies express a *collective will* for self-preservation and establish a primacy of politics in the regulation of the economy.

This thesis is based on a view of Engels's regarding the effects of capitalist socialization:

> Capitalist production by *joint-stock companies* is in itself no longer *private* production but production for the *associated* account of many. And if we move on from the joint-stock company to the trust, not only *private production* but also the *lack of planning* end.[24]

Monopolization in the economic sector and the systematic planning of production arising from this appear as the basis for state programming. The concentration in a few monopolies, so it is argued, increases the chances to survey and forecast, which are the pre-conditions for a 'forward regulation' of production and demand. This is accompanied by the relative independence of global guidance by the state, which in turn leads to emphasizing political considerations.[25]

In *Imperialismus heute* the increasing complexity of state and supra-state apparatuses is considered to constitute a *restriction of the power of the monopolies*. The correlation between the growing power of the monopolist bourgeoisie and the expansion of the state-apparatus, breaks up at the point where the latter becomes so complicated that it can no longer 'be absolutely controlled in every detail'. 'As it grows and becomes progressively more ramified, this organism becomes more susceptible to public pressure and to the influence of the social forces struggling for democracy'.[26] Its susceptibility stems mainly from the fact that national and supra-national organs 'while regulating more and more social sectors [have to] take issue with the opposition present in more and more areas'. Wirth quite rightly remarks here that 'this does not [say] anything about how successful the opposition can be in sub-areas'.[27]

In much the same way as according to this conception the spontaneity of capital within the states is curbed by political considerations, it is regulated on the supra-state level in

> an attempt to create an anti-national sovereignty of the leading monopolies through the establishment of a mammoth-state and a central executive organ of collective imperialism vested with extensive powers.[28]

These views which are reminiscent of 'ultra-imperialist' ideas,[29] are extrapolations of the integrational progress made in the European Community, above all in the attempted trans-national mergers of European firms.

If the fusion of the monopolies into multi-national concerns of the type

Agfa-Gevaert, Fiat-Citroën, Dunlop-Pirelli continues, it will only be possible to defend the special interests of these monpolies by means of a supra-national European Federal State.[30]

Since 1965 and in the course of the crises of the European Community and the world monetary system conceptions of this kind are being supplemented or disproved in a number of points in the Soviet and East German literature on political economics and in Marxist writings in the West. The following theses have since dominated the discussion:

1. *'In the present world monetary system . . . it is precisely nation-state crises that are externalized by the policy of regulation . . .'*[31]

An externalized recession reacts on the national economies in the form of a monetary crisis. As a result of this interdependence the national systems within the European Community become unstable and crisis-prone.

It would seem obvious to suppose that the possibility of simultaneous recession phenomena in several capitalist countries is growing and that thus the chance is decreasing of absorbing this kind of recession on a national level via exports as, for example, the Federal Republic of Germany still managed to do in 1966-67. Hence more severe national recessions are to be expected in future.[32]

2. *The integration of guidance in a few economic sectors increases the crisis-proneness of the overall system.*

It is argued that although the intensive extension of monopolistic regulation by the state in sub-areas leads to a growing degree of integration, this nevertheless – on account of unequal development in the different areas – all the more frequently plunges the overall process of integration into crises. The contradictions are transferred into the global guidance itself so that the integration-structure 'itself becomes the subject of the contradictions between the powerful monopoly-groups and the imperialist states, and also the stage on which these contradictions are fought out.'[33]

3. *The economic interest of business in a supra-state is not uniform.*

The replacement of nation-states by supra-national structures according to this argument not only meets the firms' interest but also their opposition.

. . . Within the national framework the monopolies on the one hand seek economic support from the state but on the other obstruct the transfer of new economic levers to the state; this tendency is equally typical for their relations with the international associations of state-monopolies, with the sole difference that the already-mentioned contradiction appears many times more sharply in the latter case.[34]

One of the causes of the firms' opposition is that

> without appropriate safeguards there [cannot] be a complete lifting of trade
> restrictions. As soon as the unemployment figures rise sharply in individual
> imperialist countries on account of increased exports by other countries,
> restrictive measures would doubtless be taken. In this sense the domestic
> economy thus continues to take precedence.[35]

As long as the national associations and authorities are the main opponents in
industrial struggles, the transference of state powers to a supra-national 'collective
capitalist' will be conducted with delaying tactics.[36]

4. *Finally, an answer to the question of whether supra-national regulation can be
effective is attempted on the basis of the behaviour or actions of the workers.*

In the opinion of Soviet authors supra-state regulation is accompanied 'by an
increasing international solidarity of the working class'.[37] In view of this trend the
ruling circles endeavour to tackle the social component 'of integration in order to
be able to channel and absorb incipient conflicts and class struggles'.[38] Whether
they succeed in doing so or not depends on how they employ the guiding
mechanisms. One should ask in this context, as M. Wirth, does

> whether the frequently advocated theory that the intensity of reactionary forces
> increases as a result of state-monopoly capitalism does not skip over precisely
> the initially greater flexibility in the methods of government which confers on
> the ruling class the assumption of economic functions through the state
> apparatus.[39]

It would in fact be conceivable 'that as a result of the greater flexibility the
reactionary forces may be intensified (e.g. on an international level) without also
resulting directly in a similar intensification inside the capitalist states'.[40]

This should complete the presentation of the most important controversial
theses contained in the Marxist-Leninist literature on the trans-national conditions
for economic guidance in Europe. These are now to be tested in the light of
empirical data and observations.

II POSSIBILITIES AND LIMITATIONS OF GLOBAL
GUIDANCE IN THE EUROPEAN COMMUNITY

In this section the 'contradictions' and conflicts[41] arising in the European
Community particularly with respect to global guidance are to be investigated to
see whether they (inevitably) have an integration-inhibiting, indeed a disintegrative
effect − as assumed in the Marxist-Leninist theses − or whether they do not rather
indicate a process of integration which, although not in a straight line, is
nevertheless progressing towards its goal despite (or perhaps because of) the crisis

situation. In other words: the 'objective limits' of capitalist integration asserted by the Marxist-Leninists in the above-mentioned theses are to be looked at more closely.

1. The interdependence of national business-cycles and the beginnings of supra-national guidance in the European Economic Community.

The 'hour of truth' for European integration will come in the opinion of all its observers in a depression. Only then, they say, will it become evident whether the EEC has reached the point of no return[42] or whether it will disintegrate. It is difficult to make appropriate forecasts. However, the business cycles of the EEC countries or the guidance of them provide a number of clues.

The economic theory of integration (on which the EEC Treaty is based) proceeds from the assumption that conditions similar to those of a domestic market can only be established in Western Europe when the *business-cycles* in the countries involved display steadily decreasing differences.

The views on actual business trends in the EEC differ little. In Marxist-Leninist writings,[43] along similar lines to those found in bourgeois analyses, it is shown that after the Second World War the Western industrial nations 'display similar fluctuations in economic activity, although various degrees of similarity and also deviating trends can be discovered.'[44]

EEC officials and experts assess the extent of the disparities still existing according to the autonomous, national alterations of the exchange-rate and the non-existence of a European capital market,[45] and come to the conclusion that an approximation of business trends has not taken place during the transitional phase of the EEC. Admittedly, the EEC countries are highly integrated with each other as regards trade, and the regional foreign trade structure in the Common Market does produce a mutual influencing of business trends, but the *interplay* of business cycles has not yet been superseded by a (predominant) *synchronic and parallel development.*

An extrapolation of the nationally guided business cycles for the seventies produces the result that in places and between individual countries they will run synchronic and parallel while elsewhere a counter-trend of flattened cycles in the EEC countries will occur. Here the interplay of business cycles could have a stabilizing effect.

Thus there exists in the EEC a 'functional harmony of business trends' which is stimulated internally by the foreign-trade integration and co-operation of the firms in the EEC and externally by US business. Figuring among the important interference factors are national business-trend policies, exchange-rate policies of the individual countries, and extra-economic factors which are reflected, for example, in social conflicts.

As far as trade integration is concerned, it is *over-proportionately* affected by business trends. In a slump the internal exchange of goods within the EEC drops heavily and in a boom it rises steeply. It is not difficult to deduce from this that a collective boom is of advantage to the progress of integration.

As already mentioned, the Common Market itself cannot, under the terms of the

Treaty, spontaneously solve the problem of the optimal allocation of the means of production and the distribution of the goods produced to the customers; it rather brings about distortions and impediments through monopolies etc. which demand political decisions.

The EEC Treaty provides the basis for collective guidance in the terms laid down in Articles 23, 103, 104 (magic triangle), and 105. A series of committees deal with business policy and medium-term economic and monetary policies.[46] In this context the resolutions to establish a European economic and monetary union should also be mentioned.

Taken as a whole, however, the Treaty leaves economic policy within national jurisdiction and merely indicates the possibility of co-ordinating objectives.

Despite the supplementary commitments of the member-states to bring into line and co-ordinate their economic policies no form of common global guidance has yet been developed although the integration of markets and the tendencies towards the integration of business trends pressed for it.[47]

In one or two spheres state intervention has been replaced by Community intervention: in the spheres of agriculture and, to a more limited degree, transport. These are state-intervention markets in underdeveloped or distressed sectors which are more accessible to supra-state regulation than free market sectors.[48] But it is precisely these sectors which display a tendency towards the 'encapsulation'[49] of their supra-national form and are thus unsuitable to effect a spill-over into neighbouring sectors of the economy; on the contrary, they increase the difficulties in guiding both the national economies and the European Economic Community as a whole.

Apart from the encapsulation effect of underdeveloped or distressed sectors further reasons for the failure of any coherent, European global guidance would be above all the regression to welfare-state sovereignty, in particular to autonomy in business-trend policy alongside increasing integration, and the diverging interests which are appearing in the face of the complex structure of the developing economic and monetary association.

The Common Market has led to economic developments and imbalances which in some cases can *no longer* be directly influenced by governments. A responsible, i.e. politically legitimated, supra-national authority does *not (yet)* exist. Since, however, the election-dependent governments continue to be held responsible on a national level for the overall economic equilibrium, they try to assert their jurisdiction in business-trend policy but at the same time endeavour not to close the open internal borders within the Community or to shield national markets in a conspicuous way. These paradox objectives bring about 'the tendency towards particularly harsh interventions, which often have to be paid for with corresponding losses of productivity'.[50]

Von der Groeben and Mestmäcker maintain that it is 'in the nature of things that the drawing up of Community policies lags behind the measures for producing a free internal market in both importance and volume'.[51] This statement gives a hint of the contrasts that exist between the states with their respective capital interests in integration. The structurally weaker capitals in particular — especially those of France and Italy — act as brakes on a European business-trend policy. The more strongly placed capitals, on the other hand, advocate a supra-national guidance mechanism to promote uniform conditions for the realization of value. The more serverely the balance of payment crisis and monetary crises, and also the structural crises, shake the EEC system, the greater is the regression to national thinking among the weaker countries.

The 'Economic and Monetary Union' was planned as a form of absorbing these national divergencies; it is seen as being at the same time

a. an economic area with a free exchange of goods and factors under a uniform currency,

b. a business cycle association for the joint guidance of short- and long-term economic policies, and

c. a social-policy union with the aim of structural and regional compensation.

This complex structure is based on the insight that any economic policy has consequences for growth, distribution and structure policies and affects the realization of social policies.[52] It is, however, open to question whether governments and firms are prepared and able to act in accordance with this insight.

In order to remove or alleviate the disparities in socio-economic development in Europe a series of co-ordinated measures would have to be taken in the field of economic and monetary policy which would bring widely differing advantages and disadvantages for the EEC-member countries.

The experiences with economic and monetary union since 1971 have shown that in the face of possible sacrifices governments choose the course of least resistance even when it is costly on a long-term basis. Thus, for example, the medium-term advantages of partial monetary integration in the 'European Currency Snake' (restrictions on exchange-rate fluctuations) were linked with financial aid, an exchange-adjustment fund, etc., which were to come to an end if no consensus could be achieved on parallel economic-policy steps in the second stage of the economic and monetary union. This did not work out. The agreement did lead to more intensive contacts between the organs of the governments and the European Community responsible for monetary and credit policies,

but it did not exert sufficient pressure to alter the major trends and structural causes of the imbalances of payments between the countries participating in the agreement. Without transferring a considerable degree of jurisdiction in economic policy to supra-national authorities it is only possible to achieve a smooth functioning of such a system between economies displaying similar productivity and stability features.[53]

However, the EEC is not such a homogeneous economic area. Neither are the instruments of economic and monetary policy attuned to one another, nor does a break-through in harmonizing one sector necessarily have a spillover effect (Haas) on the others. On the contrary, the pressure resulting from the unequal development of two closely associated sectors has a spill-back effect, a regression to the national level.

> Instead of an adequate transference of economic-policy powers to the European level parallel to the monetary integration . . . the regressive trend in monetary policy will sweep other sectors — for example, agricultural policy — along with it . . .[54]

2. *Business concerns, supra-national integration and global guidance.*

The European Community Treaty proceeded from the assumption that a fusion of the six markets into one would bring about a better distribution of labour and thus, automatically, a more profitable utilization of production factors, which would consequently lead to improvements in productivity, to a higher standard of living and to more efficient investment activity. The monopolies, cartels or market-dominating business concerns did not at first figure in this concept. In the meantime it has become clear who the 'true bosses' in the EEC are, namely — in the opinion of Sicco Mansholt, who retired from office in 1972 — not the governments but the multi-national firms.[55] It is they who play an active rôle in integrating allocative transactions across national frontiers, who penetrate the developed countries through direct investments and link up their industries in the distribution of labour. The greater this intermeshing becomes, the stronger the negotiating positions of business concerns become compared with the governments, the more their special interests in profit, productivity and efficiency conflict with the collective political and social objectives established by the election-dependent governments. In view of this constellation the question arises as to the way in which business firms influence regional integration in Europe.

The multi-national firms are undoubtedly better adapted to large-area production with an efficient division of labour than national business firms or governments. They are potentially able to organize people of different nations, to mobilize resources trans-nationally, and to employ the most modern production techniques. In other words, the multi-national concerns practise what can only be realized with great difficulty by the European governments: the free movement of people, goods and capital. However, the freedom of movement of the multi-national firms primarily serves the purpose of improving the utilization of resources in private interest, whereas the peoples' interest in a better supply of goods is merely derived from this. For a number of reasons directly attributable to the private interests of the firms the integrative force of the multi-national concerns is called into question:

1. They take too much from their host countries and leave them too little. This applies to technology, profits and re-financing as well as to the fact that labour costs are lower in the host countries than those of the firms in their countries of origin.

2. Managerial capacities are not distributed multi-nationally; the final decisions continue to be taken in the parent company. This expresses the fact that the multi-nationals do not practise integration but rather penetration.

3. The profit-maximization strategies are designed internationally but do not necessarily secure integration of the collectives. For multi-national companies are 'companies with their administrative centre located in one country, their production located in other countries where labour is cheap and their profits declared in countries where taxes are low'.[56]
The corresponding techniques are based on the existence of nation-states. Co-ordinated behaviour on the part of the national governments would make this manipulation a great deal more difficult.

4. Autonomous (or even concerted) action on the part of governments is impeded by the attempts of multi-national firms to make their host countries dependent on their raw materials or technologies. Once this dependence is established, opposition to foreign policy influencing on the part of the government of the parent company dwindles.

5. As was shown by the interference of the American Government and trade unions in the German debate on co-determination in management, attempts are made at curbing social reforms which seem detrimental to capital profits.

6. The 1969-73 monetary crisis is to be traced back to, among other factors, the speculative movement of the financial resources of the multi-nationals, which are exerting a de-stabilizing effect on the international monetary system.

These points of criticism should make the imperial integration concept of the multi-national firms clear: the firms govern the production of the world, or of certain regions, from a few capitals in the developed countries while the world periphery is confined to subordinate activities: it is being provided with wages, patterns of behaviour and consumption, by which it loses more and more of its independence.[57] American patterns of production and consumption are copied in Europe and elsewhere, and a turning-away from Americanism is not likely to be an easy matter on account of the influence of the multi-national firms in the respective governments. The estimated share that US firms have in the total GNP of the European Community amounts to between 15 and 20 per cent.

If the GNP growth rates can be used as an indicator of the overall performance of an integrating economy — as they often are — then the Europe-based US corporations comprise the total *relative* growth of Western Europe as compared to the growth of the US economy from 1950 to 1968.[58]

The power-potential of the multi-nationals is in addition indicated by the fact that they control greater portions of the GNP than the governments do through public expenditures.[59]

In order to resist this external determination or penetration of their own collective interests the governments in the EEC are taking various measures:

1. They, or the EEC Commission, are conducting the re-structuring of the European economy by promoting strong, cross-frontier European companies.

> The (EEC) memorandum (on industrial policy) regards Europe as a possible basis of concentration thus enabling the business firms of the Community to compete (with American firms) with the same weapons. The power aspects of this measure can be detected in its protectionism: the preferential allocation of commissions in trans-European firms and the supervision of third-country investments.[60]

The integration theory derived from these political considerations holds that trans-national (European) amalgamations of firms need protection and promotion by a supra-national business policy in order to remain competitive and would therefore demand corresponding supra-state norms and authorities. European mergers are thus seen as the motive force for supra-national institutionalization, which, for its part, in turn advances economic integration. This theory is held equally by the Marxist-Leninists and the practitioners in the EEC.

Doubts remain with regard to the degree of trans-national integration that makes the creation of a 'supra-state collective capitalist' necessary and to the possibility and expediency of a supra-state. According to Mandel the development towards a European Federal State will begin

> as soon as . . . the international capital integration within the EEC has advanced so far that at least a significant proportion of the large-scale means of production and circulation is no longer the special property of each national bourgeoisie but has become the property of capitalists from several European nations. Then an *overwhelming pressure arises in favour of a new state* which can effectively defend this new private property . . . 'European capital ownership' demands a 'European' bourgeois state as an adequate instrument to promote, guarantee and defend it.[61]

The compulsion to establish a supra-state results, according to Mandel, from the fact that

> the *radius of action* of the bourgeois state has to . . . *conform* with that of the production forces and production conditions. As long as the most important means of production of a country are in the possession of the bourgeoisie of this country, the nation-state is an adequate instrument of self-defence for the large-scale business enterprises. However, if the situation begins to *change,* if a tendency towards the international integration and interlacing of capital ownership starts to develop, then the nation-state ceases to be an effective instrument for defending the interests of these large-scale business enterprises as they

become more and more internationalized. A *new form of state* must then correspond to the new economic-social reality. This is the historic chance of the supra-national European institutions.[62]

The question is whether the new 'collective capitalist' can and must enter a supra-national form of state in order to adapt to the 'radius of action' of capital. Mandel's critics maintain, for example,

> that the capitalist nation-state is and will remain the basis for capital development, for it alone, as an ideal collective capitalist, is the political guarantor of the survival of capitalist methods of production.
> Under conditions of antagonistic production relations international capital cannot undermine the sovereignty of the respective nation-state to any great degree at all − i.e. transfer too many powers to international authorities − without noticeably weakening the political power acting as a guarantee of antagonistic production conditions.[63]

In both views the regulation of relations between business concerns and political authorities is made dependent on a state or supra-state. As is to be shown in Section III, a European constitutional structure in keeping with the present degree of capital integration is not, however, necessarily associated with a removal of national guidance mechanisms to supra-national organs. But this also means that mergers of business firms do not necessarily create political responsibilities. The practices of EEC industrial policy indicate rather that the legitimation of supra-state regulation could be increasingly *uncoupled* from the organs responsible for it.

> For if the demanded organization of trans-national business concerns with European control-centres were to bring about the replacement of European competitive policy by a policy of co-operation, then economically powerful business concerns, instead of the democratically legitimated Community institutions, might determine the image of the Community. The system based on the ideas of a constitutional state and the pursuit of freedom, which is intended to be safeguarded and further developed by the EEC Treaty, would be jeopardized to a considerable degree if a non-parliamentarily controlled executive were to seek political support primarily among the economic groups affected by its decisions.[64]

This process is, however, a result of the EEC's policy, which is characterized by 'delegating the main burden of decisions to the participants in the market once the framework for liberalisation has been created by the lifting of national barriers, by legal harmonization or European Law'.[65]

Since national intervention policies are not *pari passu* co-ordinated, the business firms can extend their scope of action. In the present state of foreign-trade and capital integration in Europe they are pursuing a double-strategy on the national and on the international level to assert their interests. In cases where the nation-state demands a certain kind of behaviour of them in order to guarantee stability and welfare, they try to escape to the supra-national sphere where political responsibility is not yet established; however when the safeguarding of profits is concerned, they fall back on the nation-state or on trans-national procedures (Community or preferably inter-governmental ones).[66]

The difficulties of a co-ordinated global guidance in the EEC resulting from this 'double-strategy' are evident. Their effects are felt particularly because

> the business-cycle association between the Community countries has become closer, thus rendering integration as a whole more susceptible to business-trend fluctuations than it was during the first two phases of the process of integration.[67]

In view of this development a noticeable gap has arisen between the loss of national guidance-capacity and the absence as yet of Community action, and it is from this gap that the firms are trying to reap advantages in the areas not covered by the State and the Law.

In other words, on the one hand they are not interested in Community organs which make their transactions conditional on tax and currency discrepancies more difficult. They would regret if the possibility of benefitting from the different price-policies they have hitherto been able to pursue because of the fragmentation of the market were to be reduced in an economic and monetary union. On the other hand, however, the multi-national firms also see an economic and monetary union as an element for the stabilization of the Common Market and for the improvement of their legal security.

> The gradual removal of the technical impediments to trade (the harmonization of security and environmental regulations, norms and standards) opens up new opportunities for large-scale mass production. Whereas, on the one hand, competition might become keener, the business concerns hope, on the other hand, to derive advantages from regional-fund measures. The establishment of a European Community Law is likely to facilitate cross-frontier mergers. In view of the present emphasis on conservation of the environment the business concerns hope that uniform norms will be established on a Community level so that they do not suffer any disadvantages as compared to their European competitors.[68]

The hopes the integrationists and Communists had set on the increase of European mergers in the sixties have in the meantime been disappointed. The number of European firms can be counted on two hands and they are far from coming up to the American-dominated multi-nationals in capital assets.

The reasons for the failure of the European companies[69] which have been planned or founded indicate without exception that national loyalties and collective social actions (strikes, protests, for example, against shut-downs) noticeably weaken the urge to amalgamate. Furthermore, European business concerns are forced — on account of their belonging politically to the EEC and being much smaller in size compared to the Americans — to submit to sovereign acts of the EEC authorities. In the long run, however, they could benefit from the fact 'that they have to be less afraid of political complications in connection with their activities (than the Americans)'.[70]

2. Further measures taken by the European governments consist in controlling the American-dominated, multi-national firms by means of national or international instruments.[71] On account of the already mentioned power-potential accumulated by the US-firms within the EEC it is, however, difficult to imagine these controls being exercised without retaliatory measures — losses of productivity and jobs. It is further to be observed that national and international authorities shirk the control-problem because they do not possess sufficient reserves of power. 'They [come to an arrangement] with the multi-national firm or [overcome] the conflict between the firm's interests and the public interest by adjusting the public to the private interest.'[72] From this Biedenkopf draws the conclusion that only a powerful, democratically legitimated organ would be able to exercise control. Here the questions arise as to how suitable organs could come into being and whether control and democratic legitimacy are necessarily conditional on each other.

With reference to the second question Dahrendorf[73] has already pointed out the discrepancy between the internationalization of economic and political power on the one hand and procuring of legitimacy on the other. There is no necessary economic and political compulsion to organize control internationally in the EEC. Initial steps towards supra-state organization could at most come about if the profit-maximization or profit-safeguarding of the multi-national firms are jeopardized by insoluble social conflicts in all the EEC countries, or if crises could no longer be avoided.

3. *The 'social component' of global guidance in the European Community.*

In view of the regional and social disparities and the increasing demands of the economically discriminated and weakened groups which have grown up in the course of economic integration 'a central rôle [devolves on] a broadly-conceived social policy in the building of a Community which can stand up to stress and is capable of taking action . . .'[74]

The ability of the countries to practise guidance in the national and supra-national sphere depends decisively on the way in which the working populations and their organizations participate in determining integration. Before the Paris Summit Conference in October 1972, at which social-policy measures were introduced into the package of objectives of the economic and monetary union, the social policy of the EEC — like that of the nation-states — had been primarily orientated to economic categories such as the avoidance of distortions of competition or the removal of obstacles to mobility.[75] In 1973 an independent social policy, (which is 'not a mere appendage to economic growth'[76]), was set down in the 'Social Action Programme'[77] of the EEC. This programme has three main objectives: the safeguarding of employment, the improvement of living and working conditions, and the co-operation of employers and employed in dealing with tasks in the field of economic and social policy in the EEC. It falls far short of the intentions of the Paris Summit inasmuch as the latter spoke of the parallel advancement of the economic and monetary union and the social union, whereas in the Social Action Programme economic integration continues to dominate. Thus, the EEC's deficit in social policy is continually growing. The governments are faced with the question of what measure of regional or social compensation and harmonization is sufficient to stave off dissatisfaction. This measure (expressed in the funds available) is also determined by the strength of the solidarity that the trade unions mobilize and organize in order to exert pressure to decrease the social differential.[78]

The level of solidarity among the employed populations in the EEC is extremely low and, for various reasons, will not be raised to any great extent in the short or medium term.

1. The social and community disparities in the EEC do not strengthen but rather diminish it; any encroachment on national welfare-state advantages in favour of workers of a different nationality is rejected. Employees display political loyalty wherever their jobs are safeguarded by sovereign authorities.

2. Furthermore, the difficulties experienced by the trade unions in the state sphere anyway are increased in an international area of integration.

   'If the trade unions make full use of the great negotiating power they have derived from the strain on the labour-market, and if they threaten the profit-expectations of the firms, which in the last analysis determine business trends, then the latter will react with two strategies, both of which could doom the success of a militant wage policy:

   If the situation on the export market allows, they will raise their prices. If this is impossible, they will go on an 'investment strike' and endanger growth with negative consequences for full-employment.

   Thus rising prices and growing unemployment can be the results of an [expansive] wages policy aiming at distribution of wealth. . . . However, if the trade unions do not make use of their negotiating power, relations between organization and members can become strained: distortions in the distribution structure to the advantage of the capitalists can lead to spontaneous strikes, legitimation-crises of the trade-union leadership, and an expanding wages drift, which estranges the trade unions in the plants. This principally describes the dilemma of the trade unions' distribution struggle in state-interventionist capitalism.'[79]

If the trade unions agree to a 'peace formula' — which is today the case in all the West European countries[80] — i.e. if the wage increase is determined according to the average increase in productivity in the economy as a whole, then the trade unions consider the result of the distribution struggle (measured in absolute wages, not according to the wage quota) to be positive. However, in this process the stability of the overall economy is decisively determined by the profit expectations of private investors.

Since the raising of nominal wages ranks first among the objectives of most labour organizations in the EEC, it is only with difficulty that — in view of the different economic structures and developments — any solidarity can emerge on an international level regarding objectives which are paid little attention on a national level: e.g. participation in management, equality of opportunity, monopolies and mergers control. It is precisely on these concepts that the interests of the various national trade unions diverge, as became evident in the unholy battle over co-determination within the European joint-stock company.[81]

Tudyka[82] argues that the various groups of workers in the EEC have become divided into the following factions:

a. between those in countries with a high standard of working and production conditions and those in the so-called low wage countries;
b. on a national level, between extensively internationalized and highly capitalized branches on the one hand and stagnating or regressive branches on the other;
c. within the various branches, between multi-nationally operating firms on the one hand and national investors and suppliers on the other;
d. within the multi-national firms, between the management and supervisory personnel and the broad mass of semi-skilled and un-skilled workers.

Whether the future development will tend towards an aggravation of the contradictions or to a levelling out of the differences between these groups depends, for example, on whether the employers succeed in using above-average wages to create the kind of 'labour aristocracy' through which the 'revolutionary energy' in the whole labour force of the EEC would 'evaporate' — as Marx[83] put it — or whether they succeed in attracting trade unions which are willing to compromise and which help them to stem internal or trans-national conflicts.

Another decisive factor is the behaviour of the workers during crises. Contrary to generally accepted opinions, it has turned out that a lowering of wage levels, a cutting of the company's social contributions, and a lessening of the workers' influence on work procedures in the company and an organization for the recovery of the national working power (e.g. by means of re-training, provision for the sick, continuation training, etc.)[84] contribute little towards producing solidarity: the effects of integration on the collective struggle of the workers express themselves in the fact that the employers settle unrest in branch-works by threatening partial lay-offs, investment-freezes, transfer of production, etc.

As a result of their different locations the multi-national firms are in a position to compensate the effects of strikes: they can, for example, send foreign workers as blacklegs into the parts of the concern where a strike is taking place, which means that the workers have difficulty in formulating uniform demands for the whole of the concern and its total labour force. In the face of the multi-national firm the workers in the individual national and supra-national trade unions appear hopelessly disunited and not very amenable to international organization.

What is to be observed, then, is the emergence of a 'European Gesamtarbeiter' who, without an articulated and organized interest of his own, contributes to the fact that social policy and industrial law are only very hesitantly considered and tackled in the supra-national organizations. He even impedes the relatively progressive, welfare-state measures taken by national governments inasmuch as the activities of the multi-national firms have the effect that the overall reproduction of the national workers can no longer be guaranteed nationally, while supra-national action is not (yet) possible. The conservative critics of the present development of the EEC attribute the deficiencies in social policy to the Community's structure and consider that a conflict-front has opened up between workers, industrialists and supra-national bureaucracy.

All demands for more direct democracy and for the democratization of society are bound to come into conflict with the present structure of the Community. Consideration of the social implications of decisions regarding economic policy runs up directly against the limitations of the Community. The question of whether and in what way workers' co-determination should be provided for in the organs of the capital company is an impediment to the process of legal alignment in the field of Company Law because an adequate political basis is lacking for the development of a European model of participation in management.[85]

Up to now the level of solidarity has still been controlled by the EEC governments.

They decide the extent to which associations and parties participate in the European decision-making process and thus determine the degree of diversification of the bodies responsible for integration. The effort to solidarily smoothe out inter-regional and inter-state disparities also falls within the competence and the 'will' of the governments. Thus community solidarity is identical with loyalty-relationship of the political élites to the EEC.[86]

The investigations on global guidance in the EEC show that it is not functioning as planned. It creates considerable conflicts which are, however, distinguished by the fact that they are fought out in overlapping fields: between states, between these and other associations, etc. However, depending on the respective economic situation, coalitions also come into being, for example, between states and business concerns against the trade unions, between trade unions and business concerns against the states, etc. The effect of this is that the conflicts scarcely lead to polarizations but at most to changed constellations of interests which are likely to increase rather than to decrease the stability of the overall system.

III DE-NATIONALIZATION OF STATE
POWER AND CRISIS-AVOIDANCE

In this section the questions are to be investigated of what political form the increasing integration or disintegration of the European states leads to and of what influence it has on crisis guidance. In other words:

a. Is the self-transformation and self-preservation of the capitalist systems in Europe succeeding, and what rôle do the supra-national amalgamations play in this?
b. Are economic crises rather encouraged or avoided by supra-national organizations?
c. Provided that a European depression comes about, will it then encourage deviant social and political behaviour which leads into a revolutionary class struggle?
d. Are there signs that a general crisis is being 'postponed' or transformed into a variety of crisis tendencies? 'Does the anomous potential to be expected allow of purpose-orientated political action or does it rather lead to the non-directed dysfunctionalization of sub-systems? '[87]

In Marxist-Leninist literature depression, crisis, the disintegration of the European Community and the collapse of the capitalist systems in Europe are brought into relation with each other, if not identified altogether. The above mentioned, continually growing contradictions within the EEC are taken as indicators of capitalist crises. Although these contradictions could theoretically be settled by a European Federal State, this state is hardly to be expected to come into being on account of the lack of political consensus — which in turn is due to the contradictory economic interests.

Accordingly, the EEC will continue to be threatened by crises as long as, firstly, a certain volume of capital is not socialized to a degree that disintegration would bring incalculable costs in its wake and, as secondly, the supra-national firms do not demand public — more specifically, supra-state — promotion and safeguarding which would also provide starting-points for European global guidance.

According to this view — which, incidentally, is to be found both among the Marxist-Leninists and among the supra-nationalists — the EEC is in an exceptionally unstable condition on account of the growing harmony of business trends and on account of the control-gap[88] which has arisen between the loss of grip by the national stabilization instruments and the not yet applied supra-national guidance levers.

The theses underlying these premises are open to attack. It has already been pointed out that an increasing harmony of business cycles would only appear over a long period. Up to then the divergent national business trends create for the governments possibilities for compensation which they are unwilling to renounce.

The idea prevailing among supra-nationalists and Communists that transnational economic activity 'is only to be regulated on an EEC level by an 'ideeller Gesamtkapitalist' (Marx) furnished with all the means of state power'[89] does not correspond with the developments to be observed in the European Community. Since both fix their gaze on supra-national authorities and the development of these towards a supra-state, they judge the 'council constitution' emerging on the inter-governmental level to be a 'mis-development', a national regression and stagnation of the EEC, or the expression of capitalist contradictions. They do not ask whether these new forms and functions of sovereign power do not possibly correspond to present capital interests and their amalgamations better than supra-nationality would.[90]

A European constitutional structure which corresponds to the present degree of capital integration[91] is not necessarily associated with a transference of national guidance mechanisms to supra-national organs. It needs rather to be examined whether the guidance of trans-national relations could not be carried out more efficiently by making competitive or synchronic use of national and possibly also supra-national instruments. Admittedly, the economic and monetary union is based on the idea that the transference of instruments of economic and monetary policy to supra-national authorities is to be combined with their gradual incorporation into a responsible 'European Government'. However, one must ask in this connection whether the 'state-like nature' of a government is an indispensable pre-requisite for its guidance activity.

The rapid trans-national concentration, centralization and socialization of capital without doubt demand greater possibilities for sovereign control and guaranteeing activities. It is not certain whether they also demand a larger state-unit[92] on which the national governments would have only an indirect influence. It would be conceivable that the state-mechanisms become differentiated and partially fused on an inter-governmental level (i.e. responsible to the governments as opposed to being supra-national, i.e. European-technocratic). Against this the following objection is to be taken into consideration:

> This process, however, is in contradiction with the state's role as a factor of social cohesion, which is increasingly called into question. It would seem that the development of integrated European capital will come into conflict with the need to maintain adequate state institutions at national and social level to fulfill the varied social functions summed up by Murray as 'intervention for social consensus'. In fact these 'economic' and 'social' state functions are not separable, and the attempt to carry out state functions through different mechanisms and at different levels of international integration will impose great strains on the state . . .[93]

The thesis of the inseparability of state functions contained in this statement would require discussion.

In fact a 'de-nationalization of state power'[94] is taking place without a new state super-system coming into being. It is expressed rather in the progressive integration of national and supra-national bureaucracies, through which the feed-back processes become a great deal shorter. Von der Groeben and Mestmäcker charge this system with possessing a very small possibility of correcting decisions once they have been made.

In the institutional system of the Community political constraints and possibilities to correct decisions are extremely small: the most important example of this is provided by agricultural policy. If a supreme decision-making organ of the Community orientated at the principle of unanimity were to tackle a great amount of common economic planning, this would be bound to increase the inadequacies of the present structure of the Community. A danger of this kind is indicated in the recommandations of the Commission on the Industrial Policy of the Community.[95]

The standpoint of the critics of the inter-governmental 'council constitution' is clear, determined as it is by the idea of a supra-national Community equipped with democratic-parliamentary organs. In fact the question arises as to whether economic stabilization can be achieved without formal democratic institutions and procedures since they after all make sure that

the decisions of the administration can be reached to a great extent independently of specific motives of the citizens. This is achieved via a legitimation process which furnishes generalized motives — i.e. diffuse mass loyalty — but avoids participation.[96]

The more closely the feed-back of the economic system is linked to the political system, the greater the need for legitimation becomes.[97]

Because their reproduction is based on the privileged appropriation of socially produced wealth, all class societies have to solve the problem of how to distribute the surplus national-product unequally and yet legitimately.[98]

This purpose is served by the legal procedures in parliament and government, whose legality is advanced as a sign of legitimate distribution. This form of procuring legitimacy, does not yet take place in the EEC although the constitutional superstructure for it has already been established as an empty form. As emerges from the discussion on the European elections,[99] the governments are faced with the difficult task of creating institutional pre-conditions for participation and at the same time reducing the risk of this chance being taken. Accordingly, they propagate democratic elections but also endeavour to delay them as long as possible. Furthermore, even if European elections should materialize, the physical distance between the citizens and the international decision-making authorities and the complexity and size of the integrated West European area would enable them to maintain the 'civic privatism' (Habermas) of the citizens in the future, too. In bottlenecks of welfare-state programming it is possible to hold up system-constraints as scapegoats, such as, for example, the different economic systems in the EEC, the threat from the East, or the trade war with the USA. As a result of the fact that the instruments for global guidance are no longer connected with authorities but in part lie in the intermediate area between the governments, the legitimation-claims or legitimation-deficits can furthermore be averted or avoided by pointing out that the limits of the political system or of its jurisdiction have shifted.

Even though it is still questionable whether supra-national integration can serve 'to prolong the business-cycle and transform the periodic bursts of capital depreciation into a permanent inflationary crisis with milder business trend fluctuations',[100] the possibility at all events remains of spreading the consequences of the intercepted crises over a broad area in the European Community, i.e. trans-nationally. The low degree of organization of the groups concerned — so far as they are not industrialists — makes this possible. It can be guaranteed that social protests will not turn into the political form of a class struggle but will be processed or regulated administratively or politically.

This regulation is further facilitated by a new dimension of integration between states and economies, namely by the *East-West co-operation between the antagonistic systems in Europe.* This not only serves to protect production and marketing against the swings in capitalist business trends; it also opens up ways to co-operation with the Third World, by which the commercialization difficulties in the capitalist countries can be lessened; but finally inter-system co-operation creates for the states and business firms (especially for American, European, and Soviet multi-nationals) uncontrolled areas in which co-determination or even self-management of the production in East and West has little chance to develop.

NOTES

1. Friedrich Engels: *The Festival of the Nations in London* (On the Celebration of the Establishment of the French Republic, 22 September 1792) quoted originally from the German *Nachlass*, edited by Mehring, vol. 28, 406.

2. R. Hilferding: *Das Finanzkapital*, (Vienna: 1910), 420.

3. Hilferding, op. cit., 477.

4. Hilferding, op. cit., 428.

5. Cf. below.

6. K. Marx: *Capital.* Quoted from the German edition, vol. 1, (Berlin: 1951), 803. (The italics are mine.)

7. K. Marx and F. Engels: *The Communist Manifesto,* (German, Stuttgart: 1953). Cf. in this connection the controversy between K. Tudyka and F. v. Krosigk ('Marx, Universalism and Contemporary World Business', in: *International Studies Qu.,* Dec. 1972). In German in: K. Tudyka et al.: *Transnationale Konzerne und Interessenvertretung der Lohnabhängigen.* 1. Zwischenbericht für die DGFK, April 1973, Nijmegen. Mimeo S.10.

8. K. Kautsky: 'Zwei Schriften zum Umlernen', in: *Die Neue Zeit,* 1915, vol. 2, 144.

9. Kautsky, op. cit., 144.

10. K. Kautsky: 'Der Imperialismus', in: *Die Neue Zeit,* 32nd year, vol. 2, 1914, 922.

11. Kautsky: 'Zwei Schriften . . .', op. cit., 145.

12. K. Kautsky: *Habsburgs Glück und Ende,* 1918, 78. This contains the beginnings of the theory of spill-over effects of regional and functional integration which was further developed in American integration research after the Second World War. Cf. the works of E. B. Haas and A. Etzioni.

13. Kautsky, op. cit., 78.

14. L. Trotsky: *Europe and America,* (in German, Berlin: 1926) 92ff.; E. Bernstein: Völkerbund und Staatenbund', (Berlin: 1918), 7; R. Luxemburg, *Die Akkumulation des Kapitals* (Berlin: 1913), and quoted by R. Fischer: *Stalin and German Communism* (Cambridge: 1948) 24f.

15. Luxemburg, op. cit., 423ff.

16. V. I. Lenin: *On the Slogan of the United States of Europe,* in German in: *Ausgewählte Werke in 2 Bänden,* Bd. 2 (Moscow: 1946), 750-54; Lenin's argumentation lacks any reference to capitalist federal states which had disbanded again after a while.

17. Lenin, quoted in E. Mandel: 'Die Widersprüche des Imperialismus', in *Internationale Marxistische Diskussion 13* (Berlin: 1971) 155.

18. N. Bucharin: *Imperialism and World Economy,* 1929, quoted in S. Picciotto and H. Radice: 'Capital and State in the World Economy', in: Kapitalistate, 1/1973, 57f.

19. Op. cit., 60.

20. In the Moscow Theses on the EEC of August 1962.

21. A. Arsumanian in Pravda, 23 May 1962.

22. *Imperialismus heute* (Imperialism Today) (Berlin (East): 1965).

23. Quoted in M. Wirth: *Kapitalismustheorie in der DDR* (Frankfurt: 1972).

24. F. Engels: *Zur Kritik des sozialdemokratischen Programmentwurfs 1891* (Critique of the Plan for a Social Democratic Programme 1891), quoted in: *Imperialismus heute,* op. cit., 431.

25. Wirth, op. cit., 96.

26. *Imperialismus heute,* op. cit., 184.

27. Wirth, op. cit., 124f.

28. K. H. Domdey, quoted in Wirth, op. cit., 60.

29. Formulated as a reproach against Mandel by Nicolaus, in: Die Objektivität des Imperialismus. Anti-Mandel: *Internat. Marx. Diskussion 13,* Berlin 1971, 85ff.

30. Mandel, op. cit., 156.

31. E. Altvater: *Die Weltwährungskrise* (Frankfurt: 1969) 75.

32. Wirth, op. cit., 142.

33. *Der Imperialismus der BRD,* (Berlin (East): 1971) 426.

34. *Politische Ökonomie des heutigen Monopolkapitalismus* (Frankfurt: 1972) 610.

35. Gündel, quoted in Wirth, op. cit., 60f.

36. Cf. Section III below.

37. *Politische Ökonomie . . .,* op. cit., 613.

38. *Der Imperialismus . . .,* op. cit., 411.

39. Wirth, op. cit., 77.

40. Ibid.

41. In order to make an empirical investigation of the 'contradictions' of capitalism or the conflicts arising from it in global guidance it would be necessary to first differentiate them according to cause, course and effect in the process of integration. Only a procedure such as this would also give the term 'crisis' precision in depth. An unreflected use of the terms 'conflict' and 'crisis' leaves out of consideration for example, that there can be system-stabilizing conflicts or that the open expression of a conflict can have a crisis-alleviating (or even crisis-avoiding) effect.

42. Cf. Section III below.

43. E.g. *Politische Ökonomie . . .*, op. cit., 861, and *Der Imperialismus . . .* op. cit., 293ff.

44. Colloquium on selected problems of business-trend theory, under Prof. Dr A. E. Ott in the summer term 1971. Printed in Germany by the Univ. of Tübingen, 394.

45. Cf. on this H. von der Groeben and E.-J. Mestmäcker (eds): *Ziele und Methoden der europäischen Integration* (Frankfurt: 1972) 81, and also the controversy between Mandel and Nicolaus in: Die Objektivität des Imperialismus. Anti-Mandel: *Internat. Marxist. Diskussion* 13 (Berlin: 1971), 38ff.

46. v. d. Groeben and Mestmäcker, op. cit., 83.

47. Ibid., 17.

48. Ibid.

49. Cf. E. B. Haas on the encapsulation of international organizations in: 'The Study of Regional Integration', in *International Organization*, 24, 615.

50. Ibid., 98.

51. v. d. Groeben and Mestmäcker, op. cit., 98.

52. Bildungswerk Europäische Politik: Bericht der Deutschen Studiengruppe 'Übergangsphase zur Wirtschafts- und Währungsunion' (Draft) mimeo, 32. This is a report by the German Study Group on the "Transitional Phase towards the Economic and Monetary Union" produced for the Bildungswerk Europ. Politik. Bonn.

53. Chr. Lutz: 'Nachruf auf die europäische Währungsschlange', in: EA, 9a/1974, 290.

54. Lutz, op. cit., 290.

55. H. Hveem: 'Integration by Whom, for Whom, against Whom?' in: *Cooperation and Conflict*, 4/1974, 271.

56. Hawker-Siddley quoted in Bruno Colle: 'Private Supranational Power', in: *Lo Spettatore Internazionale*, 1/74, 34.

57. S. Hymer quoted in Colle, op. cit., 47.

58. Hveem, op. cit., 271.

59. Ibid.

60. v. d. Groeben and Mestmäcker, op. cit., 77.

61. E. Mandel: *Die EWG und die Konkurrenz Europa-Amerika* (Frankfurt: 1968) 46.

62. Ibid., 45.

63. D. Goralcyzk: Möglichkeiten und Grenzen der ökonomischen Integration kapitalistischer Staaten, in: *Blätter für deutsche und internationale Politik*, 1972, 1287.

64. v. d. Groeben and Mestmäcker, op. cit., 179.

65. Op. cit., 114.

66. Cf. on this for example, the attempts of the industrial associations to influence the Ministries in order to prevent the amendment of West German Cartel Legislation by pointing to the development of a (much more laxly administered) European Cartel Law; further the lobby of the German cosmetics industry on: the European harmonization of legislation on foodstuffs.

67. Item 46 of the 'Jahresgutachten 1972-73 des Sachverständigenrats zue Begutachtung der gesamtwirtschaftl. Entwicklung "Gleicher Rang für den Geldwert" ', (Stuttgart: 1973).

68. Bericht der Deutschen Studiengruppe, op. cit., 92. Cf. note 52.

69. Factors mentioned are: 1. the lack of a European Company law; 2. the lack of a European capital market; 3. the lack of a uniform currency; 4. the differences in social legislation; 5. the differences in tax legislation; 6. the national loyalties of the business concerns; 7. differences in social policies; 8. shut-downs after amalgamation.

70. H. Bößenecker: *Europa in der Stunde der Entscheidung* (Munich: 1974), 60.

71. On the measures in detail cf. G. Langer: 'Können multinationale Unternehmen international kontrolliert werden?' in: D. Kebschull and O. G. Mayer (eds) *Multinationale Unternehmen, Anfang oder Ende der Weltwirtschaft* (Frankfurt: 1974) 2.

72. K.-H. Biedenkopf, quoted in Langer, op. cit., 243.

73. *Plädoyer für die Europäische Union* (Munich: 1973).

74. R. Rummel: *Die soziale Komponente in der Europäischen Union.* Stiftung Wissenschaft und Politik, 224 (Ebenhausen: 1974) 35.

75. v. d. Groeben and Mestmäcker, op. cit., 117.

76. Ibid., 135.

77. Brussels, October 1973.

78. Cf. on the tying up of social expenditures in the European states, Rummel, op. cit., 67ff.

79. W. Meißner and L. Unterseher (eds) *Verteilungskampf und Stabilitätspolitik* (Stuttgart: 1972), 17.

80. G. Zellentin: *Europa 1985* (Bonn: 1973), 65.

81. Described in K. O. Hondrich: *Mitbestimmung in Europa* (Bonn: 1971).

82. K. Tudyka, op. cit., 63.

83. K. Marx and F. Engels: *Correspondence,* quoted from the German edition vol. III, Berlin 1950, 124.

84. Tudyka, op. cit., 65.

85. v. d. Groeben and Mestmäcker, op. cit., 107.

86. Rummel, op. cit., 102.

87. J. Habermas: *Legitimationsprobleme im Spätkapitalismus* (Frankfurt: 1973), 59f.

88. Cf. above 00.

89. Goralczyk, op. cit., 1287.

90. The fixation on supra-nationality or on the Commission leads to false judgements. Thus the (young) Leftists are jubilant, for example, that the Commission and the European Parliament have gone over to demanding a greater democratization of EEC-institutions, a Community policy on the conservation of the environment, a revision of development and agricultural policy, the guaranteeing of a minimum wage in Europe, the introduction of local voting rights for foreign workers, and a social and regional policy in the development of the economic and monetary union. What they fail to see is that these 'left-wing' demands indicate exactly the distance of the Commission from the centres of power. (E. Häckel and W. Elsner: *Kritik der Jungen Linken an Europa* (Bonn: 1973). The Commission is able to put itself on the same level as the critical young Leftists because it has to a great extent lost its institutional importance as a supra-national organ compared with the inter-governmental organs.

91. It remains to be seen whether the degree of integration delineated by Mandel demands supra-national authorities. For the time being, however, – provided that US-investments in Europe are not decreasing – the American firms will remain by far stronger in volume than the European ones. Cf. on this the table and chart in Zellentin, op. cit., 88 and 89.

92. Cf. Picciotto and Radice, op. cit., 64.

93. Ibid., 64.

94. Ibid., 65.

95. v. d. Groeben and Mestmäcker, op. cit., 103.

96. Habermas, op. cit., 55.

97. Ibid., 54.

98. Lenski quoted in Habermas, op. cit., 132.

99. B. Kohler: 'Integration und Verflechtung durch Europäische Wahlen? ' in: *Regionale Verflechtung der Bundesrepublik Deutschland* (Munich: 1973) 247ff.

100. Habermas, op. cit., 58.

Conditions for Economic and Technological Exchange in the Co-operation between East and West

Ulrich Albrecht and Udo Rehfeldt

ON THE DEVELOPMENT OF ECONOMIC RELATIONS BETWEEN EAST AND WEST EUROPE

THE BREAKING UP OF THE COALITION of the victorious powers[1] through the American rejection of a settlement of interests with its former wartime ally, the USSR, led to a parallel politico-military confrontation and, also, to an almost total collapse of economic relations between the capitalist 'West', on the one hand, and the Soviet Union and the East European countries in its 'influence zone', on the other. The decisive factor in this was the economic offensive weapon used in the 'Cold War' corresponding to the American global strategy of 'roll back' and 'containment': the setting up of an economic blockade against the East European states. From 1947 on, the US administration had been developing plans to force down Soviet growth-rates by means of a strict control on Soviet imports. Thus, the economic and military supremacy of the United States would be ensured. In 1949, these plans culminated in a 'gentlemen's agreement', in which the American government forced its Western allies de facto to join in the embargo measures already decided on by the American Congress.[2] A Co-ordinating Committee (COCOM) was established, which comprised all the member states of the newly formed NATO (except for Iceland), plus Japan. COCOM's function was to draw up lists of 'strategic goods' which it was forbidden to export to the Eastern Bloc and to supervise the implementation of the regulations. The West European governments opposed from the outset an excessive interpretation of the embargo and wanted to see it limited to strategic goods in the strictest sense. During the Korean War, however, they were forced to fall into line with American conceptions, with the result that, at the height of the Cold War, the COCOM lists covered about 50 per

Translation: Susan Johnson

cent of all the types of goods figuring in world trade, and included almost all armaments goods with a high level of technological sophistication.

In 1952, Stalin, in an historical abridgement,[3] summed up the consequences of these measures in his thesis of the 'two parallel world markets': 'The most important economic result of the Second World War must be seen to lie in the disintegration of the unified, all-embracing world market'.[4] However, the emphasis on the 'consolidation of the new (socialist) world market'[5] obscures the fact that it was the American embargo which, in the first place, enabled the USSR to transfer Eastern Europe's foreign trade relations to a new Soviet-dominated structure.

By 1958, inter-system economic relations had sunk to their lowest: trade between 'blocs' accounted for no more than 2.1 per cent of the foreign trade of the 'Western' states and 14 per cent of that of the East European socialist states. The significance of this change is brought out by calculations giving the corresponding figures for the same economic areas before World War II (1938) as 10 and 74 per cent, respectively.[6] It was inner-European trade which was most severely affected by this development, since West European industries lost valuable sources of raw materials and markets. The loss was particularly important for German industry, which before the war occupied a dominant position in this inner-European, centre-periphery relationship: German trade with the East was twice to three times as much as that of its competitors (USA, Great Britain, Italy) in 1938, and accounted for almost 20 per cent of the country's foreign trade.[7] However, after the war, West German industry, like that of the other West European countries, was forced on political and economic grounds (the need for American aid for reconstruction, the danger of socialization, etc.) to submit to American pressure and join in the embargo measures.[8] The losses were, however, initially offset by the fact that West Europe profited from American economic aid and from the swift upward trend in world trade (especially between the capitalist industrial states), so that the 'further worsening of the crisis in the capitalist world system' which Stalin prophesied did not come about.

For the newly established 'People's Democracies' in Eastern Europe, the economic blockade represented at the same time both a chance and a danger. A chance, inasmuch as the blockade opened up an opportunity for them to free themselves from their economic dependence on Western Europe and to develop their own industries. A danger, in that the East European countries, were on the other hand, bound to become economically and politically dependent on the Soviet Union and to be faced with a number of contradictions between their own economic development and the building up of the Soviet economy.

After Stalin's death and the beginning of the 'thaw' period in 1953, the conflict of interests within Western capitalism made a consistent application of the American embargo more and more impossible.[9] East-West trade gradually began to increase again, but, nevertheless, remained considerably below the pre-war level — primarily as a result of the structural changes which had been carried out within and between the individual East European economies and of the import restrictions imposed by the Western states.

In the early to mid-sixties, a second phase of improvement began in trade relations between East and West Europe. The reasons for this upward swing are to be found in a number of factors:

- the end of the reconstruction period of the West European economies;
- the decrease in the USA's political domination in Western Europe and, at the same time, an increase in the presence of American 'multi-national' corporations with an allied intensification of the competition between the US and Western Europe;
- the structural and business difficulties encountered by important branches of West European industry;
- the partial stagnation of industrial development in Eastern Europe; the increased demand for 'Western' technology and consumer goods;
- the political changes in the 'détente' phase; on the part of the Soviet Union, endeavours to couple a European security system with economic co-operation in accordance with the policy of 'peaceful co-existence'; on the part of the West, attempts to erode the 'Eastern Bloc' (bridge-building strategy) by means of differentiated trade relations (e.g. the strategy of isolation pursued by the Federal Republic of Germany towards the German Democratic Republic and the USSR up to 1969); on the other hand, endeavours on the part of French capitalism to support its neo-imperialist strategy of 'national independence'.

It is characteristic of this new phase in economic relations that, in addition to the pure exchange of goods, forms of individual co-operation take shape — corresponding to a tendency noted before within the capitalist world economy, in the form of mergers, cartel agreements, etc. Within the area of the private-industry system, a 'trans-national capitalism' establishes itself, which is paralleled in the East by an emphasis on the internationalistic elements of the socialist mode of production. The meeting of both internationalization trends in Europe forms the background for the increased efforts towards co-operation.

INTEREST IN ECONOMIC CO-OPERATION

East European Interests in Co-operation

The adoption of the Soviet development model — i.e. the priority development of independent heavy industry — by the socialist bureaucracies of Eastern Europe was, at first, quite compatible with the objective interests of most of the East European transition-societies, which had to make up the development backlog they had as a result of imperialist dependence.[10] Although a development of this kind initially meant a serious setback for those countries which were already industrially advanced before the war (above all, Czechoslovakia), the strong growth of industrial production in the socialist states as a whole proved, in the first instance, that the model was adequate to overcome the overall development backlog in Eastern Europe.[11]

The fact that almost all economic relations were now transacted within the socialist camp was definitely to the advantage of the USSR, which was thus enabled to supply most of its needs for industrial products from non-capitalist countries. On the other hand, the expansion of basic industries in the East European countries forced them to become dependent on the Soviet Union for raw materials. Furthermore, the USSR sold a number of products (above all, crude oil) to the Comecon-countries[12] at higher prices than to Western countries but could argue, on the other hand, that it was buying industrial products (e.g. from the GDR) at prices above those of the world market[13] as well as putting its more highly developed technology at their disposal free of charge.[14]

After initial successes in the application of the Soviet model of industrialization, difficulties in 'mastering the scientific-technical revolution compared with the developed capitalist countries'[15] gradually appeared in the course of the necessary transition from the extensive to the intensive phase of industrialization. In the early sixties, these difficulties manifested themselves in a 'temporary loss of tempo', i.e. in the stagnation of economic growth. The main responsibility for this lies with the inability of the socialist bureaucracies to continue industrial development once the first phase of industrialization had been concluded by expanding the consumer-goods industry.[16] Their retention of a policy of foregoing consumer goods, which had been necessary during the first phase, led to increasing economic obstruction and political opposition on the part of the workers, which, in turn, led to a dead-end in economic development as well as in the other spheres. In the field of the consumer-goods industry and in technologically important sectors,[17] the socialist countries continue to lag far behind the developed capitalist economies.

Thus, the newly awakened interest in economic co-operation with Western Europe can be explained by a number of factors, which are to some extent contradictory as a result of an increasing differentiation and polarization both within the dominating bloc[18] of the individual transition-societies and also between the bureaucracies of the Comecon countries. Although due to the lack of a satisfactory theory of the transition-society,[18a] any statements regarding the socio-economic development of the Comecon states are of only limited value, a certain constellation nevertheless seems to be clearly emerging since the introduction of the so-called economic reforms in Eastern Europe. Within the dominating bloc, a new class is establishing itself more and more firmly alongside the social class constituted as the political leadership (the 'bureaucracy'); this is the 'technocracy'.[19] It is made up of works superintendents, management groups, etc., and of their 'organic' intellectuals[20] (Libermann, Ota Sik . . .), who formulate their specific interests in economic decentralization and the introduction of the economic efficiency criteria customary in capitalist countries. Although the technocracy can at first only operate within the framework of the limits set down by the political bureaucracy, its influence on overall social development increases in proportion to the progress of 'reform' tendencies (as, for example, in Czechoslovakia before 1968 and today, above all, in Hungary).[21] It hopes that intensified inter-system economic co-operation will lead to an adoption of urgently needed technologies, a stimulation of its own economic development through competition and, finally, will provide a long-term prospect of indirect access to the capitalist world market by being linked up with the network of 'multi-national' corporations.

It does not appear to be coincidental that the adoption of innovative organization principles first applied in capitalism varies remarkably precisely in south-east European countries (Hungary, Rumania, and, before August 1968, also in Czechoslovakia) with an economic opening-up towards the West according to the Yugoslavian model: the countries expect an inter-system specialization to reduce their economic dependence on the USSR and to bring them additional profits since, in their opinion, the division of labour within Comecon seems either to be too insufficiently developed or to allot them a position which appears too disadvantageous. A divergence of interests between the USSR and the other East European countries also results from the fact that the further growth of the economies of these countries depends to a far greater extent on the expansion of their foreign markets.[22] After Hungary had already gone farthest among the Comecon countries in re-establishing inter-company competition, the individual companies were also given extensive autonomy in their relations with capitalist firms. A similar undermining of the State's foreign-trade monopoly is appearing in Rumania.[23]

In addition to this, Hungary has allowed Western capital investments in domestic enterprises of up to 49 per cent of the firm's capital since 1970 and Rumania since 1971.[24] In Yugoslavia, the first East European country to make direct investments of this nature possible, similar legal provisions have existed since 1967.[25] Up to now, Rumania has gone farthest in building up its foreign trade again: after the Rumanian government had become more and more severe in its opposition to the efforts to integrate the industrial Comecon states, the country in 1967 increased its imports from Western Europe to almost half its total importation — which considerably reduced Rumania's import dependence on the Soviet Union and the other Comecon-countries. However, this ran the country into payment difficulties, which, in turn, had a negative effect on its economic growth, so that this change of course had to be stopped.[26]

The hypothesis of a correlation between an increased opening-up towards the West and advanced economic reform seems belied by the fact that although the Soviet Union itself has recently been showing an interest in inter-system co-operation, no economic reform has altered its decision-making structure for foreign trade, and its bureaucracy, rather than the technocracy, still seems to be largely determining development.[27] There is, admittedly, in the Soviet Union an active acknowledgement of the principle of an international division of labour on a world scale, a demand for the application of the postulates of the Theorem of Comparative Costs,[28] and a call for Western credits and technologies with a view to developing, above all, the consumer-goods industry.[29] All these factors however, have to be seen in the context of the stagnation phenomena and social instabilities which are now appearing in the Soviet Union as well.[30]

As is underlined by the affinity between Soviet and GDR argumentation, the offer of co-operation by socialist governments seems to be employed as a means of bringing pressure to bear, in order to carry through the principles of peaceful co-existence and the recognition of the status quo in Europe by the Western powers (especially the Federal Republic of Germany).[31] According to the theorem of the constant shift of the distribution of power in world politics to the advantage of the socialist camp, West German imperialism has not -- it is maintained -- become 'stronger' but instead 'more aggressive'. Hence, what is said to be needed is to 'force' this imperialism to accept European collective security by letting it see 'that the USSR and the other socialist countries do not consider it fully fit for co-operation'. This step would inevitably lead to a restriction of its freedom of action in foreign policy and to negative effects in its economic competitiveness.[32]

The USSR's economic opening-up towards the West is by no means incompatible with its military action against the reform government of the CSSR in August 1968, which was clearly taken, not only because of the openness of the development initiated by the Czechoslovakian technocracy (more or less towards capitalism), but, above all, because of the danger of the CSSR dropping out of the Comecon division of labour.[33] The fact that the 'economic reforms' in Hungary today are already farther advanced than the corresponding measures were in the CSSR in 1968, makes it clear that the Soviet bureaucracy wishes to come to an arrangement with the Western governments as soon as possible in order to guarantee the status quo, so as to defend its position against the ascendent technocracy.

French industry has already been rewarded for the 'progressive' Gaullist foreign policy with benefits on the Soviet market, and now this strategy seems to be being successfully applied to the Federal Republic of Germany, too, as is shown by the Treaty of Moscow of 12 August 1970, and the subsequent Soviet-German trade negotiations. It remains to be seen, however, whether this strategy has been employed with similar success after the Conference on European Security in the negotiations with the USA.

West European Interests in Co-operation

In Western Europe, interest in increased economic co-operation with the socialist countries, is, without exception, commercially motivated on the surface. Nevertheless, on a secondary level of motivation, a number of specifically West European interests in co-operation can be pin-pointed which are of a genuinely political nature, although they are all related to problems of industrial reproduction. These interests in co-operation stem from the special position of the European states in world politics. At one time, they represented the hegemonial apices of extensive sub-units in the global system. Today, the European states, having lost their colonies and seen their areas of influence dwindle in the shadow of the two super-powers, are seeking an independent reproductional function. Hence, the main threat to the success of the West European countries' endeavours to achieve independence lies not in the antagonistic socialist system but in the immense strength of the USA in almost every sphere of existence. One could even defend the idea of a 'Common Market' between Western Europe and North America. This would without doubt mean the incorporation of the western half of

Europe into the US hegemonial system somewhere between Canada and Panama. According to our knowledge of balance structures in world politics, one possible method of preventing the economic transfer-differential from producing any further trend in this direction, which is viewed with horror by West European élites, would be a rapprochement with the principle rival of the super-power USA, i.e. the socialist camp led by the Soviet Union.

A more intensive co-operation with socialist countries would not only open up possibilities of politically counteracting American efforts to dominate Western Europe, but could also supply their extended reproduction-basis, in a time when current economic developments are forcing European producers to search for such a supplier. The most spectacular and frequently discussed aspect of this need lies in the 'technological gap' between Western Europe and the USA which is so often pointed to. Relieved of all their troubles as regards financing research by large orders from the Defense Department, US producers found it easy to put all their European or Japanese competitors in their places by supplying, for example, 'civilized' calculating equipment. The experience gained in building thousands of combat aircraft for the US strategic bomber command led to a production lead which secured American manufacturers a monopoly in the construction of inter-continental passenger airliners. Thanks to militarily initiated promotion drives, the world market in communications technology, from news satellites to micro-circuits on a semi-conductor basis, is dominated by American products or those manufactured by American subsidiaries. European industrialists do not stand a chance against the concentrated economic-military strength of the super-power USA. No European government puts even a tenth of what America invests in research via its armaments budget into the development of top technologies. Hence, it is all the more obvious for West European industrialists to direct their attention to the power that is forced to compete in high-level technology, if it wants to check the US claim to supremacy: the Soviet Union. In fact, the Soviet government is making considerable efforts to economize on expenditure on advanced technologies forced on it out of military considerations by finding civil applications for this technology. Since the production structure in the socialist area is, in many respects, not yet sufficiently differentiated for such purposes, co-operation with Western Europe in this sector holds a wealth of attractions. What is particularly emphasized on the Soviet side is their high-ranking position in metallurgy,[34] for example, in the processing of titanium.

Beside the question of how West European producers are to gain access to the most modern technologies with the fewest possible political controls, the supply of raw materials represents an important motive for West European interest in extending co-operation with the socialist countries. The prospects, even for the immediate future, are particularly disquieting in the energy sector. Admittedly, the situation is not so ominous that important energy-supplying bodies will break down within the foreseeable future, but the attempts of the developing countries to expand economically and fight for higher prices for their raw products can hardly be checked any longer by the former exploiters. This is becoming particularly apparent in the supply of oil. At least as far as prices are concerned, the loss of the former overseas energy bases is making itself drastically felt, so that East European sources of supply are becoming increasingly attractive. Until recently, incidentally, no American competition was to be met with there.[35]

The rapidly expanding need for energy and raw materials in Western Europe has provoked three different plans to reply to it. On the one hand, an attempt involving considerable capital expenditure was made to tap possible reserves at home or on sea-bed shelves. The success has been moderate, since the geological structures of the European Continent are sufficiently familiar. Then, rather over-hasty attempts were made to examine the white patches on the map of the world as regards energy and raw materials to see if they were worth exploiting. European firms in collaboration with the ruling élites in several countries have been impressively successful in a number of cases. It is not certain, however, how long this neo-colonial form of obtaining raw materials can be pursued. Finally, a third solution offered itself in the form of co-operation with East European countries. Before the socialist societies were established there, Western Europe had important trade relations for the supply of raw materials with East European countries. The best known were probably with the Rumanian oil fields around Ploesti. But the new co-operation between East and West, without doubt, means more than the re-establishment of delivery relations which had in the meantime been interrupted. On a long-term basis a number of useful connections are being established — and this plays a decisive rôle in the eyes of the planners — for tapping national resources in Eastern Europe and for safeguarding the supply of raw materials for Western Europe.[36]

If carried out in co-operation by the two halves of Europe, the search for new energy-supplying bodies (the nuclear power stations have become most familiar) also seems to promise results. Scientific-technological co-operation has begun remarkably early in this politically somewhat sensitive field, in particular between French and Soviet research centres.[37] The example of common research efforts in the field of energy technology brings us on to a further central sphere of interest, which is causing West European producers to turn towards the east.

This interest is most easily understood if a few basic economic facts are borne in mind. The production cost of capital goods falls as the output of a particular product rises. However, in a number of important cases — such as nuclear power stations, rolling mills, ship and aircraft building — the national and regional markets are too small to allow goods to be produced at prices which can compete with American products. The importance of the expansion and safeguarding of European markets through wider co-operation is, therefore, considerably greater than the mere function of providing a number of manufacturers with larger profits by extending their production runs. If it does not prove possible to install and utilize capacities on the required scale to produce capital goods which can compete on the world market, then, in the long run, not only the utilization of capital but also industrial production would be restricted to the consumer-goods sector and the production of cheap capital goods. It is precisely this division of labour that West European industrial planners fear. The two sectors mentioned not only have the lowest capital-accumulation rates but are, in addition, considered to be the least innovative areas of the capitalist economies.[38] If Western Europe remains limited to its complementary rôle, enormous research investments would have to be made and publicly financed before new types of goods could be produced. The reason for this is that West European producers of consumer goods are neither willing nor in a position to make suitable advance investments themselves. On the other hand, the considerable advance investments needed for the creation of innovative technologies could not be amortized if the products were to be sold at competitive prices on the world market. The answer is self-evident, if West European industrialists want at all costs to participate independently in the further development of the highly innovative production of heavy capital goods with their secondary effects: the socialist countries in Eastern Europe, with their above-average need for capital goods, are regarded by Western economic leaders as the right partners for solving their long-term problems.

The above motives, which apply to the overall economy, are joined in the case of individual private companies by important aspects of industrial cooperation with East European countries, which, can, in general, be regarded as aspects of the conditions of production. Private companies are still, above all, attracted by what are, in comparison to West European conditions, considerably lower wages in socialist countries. The utilization of this wage-differential – whether through co-operation in production or through the purchase of intermediate and semi-finished products at low wage costs – is likely to be the motive behind the journeys to the East undertaken by innumerable West European industrialists. Finally, the general external conditions of production are a point in favour of production co-operation with East European partners: there are practically no strikes or other interruptions of production activity. Furthermore, it is easier to engage in long-term planning with comparatively constant planning data such as wage costs or the price of materials in centrally administered economies than in competitive profit systems.

OBSTACLES TO ECONOMIC CO-OPERATION

The various interests in both the East and the West in a systematic expansion of economic co-operation reflect only one aspect, albeit a dominant one, of current European developments. The persisting contrasts between the systems still confronting each other harshly on a number of levels remain immense. It would be false and detrimental to the chances of achieving increased co-operation to view these factors as the residue of a state of affairs which is believed to have been overcome. The fact that it is strictly pointed out in Eastern Europe that any economic rapprochement is accompanied by a move to delimit its extent and that the West also displays demonstrable ideological reservations towards plans for co-operation which go 'all too far' shows that there are those with attitudes which are based on a more profound insight into the basic structure of co-operation development than is to be found among the co-operation enthusiasts who criticize such reservations. Any conception of all-European co-operation is appropriate only if it does not ascribe to this co-operation the magic power of replacing the competition between the systems but is, instead, understood as a means which is much more limited in scope and aims at putting into practice the concept of different variants of co-existence between the two systems in Europe, combining the most peaceable path of development with the greatest economic advantages for all concerned. The conditions continuing to form the framework of a confrontation of systems thus still represent a potential threat to the above concept, but a threat which will presumably decrease in the course of the development of co-operation. Political actions in one half of Europe which appear to the other side of be a return to traditional positions of confrontation are still basically capable of causing severe setbacks to economic co-operation between East and West.

Obstacles in Eastern Europe

There are likely to be a few obstacles of a less general nature to be pointed out in all parts of Europe, which are of practical significance for realizing the plans for co-operation. But one can mention, above all, aspects of the bureaucratic steering of the economy as being difficulties which are special to Eastern Europe. In the past, the unwieldy planning systems of the socialist economies made it practically impossible to believe in the superiority of the East European central-planning system over the methods practised in Western Europe. In view of the planning mentality and planning practices to be found there, it seems unlikely that rapid restructuring programmes of the kind quite familiar in Western Europe from the period of extensive US economic programmes will be carried out in the East European economies. It is to be expected that, in the course of putting any form of extended co-operation into practice, petty difficulties will have to be combatted daily which are likely to range from the disinclination of subordinate decision-making organs to assume responsibility down to an acute lack of adequate organization. Apart from problems of this nature which cannot be accommodated in a theory, it remains difficult to see how the establishment of new transfer-structures, the complications of obtaining potential demand and realistic supply can be carried out elastically over the State foreign-trade monopolies without a fundamental structural reform. The attempt to get both information and decision-making channels of the economy-steering apparatus in the East European countries running parallel has not even been achieved successfully enough to satisfy domestic requirements. In foreign trade relations, which have always had no more than a subsidiary function, especially as far as those with the West are concerned,[39] it is likely that an extension of East-West exchange directed at specific objectives will run into considerable difficulties in execution, above all in its initial phase, since it requires a radically redesigned set of steering instruments.

These difficulties, which can be summarized under the heading of bureaucratic inertia, arise on quite different levels. Each level demonstrates anew that the East European economic structure was established at a time of extreme confrontation. The easiest means of removing difficulties of this kind still seems to be on the level of a direct trading of goods. However, every foreign trade transaction is accompanied by a large number of derived transfer processes on different levels.

These aspects represent the most effective obstacles confronting an intensification of economic exchange. Difficult problems remain to be solved on the monetary level: the currencies of the East European countries are not convertible, the flows of goods have to be squared in the balance of payments within a short space of time. Foreign-exchange holdings for the advance financing of co-operation transactions are not available for these tasks. Even the further development of artificial currencies such as the new 'transferable Rouble' can only partially answer the financing problems that East-West co-operation on a large scale brings with it. In order to keep their foreign trade relations transparent, the East European countries, as a rule, favour an anarchic bi-lateralism which, now that the West has transferred its trade-treaty jurisdiction to the European Communities, threatens to be a futile exercise.

The differences in ownership of the means of production produce further obstacles in the way of co-operation. If there are companies which are partly owned by private individuals from non-socialist countries, this state of affairs gives rise to a whole series of legal questions which cannot be answered quickly and are thus, in turn, likely to produce retarding effects.

A topic which is openly discussed by East European economics experts is the presence of defects of a serious nature in the system of supplying economic information – the most important basis for directing domestic and, especially, foreign trade production. Senin, the Director of the Comecon Economic Research Institute has these criticisms to make: 'In individual cases, the primary data are missing, there is often little standardization of coefficients, the latest coefficients are published too late, etc.'[40] However, the organization of broad-scale economic co-operation with Western Europe, as well as the efforts to promote socialist economic integration in Eastern Europe, should produce strong incentives to overcome step-by-step the defects in the system of running the economy.

From time to time, fears are expressed by authors in the West that ideological obstacles exist which, they maintain, make it appear almost impossible to East European policy planners (quite apart from all the practical difficulties) to seriously undertake any large-scale economic co-operation.[41] Arguments such as these can be invalidated by pointing out once more the dimensions of the East-West transfer relations and the (limited) extension of them which is contemplated. The establishment of intensified exchange relations is, for the present, little more than an attempt to close the trade gaps which have been left over from the Cold War phase and whose effects are now coming to be of greater consequence in view of the rapid development of trade with other regions of the globe. Hardly anyone will expect a step towards the normalization of what has become an anachronistic trade gap to undertake the far-reaching ideological offensives reflected in the opinions referred to above. At present, it is not possible to say what the longer-term effects of an economic co-operation intensifed to, for example, the level of transfer relations between West Europe and the USA would be. Behind these ideological imputations lies the apparent assumption that it is still possible to jeopardize political rule in the East European countries simply by presenting Western goods and whatever else is transferred in these countries; but this assumption hits back directly at its authors who, in it, betray that they are still unable or unwilling to give up outdated positions.

Obstacles to Economic Co-operation in Western Europe

Even though it is possible to speak of a re-orientation of West European 'economic circles' in the matter of economic co-operation between West and East Europe, this process is nevertheless marked by contradictions stemming from the differences in economic and ideological development. The obstacles (varying from country to country) which continue to stand in the way of expansion of inter-system co-operation (customs tariff discrimination, fixing of quotas, embargo lists, credit restrictions, etc.) are due to a combination – different in each case – of the following factors:

The strength of American influence in Western Europe. To begin with, the US Government was able to enforce the regulations of the COCOM embargo on 'strategic' exports to Eastern Europe in the West European countries through exerting direct pressure on their governments. Once the legal provisions had gradually become less strict and were being no more than laxly applied,[42] the American Government favoured exerting its influence indirectly via American firms in Western Europe.[43] One particular obstacle in the way of the expansion of East-West trade was the American legislation which, even more comprehensively than the COCOM lists, forbade West European industries to export goods to Eastern Europe if they contained components manufactured under US licence. This applied to most highly technologized industries (such as aircraft construction). Today, these regulations have practically no longer any significance. After a hard fight conducted by the industrial lobby in the American Congress,[44] they have, for the most part, been lifted,[45] in view of the fact that a number of US concerns had already been getting around them via subsidiaries in Western Europe.

A particularly interesting case of the operation of the 'American lobby' in Europe is represented in the battle waged by the US-dominated 'International Oil Cartel' against the entry of Soviet oil and natural gas into Western Europe. This was best displayed in the campaign against the director of the Italian state-owned firm of ENI, Enrico Mattei, who tried to make Italy's oil-supply independent of the cartel by, among other things, importing from the Soviet Union.[46] The cartel also operated successfully, for instance, in the case of the construction of the pipeline 'Friendship', which transports Soviet mineral oil as far as Czechoslovakia, the extension of which was prevented.[47]

The influence exerted by the American oil concerns of Gulf and Standard Oil (NJ) on the American Government and hence on the NATO bodies regarding the 1962 pipeline embargo[48] must also be seen in this context. In order to prevent Soviet oil from gaining ground, Esso and Shell are, in the meantime, employing more flexible methods ranging from the granting of more favourable terms for their own supplies to buying up Soviet gas. Since the closure of the Suez Canal, quadrilateral compensation deals have even been made between the USSR and firms belonging to the international cartel.[50] Recently, the American companies have been showing a great interest in exploiting Siberian gas and oil resources, for which they are prepared to grant dollar credits. Further possible methods by which the international oil cartel can penetrate Eastern Europe are indicated in the setting up of a Shell filling-station network in Hungary.[52]

Remains of militant anti-communism. The patterns of thinking which had hardened in Western Europe, in general, during the Cold War could not be broken down from one day to the next and, certainly, not uniformly. In 'enlightened' circles of the West European middle classes, the friend-foe images characteristic of the phase of system-confrontation have given way to more flexible attitudes influenced by convergence-ideology,[53] but, all the same, large segments of the middle classes have retained forms of thinking belonging to the militant anti-Communism which is even prevalent among the majority of the working class in some countries.[54]

Contradictions between export-oriented modern sectors of industry and protectionist traditional ones.[55] The most lucrative orders from Eastern Europe were initially concentrated, above all, on high-value investment goods. The volume of orders was mostly, even by Western standards, considerable, including as it did the delivery of ready-made factories. Hence the interest in East-West trade was accordingly restricted to those firms which a) were technologically highly developed, b) were large enough for development and production, and c) had their own systems of distribution through which the products likely to be offered in return could be marketed. This, incidentally, explains why the four largest West European industrial countries (West Germany, France, Great Britain and Italy), which are the main locations of such industries, have a disproportionately large share in exports to Eastern Europe, which they have even been able to increase over the years.[56] A further explanation lies in the fact that these industries are able to fall back on a strong banking system to finance their exports.

This picture becomes more relative when we see that a number of efficient smaller engineering firms are entrusted with equipping East European production plants; however, the firms in question are mostly 'off-shoots' of larger concerns. On the other hand, on account of the bilateral foreign trade structure of the Comecon states, any expansion of exports to the West is conditional on a similar increase in imports. The Comecon states are, however, only prepared to engage in this if they see a chance to improve the goods structure of their exports, i.e. if the discriminating restrictions on imports of finished products existing to varying degrees in Western Europe are lifted. But this move is opposed, above all, by representatives of the traditional small and medium-sized enterprises, which can, in any case, profit only to a very limited extent from orders from the East. They fear added competition from East European goods and, therefore, make a great deal of publicity about a 'flooding' of the home market by cheap East European products. But anti-Communist phrases, dumping imputations,[57] the suspicion of licence-theft,[58] etc. are usually only the ideological vehicle for covering up their own structural weaknesses and lack of competitiveness. The fixing of liberalization-quotas for foreign trade with Comecon countries is, hence, often the result of a difficult compromise between individual sectors of the economy, in which the modern sector mostly has to accept the fact that the state apparatus assumes the role of mediator. This state role in the settlement of conflicts of interest with a view to expanding exports is particularly effective in countries with a fairly large state-owned sector of industry (France, Italy) and in which the state can negotiate detailed delivery contracts directly with East European foreign-trade organizations.[59] The state passes on a share of the delivery contracts on the national level to private firms, including smaller enterprises. In this way, those countries more or less buy the agreement of medium-sized and small enterprises to an increase in trade with the East.

The state continues to play an important role in the matter of allocating credits for the export of manufactured goods (above all, production plants) to East European countries. State-provided guarantees are of great importance since private banks are not prepared to grant such guarantees on exports to Eastern Europe, on account of the lack of 'efficiency criteria'.[60] Of equal importance is the fact that the particularly favourable credit terms granted for business with the East can be financed via state taxes, as was done in the case of the construction of the Togliattigrad FIAT-works (the first large delivery of this kind).

An expansion of West European exports was, for a long time, hampered by an inter-governmental agreement, the Berne Union, and a corresponding EEC agreement in 1962, which stipulated that credits for manufactured goods supplied to 'non-developing countries' might not run for more than five years.[61] This provision was intended to prevent competition in the field of credit-conditions and avoid an 'interest rate war'. However, it was broken in dealings with Eastern Europe in 1964, first by Great Britain and then by France. The German federal government, which strongly criticized these decisions at the time on foreign policy grounds, today feels no more bound by these agreements than do the other signatories to the Berne Union, and even covers credits over a period of twelve years (as in the case of Mannesmann's contract with the USSR in 1971 for natural-gas pipes).[62] The GDR alone continues to be discriminated against in matters of credit by the Federal Republic of Germany, which succeeded in getting its EEC partners to pledge themselves to retain the 5-year rule in trade with the GDR.[63]

Proceeding from the assumption that, on a long-term basis, East-West trade can only be expanded by increasing the proportion of manufactured goods in the exports of the East European countries — which is what the Comecon governments demand and also what the UN Economic Commission for Europe supports, on the basis of trend-analyses of Western trade[64] — one cannot help observing that an expansion of this kind is at present restricted by the discriminating EEC customs-tariff structure alone,[65] quite apart from all other factors (inferior quality and inadequate marketing on the part of the Comecon countries and protectionist measures by individual West European governments, etc.). Even after the cuts resulting from the Kennedy Round, the customs tariffs imposed on imports from non-member states, which rise according to the degree of processing, are still considerable. The lack of flexibility in re-exporting further-processed goods at present also stands in the way of an intensification of inter-system co-operation.

EFFECTS OF INCREASED ECONOMIC CO-OPERATION

The Effects of Increased Economic Co-operation in Eastern Europe

Reflections on the probable effects of industrial co-operation on socialist countries meet with strong resistance in Eastern Europe, even when they are free from all ideological aims and try to restrict themselves to the main economic issue. It is generally considered the task of the State Security organs, although not publicly stated, to deal with the fact that more intensive co-operation with the West may also have disquieting effects. The thinking of the responsible planners is governed by the positive effects expected, but, even here, with a characteristic shift of emphasis. One of the basic assertions necessary for the East European economic system to hold its own has always been and still remains that the centrally planned economy, as a general principle, does not display any insufficiencies compared with the Western competitive profit system but rather, represents the superior economic system. Divergent opinions widely publicised in the West, such as the statements made by the Soviet economist Liberman or the Czech reformer Sik, in which the adoption of 'Western' elements into the running of the economy was discussed, have always been considered in Eastern Europe to be outsider positions. If significant changes really were to take place in individual areas in the course of increased East-West co-operation, they are likely to be interpreted in those countries as the fruit of socialist progress rather than, of all things, the result of Western influence.

It is difficult to say what repercussions in social policy increased economic co-operation may bring with it. It would not be surprising if certain Western production planning or even distribution techniques in the consumer-goods sector were to be tacitly introduced into the socialist economic system. This could even come about in the manner called for by Liberman and Sik. However, one should beware of the temptation in the West to make spectacular use of changes in Eastern Europe as expressions of a 'transformation' of Socialism. At least in part, we are definitely dealing with techniques of organising the economy which are simply being introduced later by the East European nations, as a result of their becoming industrialized at a later date than the Western countries. In that case, East-West co-operation would have the limited but nonetheless useful function of speeding up processes of industrial ascent which are already operative.

The main thing that East European economic planners are hoping for from increased co-operation with the West is that it will help them to achieve their primary aim; an increase in productivity. 'Productivity is, in the last analysis, the all-important, the decisive factor for the victory of the new social system'. Lenin's central statement[66] is to be heard in many variations in the East European socialist states from Party leaders and members of the government to anyone in the street as a result of a large number of cheap brochures. The propaganda for increased productivity is not aimed at improving some abstract coefficient: on the contrary, political leaders and workers agree that corresponding improvements would result directly in the fulfilment of all desires for a higher standard of living, increased consumption, better public services, etc. which they have been waiting for for so long in those countries. Indeed, it is in comparing international productivity statistics that East European politicians speak openly of a deficit compared with the West, and hope for the most effective remedy through their co-operation efforts.

Besides its economic key-functions, co-operation on a general European level is hoped to have other effects, as can be deduced from public statements made by East European politicians. They go as far as to assume that in a Europe drawn closely together by innumerable economic and other links, armaments expenditure could be considerably reduced on both sides. Since the arms race imposes relatively far heavier burdens on the lower economic potential of the socialist system than it does on the West, Eastern Europe would profit particularly from reduced armaments burdens. It will, however, remain to be seen over fairly long periods of time exactly how such hopes can be fulfilled.

Effects of Increased Co-operation in Western Europe

On account of the very small share that East-West trade has had up to now in the total foreign trade of the West European countries, it has hardly been possible, as yet, to generalize about the effect of increased inter-system economic co-operation. This is all the more true of the industrial co-production stricto sensu which has been developing since the mid-sixties and whose share in total trade cannot even be exactly estimated.[67] Nevertheless, the small percentage of overall trade accounted for by East-West co-operation should not lead us to conclude that it is economically insignificant.

Firstly, there have already been enough instances of orders from the East saving the firms concerned from acute business or structural difficulties, which thus rule out any reduction of the slogan 'Super-deal East-West trade' to its propaganda components. Since intra-system specialization within Comecon is considerably less advanced than in Western Europe,[68] an intensification of inter-system co-operation would offer still largely unexploited chances to create a broad 'inter-system division of labour', which would help West European industries achieve significant economies of scale.

It need not be emphasized that orders placed with particularly exposed sectors of the economy (i.e. above all, the investment goods industry) have also a business-stabilizing effect on the overall economy. Examples of this would be large orders given by the USSR to the French mechanical engineering industry following a recessive phase from 1963 onwards,[69] to Italian industry when it was struggling with regional structural problems,[70] or recently to certain West German mechanical engineering firms just when Volkswagen orders, the German concern with the highest turnover, were beginning to drop off.[71]

The greatest advantage from East-West business is, however, without doubt derived by the large-scale enterprises simply on account of their enormous bargaining power as a result of their size and the close ties between them as well as with the state apparatus and the large banks (e.g. FIAT-ENI-IRI in Italy, Renault-Peugeot in France, Mannesmann-Ruhrgas in West Germany). Trade with the East is of additional importance to research-intensive West European industries, most of which have to compete economically and technologically with American-dominated concerns. They can secure themselves large markets and possibly — through scientific and technological co-operation with East European partners — economic spin-off effects[72] (acceleration of the circulation of capital and technological renewal) as has already occurred in the case of the Franco-Soviet agreement on the SECAM colour television (valid for the whole Comecon area) or in the case of the domination of the Soviet computer market by the British electronics industry.[73] As regards the overall economy, an expansion of the top technological firms promoted in this way brings with it, in turn, a growth of the industries associated with them. In the importing East European country, on the other hand, conditions are created by certain Western exports for the further export of technologies, investment goods or finished articles with a particularly high manufacturing content.[74] The large proportion of branches with a high degree of research that are involved in East-West industrial co-operation[75] and the constantly increasing proportion of products of a high level of research among the exports to Eastern Europe[76] underline the growing importance of these factors. For individual multinational concerns, the 'universal world production agreements'[77] offered by the East European side continue to be able to help provide security for their positions on the world market.

Apart from these specifically economic functions, increased economic co-operation can also have a socially stabilizing effect. Thus, as early as 1960, the strike activity of the Communist trade union in a large French cement factory suddenly dropped the moment a Soviet order rescued the factory from a business slackness.[78] Examples of this kind provide industrialists and politicians in France and Italy — the countries with the strongest Communist labour movements in Western Europe — with additional motives to sign contracts with the Soviet Union and other East European countries. It can, in fact, be observed that, as the carrying-through of the principles of 'peaceful co-existence' and the general spreading of economic co-operation are declared to be the main tasks of the Communist labour movement, there is a proportional increase in willingness to co-operate on the part of the Communist Parties in Western Europe,[79] even though these have to reckon with opposition from the rank and file. Thus, theorists of West European Communist Parties are forced to admit, for example, that inter-system economic co-operation can be 'in contradiction' to this or that aspect of the class struggle'[79a] — e.g. if Poland delivers coal to Spain while the miners are on strike in Asturia. As in this example, which caused a certain amount of turbulence in the French Communist Party in connection with the Garaudy Affair,[80] the willingness to co-operate on the part of the West European Communist Parties and trade unions can — despite its initial stabilizing effect — quite easily give rise to opposite tendencies which can assume larger dimensions in times of social unrest (May 1968, in France, Autumn 1969, in Italy).

GLOBAL EFFECTS OF INTRA-SYSTEM ECONOMIC
CO-OPERATION AND ITS FUNCTION IN
SAFEGUARDING PEACE

Although the present data on East-West economic transactions — even if the
present trends were projected into the future — urge moderation in assessing their
effects on the world economic system and the existing division of labour in world
society, the signs which herald a change in this division of labour should not go
unmentioned; for they, in turn, form the basis for an appraisal of the chances of a
peaceful development — not only in the sense of the absence of war, but also in the
breaking-down of development disparities which could one day form the basis of
new potentially violent conflicts.

Proceeding from the fact that one of the basic rationales of the Russian October
Revolution and of the socio-economic re-structuring of the East European societies
after 1945 lay in the attempt by these countries to free themselves from imperialist
dependence on a dominating centre, the reintegration of the 'socialist' economies
into the system of capitalist world economy,[81] in other words their 'reperipherization', must be viewed as a perfectly possible alternative. Although the quantifiable
extent of such a reperipherization (the partial incorporation of Eastern Europe into
the internationalization of production embodied in multi-national corporations;
technological dependence; growing incumbrance with debts; the induction of production, consumption and infra-structure patterns, etc.) is, up to now, still small,
the rate of development can nevertheless speed up very rapidly as a result of
differential spin-off and spill-over effects. East European society could obviate the
danger of a perpetuation of dependence only by retaining the primacy of overall
social planning over and above the outside influences of private industry, and by
employing its own research programmes parallel to the import of technologies in
order to develop these technologies further.[82]

The re-structuring of the international division of labour which is suggested here
would, however, not only have consequences for the social constellations in the
European countries but would also affect Europe's relationship with the 'Third
World'. The East European market is now already appearing as an alternative
market for certain products of West European industry (machines, automobiles,
etc.), the sales of which are stagnating in the underdeveloped countries. On the
other hand, the relative political and economic stability of Eastern Europe is
considered by many Western industrialists to be a guarantee for a safe commitment,
as far as the setting-up of plant and the securing of raw materials are concerned,
whereas the dangers of revolutionary or even just nationalistic developments in the
underdeveloped countries are continually becoming greater (cf. for example, the
demands of the oil-producing countries).[83] In the long term, the general spread of
the 'scientific-technical revolution' will speed up the decline of certain industries in
Western Europe, whose products would then be replaced by imports. In that case,
imports from Eastern Europe would, in the course of industrial co-production,
compete even more than they have up to now with imports from underdeveloped
areas, to the disadvantage of the latter.[84]

In this context, we can merely raise the question of whether a complicity or complementariness of interests of the kind which is in this way beginning to develop, placing the whole of the 'North' against the 'South', would be compensated for by common capitalist-socialist industrial and infra-structure projects in the 'Third World'. Even if this cannot be answered here, a warning must be expressed against euphoric expectations such as those expressed by UNCTAD and other organizations that such 'mixed' undertakings would 'contribute to the economic growth of the developing world'.[86] This holds true at least as long as it has not been proved to what extent such (already existing) projects[87] differ from those of traditional capitalist 'development aid', the usefulness of which in overcoming underdevelopment is, at least, doubtful. The 'trans-ideological' nature of the undertakings alone is no guarantee that no negative effects will ensue for the recipient countries.[88]

There is a possibility that, in such a way, the amount of structural violence exerted on an international level would also be increased through the introduction of new dependence relationships in the West-East-South triangle. For this reason, the question must once more be brought up as to whether such a development should be tolerated or even encouraged in order to lessen the possibility of military conflict in Europe. Against the background of these considerations, the idea that socialist peace policy must 'actively promote every interlocking of business which effectively detracts from the deadly enemy ideology, and gratefully make use of every capitalist sales-interest as a stratagem of reason'[89] appears as a considerable abridgement of the problems. It expresses the naive belief that trade-relations have, a priori, a peace-promoting character, a belief of the kind which, despite having been disproved by history,[90] has not disappeared from the landscape of debate since Montesquieu.[91]

In contrast to this, one should not lose sight of the fact that economic co-operation based on inequality and dependence consolidates existing social conditions or even intensifies them and, thus, carries with it the germ of new armed conflict, if conditions for social transformation are not simultaneously created as a basis for permanent universal and peaceful co-operation.

NOTES

This is an English version of an article first published in: U. Albrecht et al.: *Durch Kooperation zum Frieden?* , (Munich: 1974), 66-99. Recent developments having only strengthened the *degree* of East-West economic cooperation, the authors did not think a modification of their argumentation necessary. However, they added a few hints to contributions that treat some of the problems mentioned in a more detailed way (cf. especially footnote 81). Out of the great number of books published on the subject in general, we shall only refer to the most recent German one: H.-D. Jacobsen, *Die wirtschaftlichen Beziehungen zwischen West und Ost,* Reinbek 1975 (with a comprehensive bibliography).

    1. Cf. J. Rodejohann 'Zum Beginn des Kalten Krieges', in: U. Albrecht et al., op. cit., 33-65.

    2. Cf. on the following G. Adler-Karlsson, 'Problems of East-West Trade – A General Survey', in: *Economics of Planning,* vol. 7, No. 2 (1967), 119-182; and by the same author,

Western Economic Warfare, 1947-1967. A Case Study in Foreign Economic Policy (Stockholm: 1968).

3. He does not mention the efforts made up to 1947 to come to an arrangement with the US. Cf. the quotation in Petrowsky, *Zur Entwicklung der Theorie des staatsmonopolistischen Kapitalismus nach 1945*, in: *Probleme des Klassenkampfs*, No. 1, 1971, 132.

4. J. Stalin, *Die ökonomischen Probleme des Sozialismus in der USSR* (Moscow: 1952), 36.

5. Ibid., 37.

6. J. Wilczynski, *The Economics and Politics of East-West-Trade. A Study of trade between developed market economies and centrally planned economies in a changing world* (London: 1969), 54. The difference between the percentage of East-West trade accounted for by Western and Eastern foreign trade is a result of Eastern Europe's lower economic potential and of the great importance of trade for capitalist centres both between themselves and with their peripheries as well as of the correspondingly less extensive participation of the East European economies in world trade. (Furthermore, as a result of the geographical size of the USSR, the foreign trade between states in Western Europe would correspond to domestic trade inside the USSR.)

7. R. Krengel, *Die Bedeutung des Ost-West-Handels für die Ost-West-Beziehungen* (Göttingen: 1967), 63.

8. *Adler-Karlsson*, op. cit., 47.

9. In 1920/21, *Lenin* made similar use of inter-imperialist rivalries to break what was historically the first economic blockade against a non-capitalist state. (See E. H. Carr, *The Bolshevik Revolution 1917-1923*, (Harmondsworth: 1966), vol. 3, 276ff.

10. On the following cf. J. Kuron/K. Modzelewski, *Lettre ouverte au parti ouvrier polonais*, (Paris: 1969), p.27ff, and C. Seranne, 'Les situations d'inégalités au sein du Conseil d'Assistance Economique Mutuelle' (Comecon), in: Etudes Internationales (Québec), vol. II, No. 2 (June 1971), 250-296.

11. This would have to be judged positively, if one shares the premise of accelerated maximal accumulation aimed at "catching up" on the developed capitalist states. For a critical examination of the priorities not gone into by the Soviet accumulation-model, especially the relation between agriculture and industry, see: S. Amin, *Le développement inégal. Essai sur les formations sociales du capitalisme périphérique*, (Paris: 1973), 328ff; R. Rossanda, 'Die sozialistischen Länder. Ein Dilemma der westeuropäischen Linken', in: *Kursbuch 30*, Dec. 1972, 1-34; A. Carlo, *Politische und ökonomische Struktur der UdSSR (1917-1975). Diktatur des Proletariats oder bürokratischer Kollektivismus*, (Berlin: 1972), 77ff.

12. On the Comecon states, see under 'European Institutions' in the German version of this book (footnote 1).

13. On pricing policy in the Comecon areas, see M. Kaser, *Comecon Integration Problems of the Planned Economies*, (2nd ed.) (London: 1967), 176ff.; Wilczynski, op. cit., 162ff.; Seranne, op. cit., 275ff.

14. The height of this scientific-technical co-operation within the framework of Comecon was reached in the fifties; since 1960, the amount of material supplied gratis by the USSR has been growing less, because the USSR has since then been demanding financial participation in the costs of research and development (J. Lagneau, *'Coopération scientifique et technique entre les pays membres du C.A.E.M.,'* in: *Economies et Sociétés*, January 1971, 286ff.

15. *Wohin geht Europa? Aktuelle Aspekte – Geschichte – Perspektiven des Problems der europäischen Sicherheit*, (Berlin (East): 1970), 81.

16. Kuron/Modzelewski, op. cit., 31ff.; Carlo, op. cit., 63ff.

17. On the 'gap' in the computer industry, cf. R. W. Judy, 'The Case of Computer Technology', in: S. Wasowski (ed.), *East West Trade and the Technological Gap. A political and economic appraisal*, (New York: 1970), 43-72.

18. The concept of the 'Dominating Bloc' was developed by Gramsci (see Antonio Gramsci: *Note sul Machiavelli, sulla politica e sullo Stato moderno*, German extracts in: *Gramsci, Philosophie der Praxis. Eine Auswahl*, Frankfurt/Main 1967, 282ff.).

18a. Cf. now a discussion of the various attempts at theories in Carlo, op. cit., and the reprint of several important articles by Chaulieu (pseudonym), which appeared in the periodical *Socialisme où Barbarie* since 1949 in: *C. Costariadis: La société bureaucratique, Les rapports de productions en Russie,* Paris: 1973, among others 205-281. On the socio-economic conditions for Soviet foreign policy cf. the contributions in: E. Jahn (ed.), *Sozioökonomische Bedingungen der sowjetischen Aussenpolitik,* Frankfurt/M. 1976.

19. The concepts of 'bureaucracy' and 'technocracy' are employed along the lines of Carlo, who took them over from Bruno Rizzi and Burnham and dealt with them critically. (Carlo, op. cit., 11ff.) On account of the special nature of the formation of Soviet society, they have a different meaning there from that within capitalist societies. Similar results are reached from the interest-group theory standpoint by Sidney I. Ploss: 'Interest Groups, in: A. Kassof (ed), *Prospects for Soviet Society,* (New York (Praeger): 1967), 76-103, Vernon V. Aspaturian, 'Internal Politics and Foreign Policy', in his book *Process and Power in Soviet Foreign Policy,* (Boston: 1971) 491-550 and J. P. Hardt/T. Frankel 'The Industrial Managers', in: H. Skilling/F. Griffiths (eds), *Interest Groups in Soviet Politics,* (Princeton: 1971), 171-208. The concept of 'technocracy' is employed in the meaning it has in Gramsci (see footnote 18).

20. The outcome of the conflict between bureaucracy and technocracy will be determined essentially by the attitude of the working-class, which is at present, however, for the most part, uninvolved and hardly articulates its own demands (Carlo, op. cit., 107).

21. Cf. on this the economic-theory works in Hungary by I. Vajda, *Internationale Arbeitsteilung und Wirtschaftsreform,* (Budapest: 1969), and T. Kiss, *International Division of Labour in Open Economies. With special regard to CMEA,* (Budapest: 1971).

22. Kiss, op. cit., 190.

23. M. Kaser/C. F. G. Ransom, 'Relations with Eastern Europe', in: G. R. Denton (ed), *Economic Integration in Europe,* (London: 1969), 69ff; M. Kaser, 'Current Problems in East-West Trade', in: H. Raupach et al. (eds), *Jahrbuch der Wirtschaft Osteuropas,* vol. 1, Munich-Vienna 1970, p.320ff.

24. CNUCED, 'Relations commerciales entre pays à systèmes économiques et sociaux différents' (Rapport du secrétariat de la CNUCED, Genève, 24 août 1971) in: *Le Courrier des pays de l'Est,* No. 145, October 1971, 83; East West (research and advisory) 1972, Industrial and Marketing Cooperation, vol. II, 1971 (A Research Report), Brussels, March 1972, 56ff.

25. OECD, *Foreign Investment in Yugoslavia,* Paris 1970. Cf. the case-study on the FIAT investments in Yugoslavia, in: East West 1972, op. cit., 50ff.

26. Kaser, op. cit., 328ff. One consequence was an economic rapprochement with the USSR and the partial abandonment of its oppositional rôle within Comecon (Seranne, op. cit., 288f.).

27. On the discontinuation and partial withdrawal of economic reforms in the USSR and the GDR in 1971, see M. Kaser, 'Planning together under Comecon's "complex programme" ', in: *The Financial Times,* 20.6.1972.

28. Cf. the directives of the 23rd Party Congress of the Soviet Communist Party, quoted in: S. Pisar, *Supergeschäft Ost-West. Der Schlüssel zum Weltfrieden* (Hamburg: 1970), 58 (originally published in English under the title *Coexistence and Commerce,* New York 1970).

29. As, for example, in the *Spiegel* interviews with the Soviet functionaries Vadim V. Sagladin (Der Spiegel 50/1971) and Zhermen Gvishiani (Der Spiegel 19/1972).

30. Such as were expressed in the 'confidential' report made by Brezhnev to the Central Committee of the Soviet Communist Party on 15.12.1969. (Cf. the article by K. S. Karol: 'Les crises de la société russe', in: *Le Monde,* 23/24.8.1970.) On failure to fulfill the plan completely in 1972, cf. Alain Jacob: 'Le retard des investissements industriels explique le marasme en URSS', in: *Le Monde,* 13.2.1973.

31. Thus, for example, Domdey in: K. H. Domdey/J. L. Schmidt (eds), *Europäische Sicherheit und internationale Wirtschaftsbeziehungen,* (Frankfurt: 1970), 73ff., and the same author in: *Wohin geht Europa,* op. cit., 283. A. N. Kosygin, 'Direktiven des XXIV. Parteitages der KPdSU für den Fünfjahrplan zur Entwicklung der Wirtschaft der UdSSR 1971-1975', in: *Presse der Sowjetunion,* 19.4.1971) formulates it more cautiously on p. 226: 'Our economic

relations with countries in the West could, of course, assume quite different dimensions, if it were possible to undertake constructive steps to solve the current problems which are at present complicating the international situation'.

32. Domdey, op. cit., 74.

33. Of significance in this connection were the efforts of the Czechoslovakian Government to obtain a Western credit of 500 million US-dollars (cf. Michael Kaser: 'Economic impact of the Czech crisis', in: The Times, 28.8.1968) and the attempt to establish a 'Common Danube Market' in conjunction with Hungary and Yugoslavia, which was to intensify the exchange of goods between these countries and with the West (cf. Michael Kaser: 'Prague – the economics of a crisis', in: The Times, 24.7.1968). On the intra-society problems of the 'New Course' in the CSSR in 1968 cf. P. Sweezy in: Chécoslovaquie, capitalisme et socialisme in: Sweezy et al., *Lettres sur quelques problèmes actuel de socialisme* (Paris, 2, 1972) and H.-J. Krahl, *Zur historischen Dialektik der nachstalinistischen Reform in der CSSR,* in a collection of works from the same author: *Konstitution und Klassenkampf,* Frankfurt/M. 1971.

34. A survey is given by T. Shabad: 'Soviet Technology for Sale', in: The New York Times, 17.9.1972.

35. On the latest developments, see 178ff.

36. Even though a warning has to be expressed against euphoric expectations especially in the field of crude oil, as the drop in the rates of increase in Soviet oil-production and export to the West in 1971 show; Poland has even gone over to importing Middle-East oil through the British concern BP, whereas the GDR has recently taken to buying oil from the Netherlands (Economic Bulletin for Europe, Vol. 24 (1973), no. 1, 32; Les Echos, 6.7.1971).

37. France already signed a contract in March, 1971, to have French uranium enriched in the Soviet Union and, now, West Germany has recently shown an interest in obtaining uranium from the USSR via the EEC Atomic Energy Authority, in order to escape from the USA's supply-monopoly and to keep the road open for European production of uranium (cf. Hans Hagen Bremer: 'Die nuklearen Erpresser', in: *Die Zeit,* 30.3.1973).

38. This state of affairs forms the heart of the stagnation-theories, cf. for example, J. A. Schumpeter, *Kapitalismus, Sozialismus and Demokratie* (Berlin: 1957), 182-197 on the 'dwindling of investment chances'.

39. The restrictively conceived function of East-West trade in the fifties led the Chinese Foreign-Trade Minister Yeh Chi-huang, whose country was at the time still pursuing the same policy as the other socialist states, to utter in 1955 the following statement, pregnant with meaning: "Exports serve imports and imports serve the country's socialist development of industry" (quoted from the Neue Zürcher Zeitung, Nr. 98, 10.4.1973, 5).

40. M. W. Senin, *Sozialistische Integration,* (Berlin (East): 1972), 21.

41. Cf., for example, the statements of two high-ranking officials in the Federal German Ministry of Defence: "They (other states) fear that a high level of knowledge – for example in the field of electronic combat – could, if passed on to their allies, come indirectly to the knowledge of their potential opponent and thus endanger their national security interests. These fears are, in part, difficult to disprove when one considers that several of the Western Allies have in the meantime not only signed agreements on technical and scientific co-operation with the USSR and other Eastern-Bloc states, but also exchange experts with them, set up co-productions, and produce whole manufacturing-plants which can also be used for producing armaments goods (for example, vehicles)". H. O. Seydel and H.-G. Kanno in: K. Carstens and D. Mahncke (eds), *Westeuropäische Verteidigungskooperation* (Munich 1972) 180.

42. But, as the example of the USA's putting COCOM into practice in order to prevent the delivery of three Anglo-French Concordes to China shows, the weapons of the Cold War can still quite easily be instrumentalized within the framework of the current economic conflict between the USA and Western Europe (cf. Philippe Simonnot: *Une "chinoiserie" de l'Oncle Sam,* in: Le Monde, 10.2.1973).

43. Pisar, op. cit., 169ff.

44. Cf., for example, the special number of The American Review of East-West-Trade, April 1969: "Business urges Congress to ease Export Controls".

45. On the opposing views within the US-Administration on how to deal with trade with the East held by the Department of State and Foreign-Trade Department, on the one hand, and the Defense Department, on the other, see Ch. Levinson, *East-West Trade and the Unions,* in the book by the same author, *International Trade Unionism* (London 1972), 153ff.

46. Ch. R. Dechert, *Ente Nazionale Idrocarburi. Profile of a State Corporation* (Leiden: 1963), p.32ff.; R. E. Ebel, *Communist Trade in Oil and Gas,* (New York: 1970), 282ff.

47. K. Zoch, *Zur Problematik neuer Formen der intersystemaren Kooperation,* in: K. H. Domdey, *Grundprobleme der Wirtschaftsbeziehungen zwischen Staaten der beiden Weltsysteme,* Berlin (GDR) 1966, 116ff.

48. Adler-Karlsson 1968, op. cit., 130.

49. *Le Monde,* 21.12.1971.

50. Ebel, op. cit., 101ff.

51. Cf. Petroleum Press Service, September 1972. After initial hesitancy, American firms have, since Nixon's visit to Moscow, been appearing on the Soviet market with such concentrated financial strength that some of their West European competitors have already given loud voice to their displeasure at this. (Marie Lavigne: *L'entente entre les deux grands menace-t-elle les intérêts des "petits" Etats européens? ,* in: Le Monde diplomatique, September 1973).

52. Pisar, op. cit., 93.

53. A representative example in the context of economic co-operation: Pisar, op. cit.; more subtly: H. V. Perlmutter, *Emerging East-West Ventures: The Transideological Enterprise,* in: Columbia Journal of World Business, 4 (5), September-October 1969, pp.39-50.

54. See under "Anti-Communism" and "Convergence Theory" in the German version (footnote 1).

55. On the following, cf. U. Rehfeldt, Französische Ostpolitik und sozioökonomische Interessen, in: *Leviathan,* Vol. 2, No. 3 (1974), 409-433, where the theses are illustrated using the French example.

56. From an average of 34 percent in the years 1953-1956, to 51 percent in the years 1965-1968 *(ECE Analytical Report on the State of Intra-European Trade* (New York 1970), 73).

57. On reproaches of this kind, see Adler-Karlsson 1967, op. cit., passim, and Wilczynski, op. cit., 138ff.

58. Since the USSR in 1965, and subsequently the other East European countries, joined the Paris Convention on industrial proprietory rights, this suspicion can be considered removed, cf. M. Hiance/Y. Plasseraud, *La protection des inventions en Union soviétique et dans les républiques populaires d'Europe,* (Paris: 1969).

59. For Italy, see A. Guthart, *Chronique de l'expansion italienne sur le marché soviétique,* in: Le Courrier des pays de l'Est, No. 77 (19 April 1967), 15-35, and No. 78 (3 May 1967), 21-35.

60. Cf. Wilczynski, op. cit., 226ff. Today, credits for capital-goods transfers are, without exception, State-guaranteed.

61. Divergencies from this norm have, however, become more frequent in recent years (cf. A. Kruse, *Außenwirtschaft,* (Berlin: 1965), 123.

62. Canada is even said to have offered Rumania a credit for a period of over 15 years (CNUCED, op. cit., 84). Between 1963 and 1970, the OECD countries granted 319 export-credits over an average period of 7.26 years, and totalling 2.6 billion US-dollars for deliveries to Comecon countries *(East West* (research and advisory), *Industrial and Marketing Cooperation,* Vol. II (A Research Report), Brussels, March 1972, 35).

63. Adler-Karlsson, op. cit., 154f.

64. ECE, op. cit.

65. See the tariff list in ibid., 144.

66. Lenin, *Werke,* vol. 29, 416.

67. The proportion of co-operation-business in Poland's trade with the West amounted to 30 percent in 1970, for example (G. Zellentin, *Europäische Friedensordnung: Zielvorstellungen, Strategien und Handlungspotentiale,* in: Jahrbuch der Arbeitsgemeinschaft für Friedens-

und Konfliktforschung, vol. II, Düsseldorf 1972, 34).

68. G. Sokoloff, *Deux stratégies d'intégration internationale: socialisme et capitalisme,* in: Economic appliquée, XXIV, No. 4 (1971), 576ff.

69. Rehfeldt, op. cit., 414ff.

70. Guthart, op. cit., in No. 78, 21ff.

71. Der Spiegel, No. 34/1972.

72. On the theorem of "differential spin-off effects" cf. J. Galtung, *A Structural Theory of Imperialism,* in: *Journal of Peace Research,* 1971, No. 2, 87ff.

73. Judy, op. cit., p.65. The advantage of the East European computer-market lay, until recently, in the almost complete absence of the US-giant IBM, which was a victim of the harsh American embargo regulations. (On the change in the situation, however, see Levinson, op. cit., p.157). The Soviet computer backlog is estimated at 5 years and ca. 12,000 computers, amounting to a total value of 12 billion US-dollars. At present, the USSR is developing its own computer of the Third Generation (RYAD), which will not, however, be ready for use until 1974. Since it is compatible with IBM computers, a fierce struggle has broken out at present between IBM, on the one hand, and Siemens and the French CII, on the other, who have also been striving for technical compatibility with IBM and would thus be in a position to supply compatible hard- and soft-ware for the RYAD-series (Le Monde, 21.6.1972).

74. Cf. the concept of "push exports" in: F. Perroux, Indépendance de la nation (Paris: 1971), 37ff.

75. S. Lodgaard, *Political Change and Economic Reorientation in Europe – The role of industrial cooperation,* in: Instant Research on Peace and Violence, Nr. 3/1972, 153ff.

76. ECE, op. cit., 81ff.

77. Domdey, (footnote 47), 51.

78. France-Observateur, 7.4.1960.

79. This is analysed for the French Communist Party in: U. Rehfeldt, *Die Rolle der KPF in den Ost-West-Beziehungen,* unpublished working paper for the meeting of the "Arbeitskreis Sozialistische Länder", Frankfurt/M., February 1975.

79a. L'Humanité, 15.10.1970.

80. Cf., Garaudy's statements at the 19th Party Congress of the French Communist Party, in: Le Monde, 7.2.1970.

81. This problem is discussed by the following authors: H. Elsenhans/G. Junne, Deformation und Wirtschaftswachstum. Die Auswirkungen der wirtschaftlichen Ost-West-Kooperation auf die osteuropäischen Länder, in: *Leviathan* 4/1974, 534-571; S. Lodgaard, On the Relationship between East-West Economic Cooperation and Political Change in Eastern Europe, in: *Journal of Peace Research,* 1974, No. 4, 325-340; W. Spohn, Die technologische Abhängigkeit der Sowjetunion vom Weltmarkt, in: *Probleme des Klassenkampfs,* No. 19-21, October 1975, 225-259 (a comment on the study of A. C. Sutton, *Western Technology and Soviet Economic Development,* 3 vol., Stanford 1968, 1971 and 1973.); H. D. Jacobsen, *Kooperation und Abgrenzung in den wirtschaftlichen Beziehungen zwischen Ost- und Westeuropa,* to be published by the Deutsche Gemeinschaft für Friedens- und Konfliktforschung; U. Rehfeldt, *Zur Struktur der ökonomischen und technologischen Austauschprozesse zwischen Ost- und West-europa. Asymmetrien und Abhängigkeiten,* mimeo 1974, to be published in: K. J. Gantzel (ed.), *Konflikt und Integration zwischen Industriegesellschaften* Frankfurt/M., (forthcoming).

82. Lodgaard, op. cit., 153ff.

83. According to the statement made by the Deputy Governor of the Hungarian State Bank, Eastern Europe is the safest place in the world for investments 'since everything is already nationalized' (The New York Times, 14.2.73, p.52).

84. M. Cabannes, *Les possibilités de transition vers une nouvelle spécialisation entre l'Est et l'Ouest,* in: Economies et Sociétiés (Cahiers de l'I.S.E.A.), VI (1), January 1972, 354.

85. Which is expressed, for example, in the fact that a Soviet insurance company in London guarantees American investments in the Third World in conjunction with Lloyds (L'Express, 10.7.1972, p.69).

86. UNCTAD, Industrial co-operation in trade between socialist countries of Eastern

Europe and developed market-economy countries. Study prepared by the UNCTAD secretariat, in: UNCTAD, 9th session, Agenda item 9, Annexes (Document No. TD/B/247), Geneva 1969, 12.

87. E.g. the building of a French-Yugoslavian electricity-work in Lebanon, the assembly of Italian-Polish Polski-FIAT in Egypt and Colombia (East West 1972, p. 41 ff), or the mining of iron-ore in Guinea by an Australian-American-Italian-Rumanian-Yugoslavian consortium (Jalée, *Le pillage du tiers monde,* (Paris: 1973), 92.

88. Samuel Pisar is of a different opinion (Un instrument de développement: la 'société transidéologique', in: Le Monde, 1.9.1973).

89. F. Vilmar/W. Möller, *Sozialistische Friedenspolitik für Europa,* Reinbek 1972, 109.

90. For example, the First World War broke out in spite of the intensive trade relations and capital ties between the European countries.

91. Cf. Montesquieu: *De l'Esprit des Lois,* book XX, chap. 1: 'Trade heals destructive prejudices; and it is almost a general rule that wherever there are friendly customs, there is also trade; and that wherever there is trade, there are also friendly customs', ibid. chap. 2: 'The natural effect of trade is to create peace'.

Bibliography of
German Political Science Literature 1973-74

Klaus v. Beyme and Volker Rittberger

LIST OF PERIODICALS AND ABBREVIATIONS

Das Argument
Aus Politik und Zeitgeschichte (Beilage zur Wochenzeitung 'Das Parlament')
Aussenpolitik   AP
Blätter für deutsche und internationale Politik   Blätter
Deutschland-Archiv   DA
Europa Archiv   EA
Kölner Zeitschrift für Soziologie und Sozialpsychologie   KZfSS
Leviathan   Lev
Osteuropa   OE
Politische Vierteljahresschrift   PVS
Probleme des Klassenkampfes   Prokla
Sozialistische Politik   SoPo
Der Staat
Sozialwissenschaftliches Jahrbuch für Politik
Die Verwaltung
Zeitschrift für Parlamentsfragen   ZParl
Zeitschrift für Politik   ZfP

MAIN SECTIONS

A   Political Science
    General Studies
    Methods, Research Techniques
    Congresses, Symposia, Associations, Curricula
    Works of Reference, Bibliographies

B Political Thought
History of Political Ideas
General Works
Ancient Times and Middle Ages
Modern Times until 1789
19th Century
20th Century
Ideological Foundations of Political Systems
General Studies
Democracy
Socialism
Marxism, Communism
Nationalism, Fascism
Totalitarianism, Authoritarianism
Liberalism
Conservatism
Theories of Political Systems (State, Power, Legitimacy)
Political Development and Change (Crisis, Violence and Revolutions)

C Government and Politics
The Political System (Theoretical and Comparative Studies)
The Political System of the FGR
Constitutional Problems
Federalism
The Powers
Executive
Legislative
Judiciary
Freedom and Civil Rights
Public Policy
Economic System and Economic Policy
Social Policy
Educational Policy and Science Policy
Environmental Policy
Infrastructural Policy
Developmental Policy
Public Administration
General and Comparative Studies
Planning
Civil Service
Local Government

D Political Process
Political Influences and Trends
Interest Groups
Trade Unions and Labour Movement
Rural Influences
Promotional Groups
Military Influences
National Minorities and Racial Factors
Political Parties
Political Socialization
Elite Recruitment
Mass Media and Political Communication

Representation and Elections
Area Studies
West European Countries
  France
  Great Britain
  Italy
  Spain
  Other Countries
The USA and Canada
Socialist Systems
Comparison of Capitalist and Socialist Systems and Theoretical Discussions of
Research on Socialist Systems
Comparisons between the two German States
The Political System of the GDR
Berlin
The Soviet Union
Other Socialist Systems
  East European Socialist Countries
  Yugoslavia
  Cuba
  China
Developing Countries
Latin America
Africa
Arab Countries and the Middle East
Asia

E **International Relations**
General Studies on Theory and Methodology
State in International Affairs: Their Foreign Relations
FRG
GDR
United States
USSR
Other Countries
International Politics
General Studies
Basic Aspects of International Politics
Configurations of International Politics
  East-West Relations
  Other
Issues of International Politics
  Armament, Arms Control and Disarmament
  Underdevelopment and Development Strategies
  Other
Transnational Relations and Politics
Multinational Corporations
International Trade Unions
Other
International Organization and Integration
General Studies
The United Nations System
West European Organizations
Other

A POLITICAL SCIENCE

General Studies

Backhaus, H. G./Bahr, H. D. (eds): Gesellschaft. Beiträge zur Marxschen Theorie. Frankfurt/M., Suhrkamp, 1974, 2 vols.

Berg-Schlosser, Dirk/Maier, Robert/Stammen, Theo (eds): Einführung in die Politikwissenschaft. Munich, Beck, 1974.

Greven, Th. Michael: Systemtheorie und Gesellschaftsanalyse. Neuwied Berlin, Luchterhand, 1974.

Grimm, Klaus: Niklas Luhmanns 'Soziologische Aufklärung', Hamburg, Hoffmann & Campe, 1974.

Konegen, Norbert: Politikwissenschaft – eine kybernetische Einführung. Düsseldorf, Droste, 1973.

Lehner, Franz: Politisches Verhalten also sozialer Tausch. Eine sozialpsychologische Studie utilitaristischen Theorie politischen Verhaltens. Bern/Frankfurt/M., Lang, 1973.

Lehner, Franz: Nostalgie einer Disziplin oder die Revolution, die nie stattgefunden hat? PVS, 245-256.

Maciejowski, Franz (ed): Theorie der Gesellschaft oder Sozialtechnologie? Neue Beiträge zur Habermas-Luhmann-Diskussion. Frankfurt/M., Suhrkamp, 1974.

Massing, Otwin: Politische Soziologie. Paradigmata einer kritischen Politikwissenschaft, Frankfurt/M., Suhrkamp, 1974.

Schlangen, Walter: Theorie der Politik. Einführung in Geschichte und Grundprobleme der Politikwissenschaft. Stuttgart, Kohlhammer, 1974.

Schmid, Günther: Funktionsanalyse und politische Theorie. Funktionalismustheorie, politisch-ökonomische Faktorenanalyse und Elemente einer genetisch-funktionalen Systemtheorie. Düsseldorf, Bertelsmann, 1974.

Schulze, Peter W.: Zum Integrationsansatz von K. W. Deutsch. Versuch einer Kritik aus marxistischer Sicht. PVS, 1973, 67-84.

Tudyka, Kurt P.: Kritische Politikwissenschaft. Stuttgart, Kohlhammer, 1973.

Vanberg, Viktor: Wissenschaftsverständnis, Sozialtheorie und politische Prgrammatik. Analyse des Gegensatzes zwischen liberalem und totalitärem Politikverständnis. Tübingen, Mohr, 1973.

Willms, Bernard: Kritik und Politik. Jürgen Habermas oder das politische Defizit der 'Kritischen Theorie'. Frankfurt/M., Suhrkamp, 1973.

Methods and Research Techniques

Alemann, Ulrich von/Forndran, Erhard: Methodik der Politikwissenschaft. Eine Einführung in Arbeitstechnik und Forschungspraxis. Stuttgart, Kohlhammer, 1974.

Eberlein, G. et al (eds): Forschungslogik der Sozialwissenschaften. Düsseldorf, Bertelsmann, 1974.

Meurer, Bärbel: Kritische Bemerkungen zur Systemtheorie. Das Argument No. 83, 1973, 883-908.

Münch, Richard: Gesellschaftstheorie und Ideologiekritik. Hamburg, Hoffmann & Campe, 1973.

Spinner, Helmut: Pluralismus als Erkenntnismodell. Frankfurt, Suhrkamp, 1974.

Wetzel, Manfred: Wider den soziologischen Behavioorismus. Das Argument No. 83, 1973, 909-926.

Vente, Rolf E. (ed): Erfahrung und Erfahrungswissenschaft. Die Frage des Zusammenhangs wissenschaftlicher und gesellschaftlicher Entwicklung. Stuttgart, Kohlhammer, 1974.

Zapf, Wolfgang (ed): Soziale Indikatoren. Konzepte und Forschungsansätze. Frankfurt, Herder & Herder, 1974, 2 vols.

Congresses, Symposia, Associations, Curricula

Doeker, Günter/Steffani, Winfried (eds): Klassenjustiz und Pluralismus. Hamburg, Hoffmann & Campe, 1973.

Grauhan, Rolf-Richard – Narr, Wolf-Dieter: Studium der Sozialwissenschaft – demonstriert an der Politikwissenschaft. Lev., 1973, 90-134.

Winkler, Hans Joachim (ed): Politikwissenschaft als Erziehungswissenschaft? Zur Lehrerausbildung und zum sozialwissenschaftlichen Unterricht. Opladen, Westdeutscher Verlag, 1974.

Works of Reference, Bibliographies

Bibliographies

Karl Dietrich Bracher/Hans-Adolf Jacobsen (eds): Bibliographie zur Politik in Theorie und Praxis. Ergänzungsband. Auswahl aus der von Juni 1969 bis Oktober 1972 erschienenen Literatur und Nachträge. Düsseldorf, Droste, 1973.

Buse, M. J./Dewitz, Dina von (eds): Bibliographie zur politischen Planung. Baden-Baden, Nomos 1974.

Works of Reference

Ballerstedt, Eike/Glatzer, Wolfgang (eds): Soziologischer Almanach. Handbuch gesellschaftspolitischer Daten und Indikatoren für die Bundesrepublik Deutschland. Frankfurt – New York, Herder & Herder, 1974.

POLITICAL THOUGHT

History of Political Ideas

General Works

Greiffenhagen, Martin (ed): Emanzipation. Hamburg, Hoffmann & Campe 1973.

Ancient Times and Middle Ages

Bien, Günther: Die Grundlegung der politischen Philosophie bei Aristoteles. Freiburg, Alber, 1973.

Tomberg, Friedrich: Polis und Nationalstaat. Eine vergleichende Überbauanalyse im Anschluß an Aristoteles. Darmstadt Neuwied, Luchterhand, 1973.

Modern Times until 1789

Brandt, Reinhard: Rousseaus Philosophie der Gesellschaft. Stuttgart, Friedrich Fromman, 1973.

Comoth, K.: Die Verwirklichung der Philosophie. Subjektivität und Verobjektivierung im Denken des jungen Marx. ZfP, 1973, 309-326.

Dangelmayr, Siegfried: Methode und System. Wirtschaftsklassifikation bei Bacon, Hobbes und Locke. Meisenheim, Hain, 1974.

Euchner, Walter: Egoismus und Gemeinwohl. Studien zur Geschichte der bürgerlichen Philosophie. Frankfurt/M. Suhrkamp, 1973.

Gralher, Martin: Demokratie und Repräsentation in der englischen Revolution, Meisenheim, Hain 1973.

Henningsen, Michael: Der Fall Amerika. Zur Sozial- und Bewußtseinsgeschichte einer Verdrängung. Das Amerika der Europäer. Munich, List, 1974.

Saage, Richard: Eigentum, Staat und Gesellschaft bei Immanuel Kant. Stuttgart, Kohlhammer, 1973.

Schmiede, Rudi: Grundprobleme der Marx'schen Akkumulations- und Krisentheorie. Frankfurt/M., Athenäum, 1973.

Sternberger, Dolf: Machiavellis' Principe und der Begriff des Politischen. Wiesbaden, Steiner, 1974.

19th Century

Herre, Günther: Verelendung und Proletariat bei Karl Marx. Düsseldorf, Droste 1973.

Henningsen, Michael: Das Amerika von Hegel, Marx und Engels. Zur Genealogie des europäischen Anti-Amerikanismus. ZfP, 1973, 224-51.

Mandt, Hella: Tyrannislehre und Widerstandsrecht. Studien zur deutschen politischen Theorie des 19. Jahrhunderts. Neuwied, Luchterhand, 1974.

Marcuse, Herbert/Schmidt, Alfred: Existentialistische Marx-Interpretation. Frankfurt, EVA, 1973.

Meyer, Thomas: Der Zwiespalt in der Marxschen Emanzipationstheorie. Kronberg/Taunus, Scriptor, 1973.

Nusser, Karl-Heinz: Hegels Dialektik und das Prinzip der Revolution. Der Weg zur praktischen Philosophie. Munich Salzburg, Pustet, 1973.

Nutzinger, Hans G./Wolfstetter, E.: Die Marxsche Theorie und ihre Kritik. Frankfurt, Herder & Herder, 1974.

Ritsert, Jürgen: Probleme politisch-ökonomischer Theoriebildung. Frankfurt, Athenäum, 1973.

20th Century

Guggenberger, Bernd: Die Neubestimmung des subjektiven Faktors im Neomarxismus. Eine Analyse des voluntaristischen Geschichtsverständnisses der Neuen Linken. Freiburg, Alber 1973.

Kammler, Jörg: Die politische Theorie von Georg Lukacs. Darmstadt, Luchterhand, 1974.

Rabehl, Bernd: Marx und Lenin. Berlin, Verlag für das Studium der Arbeiterbewegung, 1973.

Schröder, H. C.: Sozialistische Imperialismusdeutung. Göttingen, Vandenhoek & Ruprecht, 1973.

Ideological Foundations of Political Systems

General Studies

Democracy

Adam, Uwe Dietrich: Systemveränderung als Ideologie oder Vilmars Demokratisierungs- strategie. Aus Politik und Zeitgeschichte. Beilage zur Wochenzeitung das Parlament. B 51-52, 1974, 17-30.

Bermbach, Udo (ed): Theorie und Praxis der direkten Demokratie. Opladen, Westdeutscher Verlag, 1973.

Buck, Hans-Robert (ed): Demokratie. Studientexte zur Auseinandersetzung mit dem demo- kratischen System. Munich, Goldmann, 1974.

Däubler, Wolfgang: Das Grundrecht auf Mitbestimmung. Frankfurt/M., EVA, 1973.

Fetscher, Iring: Demokratie zwischen Sozialdemokratie und Sozialismus. Stuttgart, Kohl- hammer, 1973.

Fricke, Wolfgang/Geissler, Arnulf (eds): Demokratisierung der Wirtschaft. Hamburg, Hoffmann & Campe, 1973.

Greiffenhagen, Martin (ed): Demokratisierung in Staat und Gesellschaft. Munich, Piper, 1973.

Hofmann, R.: Totalisierung und Differenzierung. Die neuerliche Krise des demokratischen Prinzips. ZfP, 1973, S. 327-49.

Pelinka, Anton: Dynamische Demokratie. Zur konkreten Utopie gesellschaftlicher Gleichheit. Stuttgart, Kohlhammer, 1974.

Scholz, Rupert: Paritätische Mitbestimmung und Grundgesetz. Berlin, Duncker & Humblot, 1974.

Schlangen, Walter: Demokratie und bürgerliche Gesellschaft. Einführung in die Grundlagen der bürgerlichen Demokratie. Stuttgart, Kohlhammer, 1973.

Vilmar, Fritz: Strategie gesamtgesellschaftlicher Demokratisierung, Parlamentarische Demokratie und sozialistische Transformation. Z. Parl. 1973, 480-501.

Vilmar, Fritz: Strategien der Demokratisierung. Darmstadt Neuwied, Luchterhand, 1973, 2 vols.

Socialism

Bermbach, Udo – Nuscheler, Franz (eds): Sozialistischer Pluralismus. Hamburg, Hoffmann & Campe, 1973.

Flohr, Heiner/Lompe, Klaus/Neumann, Lothar F. (eds): Freiheitlicher Sozialismus. Beiträge zu seinem heutigen Selbstverständnis. Bonn-Bad Godesberg, Verlag Neue Gesellschaft, 1973.

Glotz, Peter: Demokratischer Sozialismus als Reformismus. Aus Politik und Zeitgeschichte, B 23/1973.

Schwan, Alexander/Schwan, Gesine: Sozialdemokratie und Marxismus. Hamburg, Hoffmann & Campe, 1974.

Steffen, Jochen: Strukturelle Revolution. Von der Wertlosigkeit der Sachen. Reinbek, Rowohlt, 1974.

Marxism, Communism

Backhaus, H. G. – et al (eds): Gesellschaft. Beiträge zur Marxschen Theorie. Frankfurt/M., Suhrkamp, 1974, 2 vols.

Bartsch, Günter: Anarchismus in Deutschland. Vol. 2 and 3, 1965-1973. Hannover, Fackelträger-Verlag, 1973.

Dutschke, Rudi: Versuch, Lenin auf die Füße zu stellen. Berlin, Wagenbach, 1974.

Ebbighausen, Rolf (ed): Monopol und Staat. Zur Marx-Rezeption in der Theorie des staatsmonopolitischen Kapitalismus. Frankfurt/M., Suhrkamp, 1973.

Frey, Bruno S./Meissner, Werner (eds): Marxismus und ökonomische Theorie der Politik. Frankfurt/M., Athenäum 1974.

Heimann, Horst: Die Kontroverse um den Wissenschaftspluralismus. Die Reaktion der Sozialwissenschaften und der pluralistischen Demokratie auf die Herausforderung der Neuen Linken.

Aus Politik und Zeitgeschichte B 26/1974.

Holz, Hans Heinz: Strömungen und Tendenzen im Neo-Marxismus. Munich, Hanser, 1973.

Kühne, Karl: Ökonomie und Marxismus. Vol. 2 Zur Dynamik des Marxschen Systems. Neuwied Berlin, Luchterhand, 1974.

Lösche, Peter: Anarchismus. Versuch einer Definition und historischen Typologie. PVS 1974, 53-73.

Schmickl, Emil: Soziologie und Sozialismustheorie in der DDR. Cologne, Wissenschaft und Politik, 1973.

Nationalism, Fascism

Haug, Wolfgang-Fritz: Faschismus-Theorie in antifaschistischer Perspektive. Das Argument 87, 1974, 537-42.

Kuehnl, Reinhard (ed): Texte zur Faschismusdiskussion. Positionen und Kontroversen. Reinbek, Rowohlt, 1974, vol. 1.

Kuhn, Axel: Das faschistische Herrschaftssystem und die moderne Gesellschaft. Hamburg, Hoffmann & Campe, 1973.

Opitz, Reinhard: Über die Entstehung und Verhinderung von Faschismus. Das Argument 97, 1974, 543-603.

Tomberg, Friedrich: Konservative Wegbereitung des Faschismus in der politischen Philosophie Carl Schmitts. Das Argument, 87, 1974, S. 604-633.

Totalitarianism, Authoritarianism

Liberalism

Langewiesche, Dieter: Liberalismus und Demokratie in Württemberg zwischen Revolution und Reichsgründung. Düsseldorf, Droste, 1974.

Conservatism

Glaser, Hermann: Die Mitte und rechts davon. Bemerkungen zur Tendenwende in der Bundesrepublik. Aus Politik und Zeitgeschichte, B 42, 1974, 14-36.

Greiffenhagen, Martin (ed): Der neue Konservatismus der siebziger Jahre. Reinbek, Rowohlt, 1974.

Kaltenbrunner, Gerd-Klaus (ed): Konservatismus international. Stuttgart, Seewald, 1973.

Lenk, Hans (ed): Technokratie als Ideologie. Stuttgart, Kohlhammer, 1973.

Saage, Richard: Konservatismus und Demokratie Zur neuesten Kontroverse über den Konservatismus. Aus Politik und Zeitgeschichte, B 42/1974, 37-47.

Schumann, Hans Gerd (ed): Konservatismus. Cologne. Kiepenheuer & Witsch, 1974.

Westarp, Michael-Viktor Graf: Konservatismus – Strategie der Vermeidung des Faschismus? Das Argument, No. 82, 1973, 830-834.

Theories of Political Systems (State, Power, Legitimacy)

Bärsch, Claus-Ekkehard: Der Staatsbegriff in der neueren deutschen Staatslehre und seine theoretischen Implikationen. Berlin, Duncker & Humblot, 1974.

Braunmühl, Claudia von et al.: Probleme einer materialistischen Staatstheorie. Frankfurt/M., Suhrkamp, 1973.

Flatow, Sibylle von/Huisken, Freerk: Zum Problem der Ableitung des bürgerlichen Staates. Prokla, 1973, No. 7, 83-153.

Geismann, Georg: Ethik und Herrschaftsordnung. Ein Beitrag zum Problem der Legitimation. Tübingen, Mohr, 1974.

Guggenberger, Bernd: Wem nützt der Staat? Kritik der neo-marxistischen Staatstheorie, Stuttgart, Kohlhammer, 1974.

Habermas, Jürgen: Legitimationsprobleme im Spätkapitalismus. Frankfurt/M. Suhrkamp, 1973.

Reinisch, Leonhard (ed): Freiheit und Gleichheit oder die Quadratur des Kreises. Munich, Bayerische Landeszentrale für Politische Bildungsarbeit, 1974.

Ulrich, Hans: Die Einschätzung von kapitalistischer Entwicklung und Rolle des Staates durch . den allgemeinen Deutschen Gewerkschaftsbund. Prokla, 1973, No. 6, 1-70.

Political Development and Change (Crisis, Violence and Revolutions)

Allerbeck, Klaus R.: Soziologie radikaler Studentenbewegungen. Eine vergleichende Untersuchung in der BRD und den Vereinigten Staaten. Munich, Oldenbourg, 1973.

Beyme, Klaus von (ed): Empirische Revolutionsforschung. Opladen, Westdeutscher Verlag, 1973.

Eichhorn, Peter: Gewalt und Friedenssicherung. Munich, Claudius, 1973.

Horn, Klaus: Gesellschaftliche Produktion von Gewalt, Lev., 1973, 310-341.

Jaeggi, Urs/Papcke, Sven (eds): Revolution und Theorie. Materialien zum bürgerlichen Revolutionsverständnis. Frankfurt/M., Fischer Athenäum, 1974.

Jaenicke, Martin (ed): Herrschaft und Krise. Opladen, Westdeutscher Verlag, 1973.

Jaenicke, Martin (ed): Politische Systemkrisen. Cologne, Kiepenheuer & Witsch, 1973.

Kepplinger, Hans Mathias: Statusdevianz und Meinungsdevianz unter Sympathisanten der Baader-Meinhof-Gruppe. KZfSS 1974, 770-800.

Lindner, G.: Die Krise als Steuerungsmittel. Lev., 1973, 342-382.

Müller-Borchert, Hans-Joachim: Guerrilla im Industriestaat. Hamburg, Hoffmann & Campe, 1973.

Narr, Wolf-Dieter: Gewalt und Legitimität. Lev., 1973, 7-42.

Papcke, Seven: Progressive Gewalt. Studien zum sozialen Widerstandsrecht. Frankfurt/M., Fischer, 1973.

Senghaas, Dieter: Gewalt, Konflikt, Frieden. Hamburg, Hoffmann & Campe, 1974.

Steiner, Jürg: Subkulturelle Segmentierung und politische Gewalt, Der Staat, 1973, 313-338.

Tetsch, Hartmut: Die permanente Revolution. Ein Beitrag zur Soziologie der Revolution und zur Ideologiekritik. Opladen, Westdeutscher Verlag, 1973.

C GOVERNMENT AND POLITICS

The Political System

The Political System of the FGR

Jaeggi, Urs: Kapital und Arbeit in der BRD. Frankfurt/M., Fischer, 1973.

Loewenthal, Richard/Schwarz, Hans-Peter (eds): Die zweite deutsche Republik. Stuttgart, Seewald, 1974.

Nicklauss, Karlheinz: Demokratiegründung in Westdeutschland, Munich, Piper, 1974.

Nolte, Ernst: Deutschland und der Kalte Krieg. Munich, Piper, 1974.

Röder, Karl-Heinz et al.: Widersprüche und Tendenzen im Herrschaftssystem der BRD. Frankfurt, Verlag Marxistische Blätter, 1973.

Constitutional Problems

Denninger, Erhard: Staatsrecht. Reinbek, Rowohlt, 1973, vol. 1.

Preuss, Ulrich K.: Legalität und Pluralismus. Beiträge zum Verfassungsrecht der Bundesrepublik Deutschland. Frankfurt/M. Suhrkamp, 1973.

Rehbinder, Manfred (ed): Recht im sozialen Rechtsstaat. Opladen, Westdeutscher Verlag, 1973.

Seifert, Jürgen: Grundgesetz und Restauration. Verfassungsgeschichtliche Analyse und synoptische Darstellung des Grundgesetzes vom 23. Mai 1949 mit sämtlichen Änderungen. Darmstadt Neuwied, Luchterhand, 1974.

Federalism

Foeltz-Schroeter, Marie Elise: Föderalistische Politik und nationale Repräsentation 1945-1947. Stuttgart, DVA, 1974.

Heckt, Wilhelm: Die Entwicklung des bundesstaatlichen Finanzausgleichs in der BRD. Bonn, Stollfuß, 1973.

Lange, Erhard H. M.: Bestimmungsfaktoren der Föderalismusdiskussion vor Gründung der Bundesrepublik. Aus Politik und Zeitgeschichte, B 2-3/1974, 9-29.

Laufer, Heinz: Der Föderalismus in der BRD. Stuttgart, Kohlhammer, 1974.

Laufer, Heinz/Wirth, Jutta: Die Landesvertretungen in der BRD. Munich, Goldmann, 1974.

Timmer, Reinhard (ed): Neugliederung des Bundesgebietes. Kurzfassung des Berichts der Sachverständigenkommission für die Neugliederung des Bundesgebietes. Cologne, Heymanns, n.d. (ca. 1974).

Political System: The Powers

Executive

Bredthauer, Karl D.: Aspekte des Regierungswechsels in Bonn. Blätter für deutsche und internationale Politik, 1974, No. 6, 559-568.

Echtler, Ulrich: Einfluß und Macht in der Politik. Der beamtete Staatssekretär. Munich, Goldmann, 1973.

Lippert, Michael R.: Bestellung und Abberufung der Regierungschefs und ihre funktionale Bedeutung für das parlamentarische Regierungssystem. Berlin, Duncker & Humblot, 1973.

Organisation der Ministerien des Bundes und der Länder. Berlin, Duncker & Humblot, 1973.

Pitschas, Rainer: Die Vertretung des Bundespräsidenten durch den Präsidenten des Bundesrates. Der Staat, 1973, 183-206.

Wahl, Rainer: Probleme der Ministerialorganisation. Der Staat, 1974, 383-398.

Legislative

Alemann, Ulrich von: Parteiensysteme im Parlamentarismus. Eine Einführung und Kritik von Parlamentarismustheorie. Düsseldorf, Bertelsmann, 1973.

Busch, Eckart: Die Parlamentsauflösung 1972. Z. Parl. 1973, 213-246.

Bieber, Roland: Organe der erweiterten Europäischen Gemeinschaften: Das Parlament. Baden Baden, Nomos, 1974.

Der Bundesrat als Verfassungsorgan und politische Kraft. Beiträge zum fünfundzwanzigjährigen Bestehen des Bundesrates der Bundesrepublik Deutschland. Bad Honnef, Darmstadt, Neue Darmstädter Verlaganstalt, 1974.

Egloff, Willi: Die Informationslage des Parlaments. Eine Untersuchung zur Gesetzgebungslehre am Beispiel des Deutschen Bundestages und der Schweizerischen Bundesversammlung. Zurich, Schulthess Polygraphischer Verlag, 1974.

Fach, Wolfgang: Koalition und Opposition in spieltheoretischer Sicht. Berlin, Duncker & Humblot, 1974.

Kaltefleiter, Werner/Veen, Hans-Joachim: Zwischen freiem und imperativem Mandat. Z. Parl. 1974, 246-267.

Kevenhörster, Paul: Das Rätesystem als Instrument zur Kontrolle politischer und wirtschaftlicher Macht. Opladen, Westdeutscher Verlag, 1974.

Magiera, Siegfried: Allgemeine Regelungsgewalt (Rechtsetzung) zwischen Parlament und Regierung. Zur Auslegung und zur Reform des Art. 80 GG. Der Staat, 1974, No. 1, 1 ff.

Pietzner, Rainer: Petitionsausschuss und Plenum. Berlin, Duncker & Humblot, 1974.

Reichel, Peter: Bundestagsabgeordnete in europäischen Parlamenten. Zur Soziologie des europäischen Parlamentariers. Düsseldorf, Westdeutscher Verlag, 1974.

Ritter, Gerhard A. (ed): Gesellschaft, Parlament und Regierung. Zur Geschichte des Parlamentarismus in Deutschland. Düsseldorf, Droste 1974.

Scheuner, Ulrich: Zur Entwicklung des Parlaments unter der Ordnung des Grundgesetzes. Aus Politik und Zeitgeschichte. B 39/1974, 3-17.

Szmula, Volker: Zum Selbstverständnis des Deutschen Bundestages. Aus Politik und Zeitgeschichte, B 39/1974, 19-37.

Väth, Werner: Zum Verhältnis von Parlament und Planung. Z. Parl. 1974, 228-245.

Wasser, Hartmut: Parlamentarismuskritik vom Kaiserreich zur Bundesrepublik. Analyse und Dokumentation. Stuttgart, Frommann-Holzboog, 1974.

Wehling, Hans-Georg and Rosemarie: Parlamentsauflösung durch Volksabstimmung. Zur Volksabstimmung in Baden-Württemberg. Z. Parl. 1973, 76-85.

Judiciary

Heyde, Wolfgang/Gielen, Peter: Die Hüter der Verfassung. Verfassungsgerichte im Bund und in den Ländern. Karlsruhe, C. F. Müller, 1973.

Hoffmann-Riem, Wolfgang: Beharrung oder Innovation. Zur Bindungswirkung verfassungsgerichtlicher Entscheidungen. Der Staat, 1974, 335-ff.

Schuppert, Folke: Die verfassungsgerichtliche Kontrolle der auswärtigen Gewalt. Baden-Baden, Nomos, 1973.

Seifert, Jürgen: Kampf um Verfassungspositionen. Materialien über Grenzen und Möglichkeiten von Rechtspolitik. Frankfurt (EVA) 1974.

Steffan, Dierk-Peter: Richterliche Rechtsfindung durch politisches Engagement? Aus Politik und Zeitgeschichte, B. 47/1974, 15-32.

Wassermann, Rudolf: Zur politischen Funktion der Rechtsprechung. Aus Politik und Zeitgeschichte. B 47/1974, 3-13.

Freedom and Civil Rights

Borgs-Maciejewski, Hermann/Martin, Ernst: Extremistenbeschluß und demokratische Verfassung. Aus Politik und Zeitgeschichte, B 5/1974, 21-25.

Borgs-Maciejewski, Hermann: Radikale im öffentlichen Dienst. Aus Politik und Zeitgeschichte, B 27/1973.

Forschungsgruppe an der FU Berlin: Zur Rolle und Funktion von Bürgerinitiativen in der Bundesrepublik und in West-Berlin. Analyse von 61 Bürgerinitiativen. Z. Parl. 1973, 247-286.

Preuss, Ulrich K.: Legalität und Pluralismus. Beiträge zum Verfassungsrecht der BRD. Frankfurt, Suhrkamp, 1973.

Kempf, Udo: Der Bürgerbeauftragte als Kontrollorgan. Aus Politik und Zeitgeschichte, B 44/1973, 17-30.

Seifert, Jürgen: Kampf um Verfassungspositionen. Materialien über Grenzen und Möglichkeiten von Rechtspolitik. Frankfurt/M., EVA, 1974.

Zillessen, Horst: Bürgerinitiativen im repräsentativen Regierungssystem. Aus Politik und Zeitgeschichte B 12/1974.

Public Policy

Economic System and Economic Policy

Adam, Hermann: Macht und Vermögen in der 'Wirtschaft'. Cologne, Bund-Verlag, 1974.

Altvater, Elmar et al: Entwicklungsphasen und -tendenzen des Kapitalismus in Westdeutschland, Prokla, 1974. No. 13, 101 ff.

Arndt, Helmut: Wirtschaftliche Macht. Munich, Beck, 1974.

Bernholz, Peter: Währungskrisen und Währungsordnung. Hamburg, Hoffmann & Campe, 1974.

Duwendag, Dieter (ed): Macht und Ohnmacht der Bundesbank. Frankfurt/M. Athenäum, 1973.

Hardes, Heinz-Dieter: Einkommenspolitik in der BRD. Stabilität und Gruppeninteressen: Der Fall Konzertierte Aktion. Frankfurt/M. New York, Herder & Herder, 1974.

Jochimsen, Reimut: Aktive Strukturpolitik – Ansatzpunkt zur Modernisierung unserer Volkswirtschaft. Aus Politik und Zeitgeschichte. B 40/1974, 3-17.

Kevenhörster, Paul: Ausländische Arbeitnehmer im politischen System der BRD. Opladen, Westdeutscher Verlag, 1974.

Kirchhoff, Gerd: Subventionen als Instrument der Lenkung und Koordinierung. Berlin, Duncker & Humblot, 1973.

Klisch, Carsten-Michael: Die Konjunkturpolitik in der Europäischen Wirtschaftsgemeinschaft. Baden-Baden, Nomos 1974.

Meier, Alfred: Systematische staatliche Wirtschaftspolitik. Ansätze zu einer Konzeption. Tübingen, Mohr 1973.

Molitor, Regina (ed): Zehn Jahre Sachverständigenrat. Frankfurt, Athenäum, 1973.

Müller, Helmut: Zentralbank – eine Nebenregierung? Opladen, Westdeutscher Verlag, 1973.

Rahmeyer, Fritz: Pluralismus und rationale Wirtschaftspolitik. Stuttgart, Kohlhammer, 1974.

Rothkegel, Christoph: Finanzplanung und Konjunkturpolitik. Stuttgart, Fischer, 1973.

Siebke, J./Willms, M.: Theorie der Geldpolitik Berlin, Springer, 1974.

Social Policy

Christmann, Alfed et al. eds: Sozialpolitik. Ziele und Wege. Cologne, Verlag Wissenschaft und Politik, 1974.

Dierkes, Meinolf: Die Sozialbilanz. Ein gesellschaftsbezogenes Informations- und Rechnungssystem. Frankfurt/M. New York, Herder & Herder, 1974.

Gladen, Albin: Geschichte der deutschen Sozialpolitik bis zur Gegenwart. Wiesbaden, Steiner, 1974.

Herder-Dorneich, Philipp/Niederfahrenhorst, Heinrich/Gerdelmann, Werner: Systemanalyse und Problemgeschichte der arbeitsrechtlichen und versicherungsrechtlichen Lösung sozialer Aufgaben. Opladen, Westdeutscher Verlag, 1973.

Isensee, J.: Umverteilung durch Sozialversicherungsbeiträge. Berlin, Duncker & Humblot, 1974.

Meyer-Harter, R.: Die Stellung der Frau in der Sozialversicherung. Berlin, Duncker & Humblot, 1974.

Metze, I.: Soziale Sicherung und Einkommensverteilung. Eine empirische Untersuchung über die Wirkungen staatlicher Maßnahmen zur sozialen Sicherung. Berlin, Duncker & Humblot, 1974.

Nicklauss, Karlheinz: Der Parlamentarische Rat und das Sozialstaatspostulat. PVS, 1974, 33-52.

Pitz, Karl H. (ed): Das Nein zur Vermögenspolitik. Gewerkschaftliche Argumente und Alternativen zur Vermögensbildung. Reinbek, Rowohlt, 1974.

Pulte, Peter (ed): Vermögensbildung. Berlin, De Gruyter, 1973.

Rummel, Reinhardt: Sozialunion – Stimulans der westeuropäischen Gemeinschaftsbildung? Aus Politik und Zeitgeschichte, B 44/1974, 31-38.

Sanmann, Horst (ed): Leitbilder und Zielsystem der Sozialpolitik. Berlin, Duncker & Humblot, 1973.

Schmidt-Regenberg,/Feldhusen,/Luetken: Sanierung und Sozialplan. Mitbestimmung gegen Sozialtechnik, Munich, Callwey, 1973.

Schreiber, Wilfrid: Um die soziale Sicherheit. Aus Politik und Zeitgeschichte B 48/1973, 3-21.

Educational Policy and Science Policy

Ackermann, Paul: Curriculumrevision im sozialwissenschaftlichen Bereich der Schule. Stuttgart, Klett, 1973.

Axmacher, Dirk: Erwachsenenbildung im Kapitalismus. Frankfurt/M., Fischer, 1974.

Briese, Volker/Büchner, Peter/Hage, Peter: Grenzen kapitalistischer Bildungspolitik. Analysen von Reformstrategien für den Ausbildungssektor. Frankfurt/M., Athenäum, 1973.

Bungenstab, Karl-Ernst: Umerziehung zur Demokratie? Reeducation-Politik im Bildungswesen der US-Zone 1945-1949. Düsseldorf, Bertelsmann, 1973.

Hearnden, Arthur: Bildungspolitik in der BRD und DDR. Düsseldorf, Schwann, 1973.

Hirsch, Joachim: Staatsapparat und Reproduktion des Kapitals. Projekt Wissenschaftsplanung 2. Frankfurt/M. Suhrkamp, 1974.

Hujer, Reinhard: Forschungspolitik und gesellschaftliche Planung. Opladen, Westdeutscher Verlag, 1974.

Lempert, Wolfgang: Berufliche Bildung als Beitrag zur gesellschaftlichen Demokratisierung. Frankfurt/M., Suhrkamp, 1974.

Lobkowicz, Nikolaus: Hochschulreform und "Hochschulreform" ZfP, 1973, 4-12.

Lohmar, Ulrich: Wissenschaftspolitik und Demokratisierung. Düsseldorf, Bertelsmann, 1973.

Naschold, Frieder: Schulreform als Gesellschaftskonflikt. Frankfurt/M, Athenäum, 1973.

Lührig, Holger (ed): Wirtschaftsriese – Bildungszwerg. Der Diskussionshintergrund zum Bildungsgesamtplan. Reinbek, Rowohlt, 1973.

Pfetsch, Frank: Zur Entwicklung der Wissenschaftspolitik in Deutschland. 1750-1914. Berlin, Duncker & Humblot, 1974.

Pfetsch, Frank/Sloczower: Innovation und Widerstände in der Wissenschaft. Bielefeld, Bertelsmann, 1973.

Prüss, Karsten: Kernforschungspolitik in der BRD. Frankfurt, Suhrkamp 1974.

Schwarz, Richard: Bildungspolitik ohne Bildung. Aus Politik und Zeitgeschichte B 51-52/1973, 21-46.

Straumann, Peter R. (ed): Neue Konzepte der Bildungsplanung. Reinbek, Rowohlt, 1974.

Titze, Hartmut: Die Politisierung der Erziehung. Frankfurt, Fischer 1973.

Voigt, Bodo: Bildungspolitik und politische Erziehung in den Klassenkämpfen. Frankfurt, Fischer 1974.

Environmental Policy

Bahrdt, Hans Paul: Umwelterfahrung. Munich, Nymphenburger, 1974.

Doran, Charles, F./ Hinz, Manfred O./Mayer-Tasch, Peter Cornelius: Umweltschutz – Politik des peripheren Eingriffs. Eine Einführung in die Politische Ökologie. Darmstadt Neuwied, Luchterhand, 1974.

Gärtner, Edgar: Wachstumsdiskussion und Umweltkrise. Blätter für deutsche und internationale Politik, 1973, 612-880 ff.

Giersch, Herbert (ed): Das Umweltproblem in ökonomischer Sicht. Tübingen, Mohr, 1974.

Hassenpflug, Dieter: Umweltzerstörung und Sozialkosten. Berlin, Verlag für das Studium der Arbeiterbewegung, 1974.

Höhmann, Hans-Hermann/Seidenstecher, Gertraud/Vajna, Thomas: Umweltschutz und ökonomisches System in Osteuropa. Stuttgart, Kohlhammer, 1973.

Scholder, Klaus: Kapitalismus, Sozialismus und die Idee der Grenze. Die Umweltkrise als Frage der Wertordnungen. Aus Politik und Zeitgeschichte, B 44/1973, 3-16.

Siebert, Horst: Das produzierte Chaos. Ökonomie und Umwelt. Stuttgart, Kohlhammer, 1973.

Infrastructural Policy

Formanek, Jan/Helms, Ekkehart: Infrastruktur 1985. Cologne, Deutscher Gemeindeverlag, 1974.

Läpple, Dieter: Staat und allgemeine Produktionsbedingungen. Grundlagen zur Kritik der Infrastrukturtheorien. Berlin, Verlag für das Studium der Arbeiterbewegung, 1973.

Linder, Wolf: Der Fall Massenverkehr. Frankfurt, Athenäum, 1973.

Merk, Bruno/Kortzfleisch, Gert von: Gemeindliche Daseinsvorsorge in neuerer Sicht. Cologne, Verband kommunaler Unternehmer, 1973.

Nowak, Werner: Der gemeinnützige Unternehmer als Instrument der Wohnungspolitik. Berlin, Duncker & Humblot, 1973.

Offe, Claus – Ronge, Volker: Fiskalische Krise, Bauindustrie und die Grenzen staatlicher Ausgabenrationalisierung. Lev. 1973, 189-220.

Sellmow, Reinhard: Kosten-Nutzen-Analyse und Stadtentwicklungsplanung. Stuttgart, Kohlhammer, 1973.

Wollmann, Helmut: Das Städtebauförderungsgesetz als Instrument staatlicher Intervention wo und für wen? Lev., 1974, 199-230.

Developmental Policy

Böll, Winfried: Entwicklungspolitik und administrative Praxis. Aus Politik und Zeitgeschichte, B 6/1973, 24-30.

Callies, Hans Ulrich: Der Einfluß von Entwicklungshilfeleistungen auf den Konjunkturverlauf und die Beschäftigung im Geberland. Tübingen, Erdmann, 1973.

Hesse, Kurt: Entwicklungshilfe. Berlin, Duncker & Humblot, 1973.

Kratochwil, German: Die Entwicklungshilfe der BRD für Lateinamerika. Stuttgart, Klett, 1973.

Küper, Wolfgang: Bildung und Wissenschaft in der Entwicklungspolitik. Aus Politik und Zeitgeschehen, B 25/1974, 15-26.

Priebe, H./Matzke, O.: Entwicklungspolitik ohne Illusionen. Stuttgart, Kohlhammer, 1973.

Public Administration

General and Comparative Studies

Derlien, Hans-Ulrich: Theoretische und methodische Probleme der Beurteilung organisatorischer Effizienz der öffentlichen Verwaltung. Die Verwaltung, 1974, 1-22.

Guilleaume, Emil: Politische Entscheidungsfunktion und Sachverstand. Die Verwaltung, 1973, 25-44.

Mäding, Erhard: Aufgaben der öffentlichen Verwaltung. Die Verwaltung. 1973, 257-282.

Narr, Wolf-Dieter: Gefragt: eine Verwaltungsökonomie. Lev., 1974, 157-178.

Siedentopf, Heinrich/Ellwein, Thomas/Zoll, Ralf: Funktion und allgemeine Rechtsstellung. Analyse der Funktionen des öffentlichen Dienstes. Baden-Baden, Nomos, 1973.

Planning

Aderhold, Dieter: Kybernetische Regierungstechnik in der Demokratie. Planung und Erfolgskontrolle. Munich, Olzog, 1974.

Buse, Michael, J./Dewitz, Dina von (eds): Bibliographie zur politischen Planung. Baden-Baden, Nomos, 1974.

Buse, Michael, J.: Integrierte Systeme staatlicher Planung. Baden-Baden, Nomos, 1974.

Gärtner, Edgar: Zur Funktion des 'Club of Rome'. Blätter für deutsche und internationale Politik. 1973, 1053 ff.

Grottian, Peter: Strukturprobleme staatlicher Planung. Hamburg, Hoffmann & Campe, 1974.

Grottian, Peter/Murswieck, Axel (eds): Handlungsspielräume der Staatsadministration. Hamburg, Hoffmann & Campe, 1974.

Häussermann, H.: Die administrative Organisation als Problem politischer Innovation. Lev., 1974, 233-262.

Hesse, Joachim: Politische Planung im Kommunalbereich. Die Verwaltung, 1974, 273-304.

Hoenisch, Hans J.: Planifikation. Recht zwischen Plan und Freiheit. Berlin, Duncker & Humblot, 1974.

Jochimsen, Reiner/Treuner, Peter: Staatliche Planung in der Bundesrepublik. Aus Politik und Zeitgeschichte, B 9/1974, 29-45.

König, Klaus: Programmsteuerung in komplexen politischen Systemen, Die Verwaltung, 1974, 137-158.

Mayntz, Renate/Scharpf, Fritz (eds): Planungsorganisation. Die Diskussion um die Reform von Regierung und Verwaltung des Bundes. Munich, Piper, 1973.

Pforte, Dieter/Schwenke, Olaf (eds): Ansichten einer künftigen Futurologie. Munich, Hanser, 1973.

Ronge, Volker/Schmieg, Günter: Restriktionen politischer Planung. Frankfurt, Athenäum, 1973.

Schlicht, E.: Die Theorie der kollektiven Entscheidung und der individualistische Ansatz. Lev., 1974, 263-280.

Schmelzer, Horst: Systemstrukturforschung und Systemsteuerung. Die Verwaltung, 1974, 159-178.

Schmidt, Volker: Finanz- und Aufgabenplanung als Instrument der Regierungsplanung. Die Verwaltung 1973, 1-23.

Waterkamp, Rainer: Interventionsstaat und Planung. Cologne, Verlag Wissenschaft und Politik, 1973.

Waterkamp, Rainer: Politische Leitung und Systemveränderung. Zum Problemlösungsprozeß durch Planung und Informationssysteme. Cologne, Frankfurt, EVA, 1974.

Wieck, Hans-Georg: Der Planungsstab im Verteidigungsministerium. AP, 1974, 178.

Civil Service

Behr, Marhild von/Schultz-Wild, Rainer: Arbeitsplatztruktur und Laufbahnreform im öffentlichen Dienst. Baden-Baden, Nomos, 1973.

Bosetzky, Horst: 'Dunkelfaktoren' bei Beförderungen im öffentlichen Dienst. Die Verwaltung. 1974, 427-438.

Guilleaume, Emil: Politische Entscheidungsfunktion und personelle Selektion. Die Verwaltung, 1974, 409-426.

Klein, Eckart: Die verfassungsrechtliche Problematik des ministerialfreien Raumes. Ein Beitrag zur Dogmatik der weisungsfreien Verwaltungsstellen. Berlin, Duncker & Humblot, 1974.

Luhmann, Niklas – Mayntz, Renate: Personal im öffentlichen Dienst. Eintritt und Karrieren. Baden-Baden, Nomos, 1973.

Ronneberger, Franz: Zum künftigen Bild des Beamten. Die Verwaltung, 1973, 129-144.

Local Government

Eisfeld, Dieter: Die Stadt der Stadtbewohner. Neue Formen städtischer Demokratie, Stuttgart, DVA, 1973.

Emenlauer, Rainer et al.: Die Kommune in der Staatsorganisation. Frankfurt, Suhrkamp, 1974.

Greger, Burkhard: Städtebau ohne Konzept. Hamburg, Hoffmann & Campe, 1973.

Gröttrup, Hendrik: Die kommunale Leistungsverwaltung. Stuttgart, Kohlhammer, 1973.

Knorr, Thomas: Gruppendynamische Methoden der Öffentlichkeitsarbeit im Städtebau. Meisenheim/Glan, Hain, 1974.

Neuffer, Martin: Entscheidungsfeld Stadt. Stuttgart, EVA, 1973.

Pfizer, Theodor: Kommunalpolitik. Praxis der Selbstverwaltung. Stuttgart, Kohlhammer, 1973.

Ribhegge, Wilhelm: Die Systemfunktion der Gemeinden. Zur deutschen Kommunalgeschichte seit 1918. Aus Politik und Zeitgeschichte B 47/1973.

Zoll, Ralf: Kommunalpolitik und Machtstruktur. Wertheim III. Munich, Juventa, 1974.

D POLITICAL PROCESS

Political Influences and Trends

Interest Groups

Bredthauer, Karl D.: Entleerter Pluralismus. Blätter für deutsche und internationale Politik, 1973, 340-342.

Ellwein, Thomas: Die großen Interessenverbände und ihr Einfluß. Aus Politik und Zeitgeschichte B 48/1973, 22-38.

Herde, Georg: Zur Aktivität der Vertriebenenverbände nach dem Inkrafttreten der Ostverträge. Blätter für deutsche und internationale Politik, 1973, 290-301.

Herder-Dorneich, Philip (ed): Zur Verbandsökonomik. Ansätze zu einer ökonomischen Theorie der Verbände. Berlin, Duncker & Humblot, 1973.

Lippold, Klaus, W.: Ansatzpunkte zur systemorientierten Betrachtung des Verbandes. Analyse der deutschen Kolpingsfamilie. Ein Beitrag zur Verbandstheorie. Berlin, Duncker & Humblot, 1974.

Mronz, Dieter: Körperschaften und Zwangsmitgliedschaft. Die staatsorganisations- und grundrechtliche Problematik der Zwangsverbände, aufgezeigt am Beispiel von Arbeitnehmerkammern. Berlin, Duncker & Humblot, 1973.

Reichvilser, Helmut: Erfolgskontrolle der Verbandsarbeit. Berlin, Duncker & Humblot, 1973.

Schürer-Wagner, Sabine/Abromeit, Heidrun: Arbeitgeberverbände und Werbung. Aus Politik und Zeitgeschichte B 15/1973, 26-29.

Steinberg, Rudolf: Die Interessenverbände in der Verfassungsordnung. PVS, 1973, 27-65.

Varain, Heinz Josef (ed): Interessenverbände in Deutschland. Cologne, Kiepenheuer & Witsch, 1973.

Trade Unions and Labour Movement

Bergmann, Joachim: Organisationsinterne Prozesse in kooperativen Gewerkschaften, Lev., 1973, 242-253.

Conert, Hansgeorg: Gewerkschaften heute — Ordnungsfaktor oder Gegenmacht? Offenbach Verlag 2000, 1973.

Dittmar, Rupprecht: Löhne und Vermögensverteilung. Göttingen, Vandenhoek & Ruprecht, 1974.

Eickhof, Norbert: Eine Theorie der Gewerkschaftsentwicklung. Tübingen, Mohr 1973.

Elsner, Wolfram: Die EWg. Herausforderung und Antwort der Gewerkschaften. Cologne, Pahl-Rugenstein, 1974.

Föhr, Horst: Willensbildung in den Gewerkschaften und Grundgesetz. Berlin, J. Schweitzer, 1974.

Gewerkschaften im Klassenkampf. Die Entwicklung der Gewerkschaftsbewegung in Westeuropa. Berlin, Argument Verlag 1974. Argument-Sonderband 2.

Höss, Dietrich: Die Krise des 'institutionalisierten Klassenkampfes'. Metallarbeiterstreik in Baden-Württemberg. Frankfurt, EVA, 1974.

Jacobi, Otto/Müller-Jentsch, Walther/Schmidt, Eberhard (eds): Gewerkschaften und Klassenkampf. Kritisches Jahrbuch '73. Frankfurt, Fischer, 1973. Kritisches Jahrbuch '74. Frankfurt, Fischer, 1974.

Kittner, Michael (ed): Streik und Aussperrung. Protokoll der wissenschaftlichen Veranstaltung der Industriegewerkschaft Metall vom 13. bis 15. September 1973 in München. Frankfurt EVA, n.d. (1974).

Leminsky, Gerhard/Otto, Bernd (eds): Politik und Programmatik des DGB. Cologne, Bund Verlag, 1974 (Sources).

Lösche, Peter: Industriegewerkschaften im organisierten Kapitalismus. Der CIO in der Roosevelt-Ära. Opladen, Westdeutscher Verlag, 1974.

Mattheier, Klaus: Die Gelben. Nationale Arbeiter zwischen Wirtschaftsfrieden und Streik. Düsseldorf, Schwann, 1973.

Mayer, Evelies: Theorien zum Funktionswandel der Gewerkschaften. Frankfurt/M., EVA, 1973.

Mückenberger, Ulrich: Arbeitsrecht und Klassenkampf. Der große englische Dockarbeiterstreik 1972. Frankfurt Cologne, EVA, 1974.

Müller-Jentsch, Walther: Bedingungen kooperativer und konfliktorischer Gewerkschaftspolitik. Lev, 1973, 223-241.

Münster, Arno: Der Kampf bei LIP. Berlin, Wagenbach, 1974.

Pätzold, Ulrich/Schmidt, Hendrick (eds): Solidarität gegen Abhängigkeit. Mediengewerkschaft. Neuwied, Luchterhand, 1973.

Peters, Jürgen: Arbeitnehmerkammern in der BRD. Munich, Olzog, 1974.

Reulecke, Jürgen (ed): Arbeiterbewegung am Rhein und Ruhr. Beiträge zur Geschichte der Arbeiterbewegung im Rheinland-Westfalen. Wuppertal, Hammer, 1974.

Rüthers, Bernd: Arbeitsrecht und politisches System. Frankfurt, Fischer Athenäum, 1973.

Schossig, Bernhard: Emanzipatorische Gewerkschaftspolitik und überbetriebliche Mitbestimmung. Hamburg, Hoffmann & Campe, 1974.

Steinhaus, Kurt: Streikkämpfe in der BRD von 1971 bis 1974. Das Argument 86, 1974, 356-408.

Triesch, Günter: Gewerkschaftsstaat oder sozialer Rechtsstaat? Stuttgart, Seewald, 1974.

Vilmar, Fritz (ed): Menschenwürde im Betrieb. Modelle der Humanisierung und Demokratisierung der industriellen Arbeitswelt. Reinbek, Rowohlt, 1973.

Weitbrecht, Hansjörg: Wirkung und Verfahren der Tarifautonomie. Baden-Baden, Nomos, 1973.

Rural Influences

Schmalz, Hellmut: Agrarpolitik ohne Scheuklappen. Cologne, Bund-Verlag, 1973.

Promotional Groups

Kühnl, Reinhard: Der 'Bund Freiheit der Wissenschaft' und sein Standort im politischen Spektrum der BRD. Ein Gutachten. Blätter für deutsche und internationale Politik, 1973, 1202-1215.

Military Influences

Bredow, Wilfried von: Die umbewältigte Bundeswehr. Frankfurt, Fischer, 1973.

Bredow, Wilfried von: Militärpolitik. Materialien zu einer Wehrkunde. Starnberg, Raith, 1974.

Ebert, Theodor et al.: Demokratische Sicherheitspolitik. Munich, Hanser, 1974.

Engelhardt, K./Heise, K.-H.: Der militärisch-industrielle Komplex im heutigen Imperialismus. Cologne, Pahl-Rugenstein, 1974.

Fleckenstein, Bernhard/Schössler, Dietmar: Jugend und Streitkräfte. Meinungen und Einstellungen der Jungen Generation gegenüber Bundeswehr und Wehrdienst in der BRD. Beiträge zur Konfliktforschung, Vol. 3, No 2, 1973, 29-72.

Kempe, Martin: SPD und Bundeswehr. Studien zum militärisch-industriellen Komplex. Cologne, Pahl-Rugenstein, 1973.

Medick, Monika: Das Konzept des 'Military-Industrial Complex' und das Problem einer Theorie demokratischer Kontrolle. PVS, 1973, 499-526.

Vetterleih, Thomas G.: Militärische Leistung und demokratische Industriegesellschaft. Stuttgart, Seewald, 1974.

National Minorities and Racial Factors

Political Parties

Alemann, Ulrich von: Parteiensysteme im Parlamentarismus. Düsseldorf, Bertelsmann, 1973.

Beyme, Klaus von et al.: Wahlkampf und Parteiorganisation. Eine Regionalstudie zum Bundestagswahlkampf 1969. Tübingen, Mohr, 1974.

Dittberner, Jürgen, Ebbighausen, Rolf (eds): Parteiensystem in der Legitimationskrise. Studien und Materialien zur Soziologie der Parteien in der Bundesrepublik Deutschland. Opladen, Westdeutscher Verlag, 1973.

Everke, Karl Friedrich: Zur Funktionsgeschichte der politischen Parteien. Baden-Baden, Nomos, 1974.

Fenske, Hans: Strukturprobleme der deutschen Parteiengeschichte. Wahlrecht und Parteiensystem vom Vormärz bis heute. Frankfurt/M., Fischer Athenäum, 1974.

Flechtheim, Ossip K. (ed): Die Parteien der Bundesrepublik Deutschland. Hamburg, Hoffmann & Campe, 1973 (Documents).

Flechtheim, Ossip K.: Der Dritte Weg in der deutschen Parteipolitik nach 1945. Aus Politik und Zeitgeschichte, B 25/1973, 3-14.

Freyberg, Jutta von: Sozialdemokraten und Kommunisten. Die revolutionären Sozialisten Deutschlands vor dem Problem der Aktionseinheit 1934-1937. Cologne, Pahl-Rugenstein, 1973.

Friedrich, Manfred: Opposition im Deutschen Bundestag: Phasen oppositionellen Verhaltens 1949-1972. Z. Parl. 1973, 392-406.

Fülberth, Georg/Harrer, Jürgen: Die deutsche Sozialdemokratie. 1890-1933. Darmstadt Neuwied, Luchterhand, 1974.

Gleissberg, Gerhard: SPD und Gesellschaftssystem. Aktualität der Programmdiskussion von 1934 bis 1946. Dokumente und Kommentar. Frankfurt/M., Verlag Marxistische Blätter, 1973.

Groh, Dieter: Negative Integration und revolutionärer Attentismus. Die deutsche Sozialdemokratie am Vorabend des Ersten Weltkrieges. Berlin, Ullstein, 1973.

Haungs, Peter: Die Bundesrepublik — ein Parteienstaat? Kritische Anmerkungen zu einem wissenschaftlichen Mythos. Z. Parl. 1973, 502-524.

Hoffmann, Wolfgang: Die Finanzen der Parteien. Munich, Praeger, 1973.

Kühr, Herbert: Probleme innerparteilicher Demokratie in der CDU. Aus Politik und Zeitgeschichte, B 34-35/1974, 3-16.

Lenk, Kurt/Neumann, Franz (eds): Theorie und Soziologie der politischen Parteien. Darmstadt Neuwied, 1972, 2 vols.

Lintz, Gerd: Die politischen Parteien im Bereich der kommunalen Selbstverwaltung. Baden-Baden, Nomos, 1973.

Miller, Susanne: Die SPD vor und nach Godesberg. Kleine Geschichte der SPD. Bonn-Bad Godesberg, Verlag Neue Gesellschaft, 1974.

Miller, Susanne: Burgfrieden und Klassenkampf. Die deutsche Sozialdemokratie im Ersten Weltkrieg. Düsseldorf, Droste, 1974.

Mommsen, Hans (ed): Sozialdemokratie zwischen Klassenbewegung und Volkspartei. Frankfurt, Athenäum, 1974.

Müller, Martin: Fraktionswechsel im Parteienstaat. Düsseldorf, Westdeutscher Verlag, 1974.

Opitz, Reinhard: Der deutsche Sozialliberalismus 1917-1933. Cologne, Pahl-Rugenstein, 1973.

Pappi, Franz-Urban: Parteiensystem und Sozialstruktur in der Bundesrepublik. PVS, 1973, 191-213.

Raschke, Joachim: Innerparteiliche Opposition. Die Linke in der Berliner SPD. Hamburg, Hoffmann & Campe, 1974.

Ritter, Gerhard A. (ed): Deutsche Parteien vor 1918. Cologne, Kiepenheuer & Witsch, 1973.

Roth, Reinhold: Parteiensystem und Außenpolitik. Meisenheim, Hain, 1973.

Rowold, Manfred: Im Schatten der Macht. Zur Oppositionsrolle der nicht etablierten Parteien in der Bundesrepublik. Düsseldorf, Droste, 1974.

Schönbohm, Wulf: Funktion, Entstehung und Sprache von Parteiprogrammen. Aus Politik und Zeitgeschichte B 34-35, 1974, 17-37.

Schleth, Uwe: Parteifinanzen. Meisenheim, Hain, 1973.

Schmollinger, Horst W.: Abhängig Beschäftigte in Parteien der Bundesrepublik: Einflußmöglichkeiten von Arbeitern, Angestellten und Beamten. Z. Parl, 1974, 58-90.

Schumacher, Kurt: Der Kampf um den Staatsgedanken in der deutschen Sozialdemokratie. Stuttgart, Kohlhammer, 1973 (The PhD Dissertation of the former SPD-leader).

Setzer, Hans: Wahlsystem und Parteientwicklung in England. Wege zur Demokratisierung der Institutionen 1832 bis 1948. Frankfurt/M., Suhrkamp, 1973.

Stephan, Werner: Aufstieg und Verfall des Linksliberalismus. Geschichte der DDP. Göttingen, Vandenhoek & Ruprecht, 1973.

Walter, Gerd: Theoretischer Anspruch und politische Praxis der DKP. Meisenheim, Hain, 1973.

Weiler, Joachim: Politische Parteien, Fraktionen und Abgeordnete im Verfassungsprozeß. Ungeklärte Rechtswege. Z. Parl. 1973, 525-533.

Wolfrum, Rüdiger: Die innerparteiliche demokratische Ordnung nach dem Parteiengesetz. Berlin, Duncker & Humblot, 1974.

Political Socialization

Ackermann, Paul (ed): Politische Sozialisation. Düsseldorf, Westdeutscher Verlag, 1974.

Ackermann, Paul: Curriculumrevision im sozialwissenschaftlichen Bereich der Schule. Stuttgart, Klett, 1973.

Ackermann, Paul: Politisches Lernen in der Grundschule. Munich, Kösel, 1973.

Behr, Wolfgang: Strukturprobleme der politischen Bildung. Aus Politik und Zeitgeschichte, B 5/1973.

Christian, Wolfgang: Problem der Erkenntnisprozesse im politischen Unterricht, Cologne, Pahl-Rugenstein, 1974.

Deichsel, A. et al.: Politische Sozialisation von Studenten. Stuttgart, Enke, 1974.

Freiwald, H. et al.: Das Deutschlandproblem in Schulbüchern der BRD. Düsseldorf, Bertelsmann, 1973.

Kogon, Eugen (ed): Rahmenrichtlinien Gesellschaftslehre. Frankfurt/M. Aspekte-Verlag, 1974.

Schäffer, Lambrou: Politische Bildung als Unterrichtsprinzip. Frankfurt/M. EVA, 1973.

Stein Gerd; Plädoyer für eine politische Pädagogik. Ratingen, Henn, 1973.

Straumann, Peter R.: Zur Vulgarisierung der Bildungsökonomie. Lev., 1973, 71-89.

Weber, Jürgen: Politischer Idyllismus. Formen, Folgen und Ursachen eines politischen Einstellungsmusters. Aus Politik und Zeitgeschichte, B 26/1973.

Wehling, Hans Georg (ed): Unterrichtspraktisches Handbuch zur politischen Bildung. Munich, Ehrenwirth, 1973.

Werder, Lutz von: Sozialistische Erziehung in Deutschland 1848-1973. Frankfurt, Fischer, 1974.

Wulf, Christoph (ed): Friedenserziehung in der Diskussion. Munich, Piper, 1973.

Elite recruitment

Kempf, Udo: Kandidatenaufstellung in Frankreich am Beispiel der Union pour la Nouvelle République und ihrer Koalitionspartner. Berlin, Duncker & Humblot, 1973.

Nassmacher, Karl-Heinz: Funktionen politischen Personals in lokalen Vertretungskörperschaften. Z. Parl, 1973, 550-566.

Mass Media and Political Communication

Becker, Wolfgang: Film und Herrschaft. Berlin, Verlag V. Spiess, 1973.

Dygutsch-Lorenz, Ilse: Journalisten und Rundfunk. Düsseldorf, Bertelsmann, 1973.

Eicke, Ulrich: 'Innere' und 'äußere' Pressefreiheit. Eine medienpolitische Zwischenbilanz. Aus Politik und Zeitgeschichte, B 24/1974, 3-13.

Geissler, Rainer: Massenmedien, Basiskommunikation und Demokratie. Tübingen, Mohr, 1973.

Koschwitz, Hans Jürgen: Kommunikation und Politik. Entwicklungstendenzen der modernen Weltpresse. Aus Politik und Zeitgeschichte B 30/1973.

Löffler, Martin: Die Darstellung der Gewalt in den Massenmedien. Munich, Beck, 1973.

Schatz-Bergfeld, Marianne: Massenkommunikation und Herrschaft. Zur Rolle von Massenkommunikation als Steuerungselement moderner demokratischer Gesellschaften. Meisenheim, Hain, 1974.

Representation and Elections

Abromeit, Heidrun/Burkhardt, Klaus: Die Wählerinitiativen im Wahlkampf 1972. Aus Politik und Zeitgeschichte, B 37/1973.

Berger, Manfred: Parteienidentifikation in der Bundesrepublik. PVS, 1973, 215-225.

Beyme, Klaus von, et al.: Wahlkampf und Parteiorganisation. Eine Regionalstudie zum Bundestagswahlkampf 1969. Tübingen, Mohr, 1974.

Bredthauer, Rüdiger: Das Wahlsystem als Objekt von Politik und Wissenschaft. Die Wahlsystemdiskussion in der BRD 1967/68 als politische und wissenschaftliche Auseinandersetzung. Meisenheim, Hain, 1973.

Eltermann, Ludolf, et al.: Drei Fragen zur Bundestagswahl 1972. Aus Politik und Zeitgeschichte B 46/1973.

Falter Jürgen W.: Faktoren der Wahlentscheidung. Eine wahlsoziologische Analyse am Beispiel der saarländischen Landtagswahl 1970. Cologne, Heymanns, 1973.

Gibowski, Wolfgang G.: Der Effekt unterschiedlicher Plazierung der Wahlabsichten im Fragebogen. PVS, 1973, 275-293.

Haungs, Peter (ed): Wahlkampf als Ritual. Meisenheim, Hain, 1974.

Kaack, Heino: Landtagswahlen und Bundespolitik 1970-1972. Aus Politik und Zeitgeschichte, B 13/1974.

Kaase, Max: Die Bundestagswahl 1972: Probleme und Analysen. PVS, 1973, 145-190.

Klingemann, Hans D.: Issue-Kompetenz und Wahlentscheidung. Die Einstellung zu wertbezogenen politischen Problemen im Zeitvergleich. PVS, 1973, 227-256.

Lehner, Franz: Politisches Verhalten als sozialer Tausch. Eine sozialpsychologische Studie zur utilitaristischen Theorie politischen Verhaltens. Bern Frankfurt/M., Lang, 1973.

Lepsius, M. Rainer: Wahlverhalten, Parteien und Politische Spannungen. PVS, 1973, 295-313.

Liepelt, Klaus/Riemenschnitter, Hela: Wider die These vom besonderen Wahlverhalten der Frau. PVS, 1973, 567-605.

Misch, Axel: Das Wahlsystem zwischen Theorie und Taktik. Zur Frage von Mehrheitswahl und Verhältnis in der Programmatik der Sozialdemokratie bis 1933. Berlin, Duncker & Humblot, 1974.

Roth, Dieter: Ökonomische Variablen und Wahlverhalten: PVS, 1973, 257-274.

Setzer, Hans: Wahlsystem und Parteienentwicklung in England 1832-1948. Frankfurt, Suhrkamp, 1973.

Area Studies

West European Countries

France

Fritsch, Adolf: Planifikation und Regionalpolitik in Frankreich. Stuttgart, Kohlhammer, 1973.

Elsenhans, Hartmut: Frankreichs Algerienkrieg 1954-1962. Entkolonisierungsversuch einer kapitalistischen Metropole. Munich, Hanser, 1974.

Goldschmidt, Werner: Frankreich vor den Wahlen. Blätter für deutsche und internationale Politik, 1973, No. 2, 111-116.

Goldschmidt, Werner/Lothar, Peter: Zur Entwicklung in Frankreich seit der Bildung der 'Union populaire' und den Parlamentswahlen 1973. Blätter für deutsche und internationale Politik, 1974, No. 8, 778 ff.

Kempf, Udo: Vom Vielparteiensystem zur Blockbildung. Das französische Parteiensystem. Aus Politik und Zeitgeschichte B 9/1973, 3-25.

Kempf, Udo: Zur Kandidatenaufstellung in Frankreich am Beispiel der Union pour la Nouvelle République und ihrer Koalitionspartner. Berlin, Duncker & Humblot, 1973.

Kempf, Udo: Strukturelle Veränderungen des französischen Parteiensystems. Jahrbuch des öffentlichen Rechts der Gegenwart, Vol. 23, 1974, 81-119.

Münster, Arno: Der Kampf bei LIP. Arbeiterselbstverwaltung in Frankreich. Berlin, Rotbuch Verlag, 1974.

Great Britain

Brendel, C.: Autonome Klassenkämpfe in England 1945-1972. Berlin, K. Kramer 1974.

Mückenberger, Ulrich: Arbeitsrecht und Klassenkampf. Der große englische Dockarbeiterstreik 1972. Frankfurt, EVA, 1974.

Oehlke, Paul: Programatische Wende der britischen Labour Party. Blätter für deutsche und internationale Politik, 1973, No. 7, 689-693.

Pickhaus, Klaus/Raulf, Dieter: Klassenkämpfe in Großbritannien heute. Frankfurt, Verlag Marxistische Blätter, 1973.

Sachs, Emanuel Salomon: Großbritannien nach den Parteitagen. Blätter für deutsche und internationale Politik, 1973, No. 11, 1151-1155.

Setzer, Hans: Wahlsystem und Parteienentwicklung in England. Wege zur Demokratisierung der Institutionen 1932-1948. Frankfurt, Suhrkamp, 1973.

Italy

Rosenbaum, Petra: Neofaschismus in Italien. Aus Politik und Zeitgeschichte. B 49/1974, 11-45.

Roth, Winfried: Zur Entwicklung der linkskatholischen Kräfte in Italien, Blätter für deutsche und internationale Politik, 1973, No. 8, 841-852.

Spain

Abendroth, Hans-Henning: Hitler in der spanischen Arena. Paderborn, Schöningh, 1973.

Deurr, Hans-Peter/Souchy, Augustin: Stalinismus und Anarchismus in der spanischen Revolution. Berlin, K. Kramer, 1973.

Maier, Lothar P.: Spanien – Agonie der Diktatur? Blätter für deutsche und internationale Politik, 1974, No. 11, 1178 ff.

Other Countries

The USA and Canada

Adams, Willi Paul: Republikanische Verfassung und bürgerliche Freiheit. Die Verfassungen und bürgerlichen Ideen der amerikanischen Revolution. Darmstadt, Luchterhand, 1973.

Becker, Klaus Bert: Die Muckrackers und der Sozialismus. Eine Untersuchung zum politischen Bewußtsein in der Progressive Era. Bern, Frankfurt/M., Herbert Lang 1974.

Gerstenberger, Heide: Zur politischen Ökonomie der bürgerlichen Gesellschaft. Die historischen Bedingungen ihrer Konstitution in den USA. Frankfurt/M., Athenäum Fischer, 1973.

Hall, Martin: Kongress contra Weisses Haus. Blätter für deutsche und internationale Politik, 1973, No. 2, 143-148.

Hochkeppel, Willy (ed): Wie krank ist Amerika? Hamburg, Hoffmann & Campe, 1973.

Kleinsteuber, Hans J.: Die USA. Politik, Wirtschaft, Gesellschaft. Eine Einführung. Hamburg, Hoffmann & Campe, 1974.

Leibfried, Stephan: US Central Government Reform of the Administrative Structure During the Ash Period (1968-1971). Kapitalistate, 1973, No. 2, 17-30.

Lösche, Peter: Industriegewerkschaften im organisierten Kapitalismus. Der CIO in der Roosevelt-Ära. Opladen, Westdeutscher Verlag, 1974.

Schultze, Rainer-Olaf: Die amerikanische Präsidentenwahl 1972. Aus Politik und Zeitgeschichte, B 10/1973, 19-47.

Trebesch, Jochen: Stellung und Funktion des Kongresses der Vereinigten Staaten von Amerika im Bereich der auswärtigen Angelegenheiten. Der Staat, 1973, 23-44.

Wolf, Dieter A.: Präsidentenkrieg in Vietnam? Kompetenz, Entscheidungsverfahren und Verhalten von Präsident und Kongreß im Indochina-Konflikt. Munich, Oldenbourg, 1973.

SOCIALIST SYSTEMS

Comparison of Capitalist and Socialist Political Systems and Theoretical Discussions of Research on Socialist Systems

Beyme, Klaus von: Methodenprobleme der vergleichenden Analyse sozialistischer Systeme. PVS, 1973, 343-378.

Damus, Renate: Vergesellschaftung oder Bürokratisierung durch Planung in nachkapitalistischen Gesellschaften. Lev, 1974, 179-198.

Furtak, Robert K.: Interessenpluralismus in den politischen Systemen Osteuropas. OE, 1974, 779-792.

Görgmaier, Dietmar: Die Konvergenztheorie – Kritik und Versuch einer Neubelebung. OE, 1974, No. 2, 83-98.

Hennicke, Peter (ed): Probleme des Sozialismus und der Übergangsgesellschaften. Frankfurt/M, Suhrkamp, 1973.

Höhmann, Hans-Hermann/Seidenstecher, Gertraud/Vajna, Thomas: Umweltschutz und ökonomisches System in Osteuropa. Stuttgart, Kohlhammer, 1973 (On the USSR, the GDR, and Hungary).

Kosta, Jiri/Meyer, Jan/Weber, Sibylle: Warenproduktion im Sozialismus. Überlegungen zur Theorie von Marx und zur Praxis in Osteuropa. Frankfurt, Fischer, 1973.

Kosta, Jiri: Sozialistische Planwirtschaft. Theorie und Praxis. Opladen, Westdeutscher Verlag, 1974.

Leipold, Helmut: Alternative Gesellschafts- und Wirtschaftssysteme. Grundzüge einer Theorie des Systemvergleichs. Hannover, Niedersächsische Zentrale für Politische Bildung, 1974.

Mansilla, H. C. F.: Systembedürfnis und Anpassung. Zur Kritik sozialistischer Verhaltenssteuerung. Frankfurt, Athenäum, 1973 (On the USSR, GDR, and Cuba).

Olle, Werner: Zur Theorie des Staatskapitalismus. Probleme von Theorie und Geschichte in Theorien der Übergangsgesellschaft. Prokla, 1974, No. 11/12, pp. 91 ff.

Osers, Jan: Forschung und Entwicklung in sozialistischen Staaten Osteuropas. Berlin, Duncker & Humblot, 1974.

Roggemann, Herwig: Volksvertretungen im Sozialismus. Eine Einführung in Strukturprobleme sozialistischer Staatsorganisation. Z. Parl, 1974, No. 3, 338-385.

Ruban, Maria-Elisabeth: Wohnungsbau und Wohnungswirtschaft in den RGW-Ländern. DA, 1973, 1312-1317.

Wädekin, Karl-Eugen: Sozialistische Agrarpolitik in Osteuropa. Vol. 1: Von Marx bis zur Vollkollektivierung. Berlin, Duncker & Humblot, 1974.

Watrin, Christian (ed): Struktur- und stabilitätspolitische Probleme in alternativen Wirtschaftssystemen. Berlin, Duncker & Humblot, 1974.

Comparisons between the two German States

Behr, Wolfgang: Bundesrepublik Deutschland – Deutsche Demokratische Republik. Grundkonflikte und Konvergenzerscheinungen. Aus Politik und Zeitgeschichte, B 36-37/1974.

Helwig, Gisela: Zwischen Familie und Beruf. Die Stellung der Frau in beiden deutschen Staaten. Cologne, Verlag Wissenschaft und Politik, 1974.

Ludz, Peter Christian: Deutschlands doppelte Zukunft. Bundesrepublik und DDR in der Welt von morgen. Munich, Hanser, 1974.

Otto-Arnold, Charlotte: Die Kosten der Lebenshaltung in der DDR im Vergleich zur Bundesrepublik an der Jahreswende 1972/73, DA, 1973, 851-855.

Roggemann, Herwig: Das Leben in Deutschland – Kriminalität und Strafrecht. DA, 1973, 518-523.

Schweigler, Gebhard: Nationalbewußtsein in der BRD und der DDR. Düsseldorf, Bertelsmann, 1973, 2nd ed. 1974.

Winkel, Harald: Die Wirtschaft im geteilten Deutschland 1945-1970. Wiesbaden, Steiner, 1974.

The Political System of the GDR

Autorenkollektiv Frankfurt: Probleme sozialistischer Kulturpolitik am Beispiel DDR. Frankfurt/M., Fischer, 1974.

Burens, Peter-Claus: Die politische Funktion der Grundrechte in der DDR. Der Staat, 1974, No. 2, 169-184.

Damus, Renate: Entscheidungsstrukturen und Funktionsprobleme in der DDR-Wirtschaft. Frankfurt/M., Suhrkamp, 1973.

Damus, Renate: Wertkategorien als Mittel der Planung. Zur Widersprüchlichkeit der Planung gesamtgesellschaftlicher Prozesse in der DDR. Prokla, Special Issue, 5, 1973.

Deutsches Institut für Wirtschaftsforschung Berlin (ed): DDR-Wirtschaft. Eine Bestandsaufnahme. Frankfurt/M., Fischer, 1974.

Die DDR vor Aufgaben der Integration und der Koexistenz. 6. Tagung zum Stand der DDR-Forschung in der Bundesrepublik 1973. DA, Oct. 1973.

Dreessen, Klaus: Die Bedeutung der landwirtschaftlichen Produktionsgenossenschaften in der DDR. Tübingen, Mohr, 1974.

Erdmann, Kurt: Der Gegenplan 1974. Ideologische und ökonomische Aspekte. DA, 1974, 734-744.

Gast, Gabriele: Die politische Rolle der Frau in der DDR. Düsseldorf, Bertelsmann, 1973.

Haller, Frank: Sozialistische Akkumulations- und Wachstumstheorie. Zur Kritik der Politischen Ökonomie des Sozialismus in der DDR. Berlin, Duncker & Humblot, 1974.

Jungermann, Peter: Die Wehrideologie der SED und das Leitbild der nationalen Volksarmee vom sozialistischen deutschen Soldaten. Stuttgart, Seewald, 1973.

Klein, Helmut: Bildung in der DDR. Reinbek, Rowohlt, 1974.

Lauterbach, Günther: Zur Theorie der sozialistischen Wirtschaftsführung in der DDR. Cologne, Verlag Wissenschaft und Politik, 1973.

Leptin, Gerd (ed): Die Rolle der DDR in Osteuropa. Berlin, Duncker & Humblot, 1974.

Leptin, Gerd (ed): Handelspartner Osteuropa. Berlin, Duncker & Humblot, 1974.

Lindemann, Hans/Müller, Kurt: Auswärtige Kulturpolitik der DDR. Die kulturelle Abgrenzung der DDR von der Bundesrepublik Deutschland. Bonn, Verlag Neue Gesellschaft, 1974.

Ludz, Christian Peter: Politische Ziele der SED und gesellschaftlicher Wandel in der DDR. DA, 1974, 1262-1271.

Mitzscherling, Peter: Der Staatshaushaltsplan der DDR. DA, 1973, 280-281.

Neugebauer, Gero: Die Volkskammer der DDR. Z. Parl., 1974, No. 3, 386-411.

Neumann, Philipp: Zurück zum Profit. Zur Entwicklung des Revisionismus in der DDR. Berlin, Oberbaumverlag, 1973.

Rausch, Heinz/Stammen, Theo (eds): DDR. Das politische, wirtschaftliche und soziale System. Munich, Beck, 1974.

Roggemann, Herwig: Die Staatsordnung der DDR. Berlin, Berlin-Verlag, 1973.

Vortmann, Heinz: Einkommensverteilung in der DDR. DA, 1974, 271-277.

Wagner, Uwe: Vom Kollektiv zur Konkurrenz. Partei und Massenbewegung in der DDR. Berlin, Oberbaumverlag, 1974.

Weber, Hermann: 25 Jahre DDR – Kontinuität und Wandel. DA, 1974, 1031-1035.

Ziegler, Uwe: Zur Diskussion um Verwaltungsrecht und Verwaltsungsrechtswissenschaft in der DDR. DA, 1974, 1036-1044.

Berlin

Mahncke, Dieter: Berlin im geteilten Deutschland. Munich, Oldenbourg, 1973.

Wettig, Gerhard: Die Rechtslage Berlins nach dem Viermächte-Abkommen aus sowjetischer Sicht. DA, 1974, 378-388.

The Soviet Union

Anweiler, Oskar/Ruffmann, Karl-Heinz (eds): Kulturpolitik in der Sowjetunion. Stuttgart, Kröner, 1973.

Barker, Enno: Die Rolle der Parteiorgane in der sowjetischen Wirtschaftslenkung 1957-1965. Wiesbaden, Harrassowitz, 1973.

Haumann, Heiko: Beginn der Planwirtschaft. Elektrifizierung, Wirtschaftsplanung und gesellschaftliche Entwicklung Sowjetrußlands. 1917-1921. Düsseldorf, Bertelsmann, 1974.

Gumpel, Werner: UdSSR – Energiepolitik und Nahostkrise. AP, 1974, No. 1, 32-41.

Leng, Hermann-Otto: Die allgemeine Wahl im bolschewistischen Staat. Meisenheim/Glan, Hain, 1973.

Meyer, Gert: Studien zur sozialökonomischen Entwicklung Sowjetrußlands 1921-1923. Cologne, Pahl-Rugenstein, 1974.

Pruck, Erich F.: Militärakademische Ausbildung in der Sowjetunion. OE, 1974, No. 2, 119.

Schulze, Peter W. (ed): Übergangsgesellschaft: Herschaftsform und Praxis am Beispiel der Sowjetunion. Frankfurt/M., Fischer, 1974.

Simon, Gerhard: Rolle und Gestaltung der Massenmedien in der Sowjetunion. OE, 1974, No. 3, pp 188ff.

Simon, Gerhard: Parteischulung und Massenagitation in der Sowjetunion. OE, 1974, No. 4, pp 335.

Simon, Gerhard: Die Wirksamkeit sowjetischer Propaganda. Einige Befragungsergebnisse in der UdSSR. OE, 1974, No. 8, pp 575.

Tecklenberg, Wolfgang: Wandel von Berufsstruktur und Arbeitsinhalten in der UdSSR. OE, 1974, No. 5, pp 351.

Winkelmann, Horst: Die Lehre vom Verwaltungshandeln in der sowjetischen Verwaltungsrechtslehre. Berlin, Duncker & Humblot, 1974.

Other Socialist Systems

East European Socialist Countries

Förster, Horst: Umweltprobleme in der Tschechoslowakei. OE, 1974, No. 3, 205.

Köhler-Wagnerová, Alena: Die Frau im Sozialismus – Beisepiel CSSR. Hamburg, Hoffmann & Campe, 1974.

Laeuen, Harald: Im Zeichen des starken Staates. Verwaltungsreform in Polen. OE, 1974, No. 6, pp 434.

Oschlies, Wolf: Umweltschutz in Bulgarien. OE, 1974, No. 3, 213.

Roggemann, Herwig (ed): Die Staatsordnung der Volksrepublik Polen. Berlin, Berlin Verlag, 1974 (Documents).

Tönnes, Bernhard: Religionen in Albanien. Enver Hoxha und die 'nationale Eigenart'. OE, 1974, No. 9, 661ff.

Yugoslavia

Conert, Hansgeorg: Gibt es einen jugoslawischen Sozialismus? Das Argument, No. 82, 1973, 735-767. No. 84, 1974, 76-103.

Hagemann, Michael/Klemencic, Alenka: Die sozialistische Marktwirtschaft Jugoslawiens. Stuttgart, Fischer, 1973.

Huebbenet, Georg: Titos Balancieren mit der Blockfreiheit. AP, 1974, No. 1, 61-79.

Ronneberger, Franz/Radovanović, Broslav (eds): Sozialer Wandel in Jugoslawien. Cologne, Verlag Wissenschaft und Politik, 1974.

Cuba

Breuer, Wilhelm: Sozialismus in Kuba. Cologne, Pahl-Rugenstein, 1973.

China

Castner, Hartmut & Thilo: Ein sozialistisches Modell. Die Volksrepublik China. Düsseldorf, Schwann, 1974.

Franke, Wolfgang (ed): China-Handbuch. Düsseldorf, Bertelsmann, 1973.

Glaubitz, Joachim: China und die Sowjetunion. Aufbau und Zerfall einer Allianz. Hannover, Nidersächsische Landeszentrale für politische Bildung, 1973.

Höhmann, Hans-Hermann/Kosta, Jiri/Meyer, Jan: China '74. Reiseprotokolle zu Wirtschaft und Gesellschaft der Volksrepublik. Frankfurt, EVA, 1974.

Kuntze, Peter: China, die konkrete Utopie. Munich, Nymphenburger, 1973.

Schickel, Joachim: China-Deutschlands Partner. Frankfurt, Fischer, 1974.

Weggel, Oskar: Die Alternative China. Hamburg, Hoffmann & Campe, 1973.

Developing Countries

Latin America

Abad, Franco Armando: Parteiensystem und Oligarchie in Ecuador. Berlin, Colloquium Verlag, 1974.

Boris, Dieter: Zu den Wahlen in Chile. Blätter für deutsche und internationale Politik, 1973, No. 4, pp 342-346.

Feder, Ernest: Agrarstruktur und Unterentwicklung in Lateinamerika. Frankfurt/M., EVA, 1973.

Grabendorff, Wolf (ed): Lateinamerika – Kontinent in der Krise, Hamburg, Hoffmann & Campe, 1973.

Harrer, Hans-Jürgen: Die Revolution in Mexico. Cologne, Pahl-Rugenstein, 1973.

Hein, Wolfgang/Stenzel, Konrad: The Capitalist State and Underdevelopment in Latin America. The Case of Venezuela, Kapitalstate, 1973, No. 2, pp 31-48.

Lühr, Volker: Chile: Legalität, Legitimität und Bürgerkrieg. Neuwied, Luchterhand, 1973.

Mansilla, H. C. F. (ed): Probleme des dritten Weges. Mexico, Argentinien, Bolivien, Tansania, Peru. Neuwied, Luchterhand, 1974.

Müller-Plantenberg, U.: Schwierigkeiten mit dem Klassenkampf in Chile. Lev., 1973, pp 419-428.

Nohlen, Dieter: Chile. Das sozialistische Experiment. Hamburg, Hoffmann & Campe, 1973.

Nohlen, Dieter: Feuer unter der Asche. Chiles gescheiterte Revolution. Baden-Baden, Signal, 1974.

Waldmann, Peter: Der Peronismus 1943-1955. Hamburg, Hoffmann & Campe, 1974.

Africa

Arab Countries and the Middle East

Elsenhans, Hartmut: Frankreichs Algerienkrieg 1954-1962. Entkolonisierungsversuch einer kapitalistischen Metropole. Zum Zusammenbruch der Kolonialreiche. Munich, Hanser, 1974.

Freund, Wilhelm S.: Das arabische Mittelmeer. Entwicklungsprobleme, Hintergrundstudien zum Nahostkonflikt. Munich, Goldmann, 1974.

Tophoven, Rolf: Fedayin – Guerrilla ohne Grenzen. Bonn, Bundeszentrale für Politische Bildung, 1973.

Asia

INTERNATIONAL RELATIONS

General Studies on Theory and Methodology

Calamaros, Arthouros-David: Theorien internationaler Beziehungen, Stuttgart, Kohlhammer, 1974.

Frei, Daniel (ed): Theorien der internationalen Beziehungen, Munich, Piper, 1973.

Gantzel, Klaus-Jürgen (ed): Internationale Beziehungen als System, Opladen, Westdeutscher Verlag, 1973.

Hein, Wolfgang/Simonis, Georg: Theoretische und methodische Probleme einer kritischen Theorie internationaler Politik, PVS No. 1, 1973, pp 85-106.

Klaczko, Salomon: Computer-Simulation von Sequenzen aus politischen Ereignissen, PVS, 1974, pp 391-426.

Krippendorff, Ekkehart (ed): Internationale Beziehungen, Cologne, Kiepenheuer & Witsch, 1973.

Rattinger, Hans: Gleichgewicht von Rüstungswettläufen und seine Stabilitätseigenschaften als Erklärungsvariablen für den Ausgang von Rüstungswettläufen: Einige vorgeordnete Definitionsprobleme. PVS, 1974, pp 471-523.

Ruloff, Dieter: Eskalation und Krise – am Computer simuliert. PVS, 1974, pp 427-470.

Seidelmann, Reimund: Simulation in Internationaler und Auswärtiger Politik. Die Inter-Nation Simulation (INS) und ihre Verwertbarkeit für Analyse und Prognose, Meisenheim, Hain, 1973.

States in International Affairs: Their Foreign Relations

FRG

Bischoff, Detlef: Franz Josef Strauß, die CSU und die Außenpolitik. Konzeption und Realität am Beispiel der Großen Koalition, Meisenheim, Hain 1973.

Braunmühl, Claudia von: Kalter Krieg und friedliche Koexistenz. Die Außenpolitik der SPD in der Großen Koalition, Frankfurt, Suhrkamp, 1973.

End, Heinrich: Zweimal deutsche Außenpolitik, Cologne Verlag Wissenschaft und Politik, 1973.

Freund, Wolfgang S./Simson, Uwe (eds): Aspekte der auswärtigen Kulturpolitik in Entwicklungsländern, Meisenheim, Hain, 1973.

Haftendorn, Helga: Abrüstungs- und Entspannungspolitik zwischen Sicherheitsbefriedigung und Friedenssicherung, Düsseldorf, Bertelsmann Universitätsverlag, 1974.

Jahn, Egbert/Rittberger, Volker (eds): Die Ostpolitik der Bundesrepublik, Opladen Westdeutscher Verlag, 1974.

Kratochwil, German: Die Entwicklungshilfe der BRD für Lateinamerika. Organisation – Ziele – Leistungen, Stuttgart, Klett, 1973.

Kuper, Ernst: Frieden durch Konfrontation und Kooperation. Die Einstellung von Gerhard Schröder und Willi Brandt zur Entspannungspolitik, Stuttgart, Gustav Fischer, 1974.

Löwenthal, Richard: Vom Kalten Krieg zur Ostpolitik, Stuttgart, Seewald, 1974.

Müller-Roschach, Herbert: Die deutsche Europapolitik. Wege und Umwege zur Politischen Union Europas, Baden-Baden Nomos, 1974.

Roth, Reinhold: Parteiensystem und Außenpolitik. Zur Bedeutung des Parteiensystems für den außenpolitischen Entscheidungsprozeß in der BRD, Meisenheim, Hain, 1973.

GDR

End, Heinrich: Zweimal deutsche Außenpolitik, Internationale Dimensionen des innerdeutschen Konflikts. 1949-1972. Cologne Verlag Wissenschaft und Politik, 1973.

Leptin, Gerd (ed): Die Rolle der DDR in Osteuropa, Berlin, Duncker & Humblot, 1974.

Lindemann, Hans/Müller, Kurt: Auswärtige Kulturpolitik der DDR, Bonn-Bad Godesberg, Verlag Neue Gesellschaft, 1974.

Rexin, Manfred: Die Außenpolitik der DDR. Eine Einführung, Düsseldorf, Bertelsmann Universitätsverlag, 1974.

United States

Küntzel, Ulrich: Der nordamerikanische Imperialismus. Zur Geschichte der US-Kapitalausfuhr, Darmstadt, Neuwied, Luchterhand, 1974.

Pütz, Karl Heinz: Die Außenpolitik der USA. Eine Einführung, Hamburg, Hoffmann und Campe, 1974.

Wolf, Dieter O. A.: 'Präsidenten-Krieg' in Vietnam? Kompetenzen, Entscheidungsverfahren und Verhalten von Präsident und Kongreß im Indochina Konflikt, Munich, Vienna, Oldenbourg, 1973.

USSR

Geyer, Dietrich (ed): Sowjetunion, Außenpolitik, Bd. 1, 1917-1955, Cologne Vienna, Böhlau, 1973.

Wassmund, Hans: Kontinuität im Wandel. Bestimmungsfaktoren sowjetischer Deutschlandpolitik in der Nach-Stalin-Zeit, Cologne, Vienna, Böhlau, 1974.

Weingartner, Thomas: Die Außenpolitik der Sowjetunion seit 1945, Düsseldorf, Bertelsmann Universitätsverlag 1973.

Other Countries

Rehfeldt, Udo: 'Französische Ostpolitik und ökonomische Interessen', Lev, 1974, No. 3, 409-433.

International Politics

General Studies

Raina, Peter (ed): Internationale Politik in den siebziger Jahren, Frankfurt, S. Fischer, 1973.

Schweitzer, Carl Christoph: Chaos oder Ordnung? Einführung in die Probleme der internationalen Politik, Cologne, Verlag Wissenschaft und Politik, 1973.

Basic Aspects of International Politics

Bredow, Wilfried von (ed): Zum Charakter internationaler Konflikte, Cologne, Pahl-Rugenstein, 1973.

Jahn, Egbert: Kommunismus – und was dann? Zur Bürokratisierung und Militarisierung des Systems der Nationalstaaten, Reinbek, Rowohlt, 1974.

Junne, Gerd/Nour, Salua: Internationale Abhängigkeiten. Ausbeutung als Regelfall internationaler Beziehungen, Frankfurt, Fischer Athenäum, 1974.

Configurations of International Politics

East-West Relations

Albrecht, Ulrich (et al.): Durch Kooperation zum Frieden? Probleme gesamteuropäischer Sicherheit und Zusammenarbeit, Munich, Hanser, 1974.

Bielfeldt, Carola (et al.): Frieden in Europa? Zur Koexistenz von Rüstung und Entspannung, Reinbek, Rowohlt, 1973.

Galtung, Johan/Senghaas, Dieter (eds): Kann Europa abrüsten? Friedenspolitische Optionen für die siebziger Jahre, Munich, Hanser, 1973.

Jacobsen, Hans-Adolf/Mallmann, Wolfgang/Meier, Christian (eds): Sicherheit und Zusammenarbeit in Europa (KSZE). Analyse und Dokumentation, Cologne, Verlag Wissenschaft und Politik, 1973.

Jaroslawska, Halina: Ökonomische Aspekte der friedlichen Koexistenz. Auswirkungen der Integrationsprozesse im Osten und Westen, Stuttgart, Klett, Munich, Kösel, 1974.

Nerlich, Uwe: Der amerikanisch-sowjetische Bilateralismus und seine Auswirkungen auf die Sicherheit Westeuropas. Bonn, Deutsche Gesellschaft für Auswärtige Politik, February 1973 (Arbeitspapiere zur Internationalen Politik, 1).

Perspektiven der Kooperation zwischen kapitalistischen und sozialistischen Ländern. Jahrbuch für Friedens- und Konfliktforschung, Bd. 3, Düsseldorf, Bertelsmann Universitätsverlag, 1973.

Slotta, Günter (ed): Chance für Europa. Aktuelle Beiträge zur Europäischen Sicherheitskonferenz, Munich, Seeliger, 1973.

Wettig, Gerhard: MBFR: Motor der Aufrüstung oder Instrument der Friedenssicherung? Aus Politik und Zeitgeschichte. B 24/73, 3-37.

Wettig, Gerhard: Das sowjetische Koexistenz-Konzept – Grundlage eines friedlichen Verhältnisses zwischen Ost und West? OE, 1974, 180-187.

Willms, Bernard: Entspannung und friedliche Koexistenz, Munich, List, 1974.

Woyke, Richard/Nieder, Klaus/Görtemaker, Manfred: Sicherheit für Europa? Die Konferenz von Helsinki und Genf, Opladen, Leske, 1974.

Other

Bechtholdt, Heinrich: Chinas Einordnung in die Weltpolitik. AP, 1973, 425-436.

Freund, Wolfgang S.: Das arabische Mittelmeer-Entwicklungsproblem, Hintergrundstudien zum Nahostkonflikt, Munich, Goldmann, 1974.

Furtak, Robert K.: Internationale Dependenzverhältnisse in West und Ost. Funktionen und Wirkungen der Monroe-Doktrin und Breschnew-Doktrin. Aus Politik und Zeitgeschichte B 30/31, 1974, 3-17.

Hampe, Karl-Alexander: Lateinamerikas Eintritt in die Weltpolitik. AP, 1974, 229-243.

Kaiser, Karl: Die europäische Herausforderung und die USA. Das atlantische Verhältnis im Zeitalter weltpolitischer Strukturveränderungen, Munich, Piper, 1973.

Seidelmann, Reimund: 'Akteur und Interesse als analytische Konzepte zur Erfassung von Beziehungen am Beispiel USA – Südafrikanische Republik', in: PVS, 1974, No. 3/4, 313-390.

Schweitzer, Carl Christoph/Nemitz, Manfred (eds): Krisenherd Nah-Ost, Cologne, Markus Verlag, 1973.

Steinbach, Udo: Türkei – Diversifizierung der Außenpolitik. AP, 1973, 436-447.

Steinbach, Udo: Saudi Arabiens neue Rolle im Nahen Osten. AP 1974, 202-213.

Steinbach, Udo: Iran im außenpolitischen Aufbruch. AP 1974, 315-328.

Issues of International Politics

Armament, Arms Control and Disarmament

Bielfeldt, Carola/Senghaas, Dieter: 'Kann die BRD abrüsten? ', Lev. 1973, No. 3, 291-309.

Bredow, Wilfried von (ed): Ökonomische und soziale Folgen der Abrüstung, Cologne, Pahl-Rugenstein, 1974.

Ebert, Theodor/Horsky, Vladimir/Niemann, Rolf/Roberts, Adam/Vogt, Roland/Wittig, Hans-Georg: Demokratische Sicherheitspolitik. Von der territorialen zur sozialen Verteidigung, Munich, Hanser, 1974.

Groll, Götz von: Die Genfer KSZE-Verhandlungen. AP, 1974, 159-166.

Groll, Götz von: Die KSZE-Debatte im Deutschen Bundestag. AP, 1974, 375-383.

Rosenkranz, Erhard/Jütte, Rüdiger: Abschreckung contra Sicherheit? Munich, Piper, 1974.

Zellentin, Gerda: Für und wider die Institutionalisierung einer Konferenz über Sicherheit und Zusammenarbeit in Europa (KSZE) EA, 1973, 147-150.

Underdevelopment and Development Strategies

Callies, Hans Ulrich: Der Einfluß von Entwicklungshilfeleistungen auf den Konjunkturverlauf und die Beschäftigung im Geberland. Tübingen, Erdmann, 1973.

Dams, Theodor (ed): Entwicklungshilfe – Hilfe zur Unterentwicklung? Munich, Kaiser, Mainz, Grünewald, 1974.

Evers, Tilmann Tönnies/Wogau, Peter von: ' "dependencia": Lateinamerikanische Beiträge zur Theorie der Unterentwicklung', Das Argument Vol. 15, 1973, No. 4-6, 404-452.

Fröbel, Folker/Heinrichs, Jürgen/Kreye, Otto: Die Armut des Volkes. Verelendung in den unterentwickelten Ländern, Reinbek, Rowohlt, 1974.

Heiduk, Günter: Die weltwirtschaftlichen Ordnungsprinzipien von GATT und UNCTAD. Baden-Baden, Nomos, 1973.

Kratochwil, Germán: Die Entwicklungshilfe der BRD für Lateinamerika. Stuttgart, Klett, 1973.

Nohlen, Dieter/Nuscheler, Franz (eds): Handbuch der Dritten Welt. Vol. 1: Theorien und Indikatoren von Unterentwicklung und Entwicklung, Hamburg, Hoffmann und Campe, 1974.

Senghaas, Dieter (ed): Peripherer Kapitalismus. Analysen über Abhängigkeit und Unterentwicklung, Frankfurt, Suhrkamp, 1974.

Senghaas, Dieter: Die Dritte Welt als Gegenstand der Friedensforschung, Bonn-Bad Godesberg, Deutsche Gesellschaft für Friedens- und Konfliktforschung, November 1974, (DFGK-Hefte, 5).

Schneider, Peter Johann: Die Bedeutung der internationalen Währungsordnung und der vorliegenden Reformvorschläge für die Entwicklungsländer. Tübingen, Erdmann, 1974.

Other

Elsenhans, Hartmut (ed): Erdöl für Europa, Hamburg, Hoffmann und Campe, 1974.

Ungerer, Werner: Auswirkungen der Ölkrise. AP, 1974, 214-228.

Transnational Relations and Politics

Multinational Corporations

Albrecht, Ulrich: 'Transnationale Rüstungskonzern in Westeuropa', Lev. 1974, No. 1, 81-107.

Busch, Klaus: Die multinationalen Konzerne, Zur Analyse der Weltmarktbewegung des Kapitals, Frankfurt, Suhrkamp, 1974.

Holthus, M. (ed): Die deutschen Multinationalen Unternehmen. Frankfurt, Athenäum, 1974.

Junne, Gerd: 'Eurogeldmarkt, multinationale Konzerne und die verminderte Wirksamkeit von Staatsinterventionen', Lev. 1974, No. 1, 109-132.

Kebschull, Dietrich/Mayer, Otto G. (eds): Multinationale Unternehmen. Anfang oder Ende der Weltwirtschaft? Frankfurt, Athenäum-Fischer, 1974.

Kreye, Otto (ed): Multinationale Konzerne. Entwicklungstendenzen im kapitalistischen System, Munich, Hanser 1974.

Krüper, Manfred: Investitionskontrolle gegen die Konzerne. Reinbeck, Rowohlt, 1974.

Mielke, Siegfried: Multinationale Konzerne – Internationale Kapitalstrategie ohne Grenzen. Aus Politik und Zeitgeschichte. B 11, 1974, 3-24.

Steuber, Ursel: Internationale Banken. Auslandsaktivitäten von Banken bedeutender Industrieländer, Hamburg, Verlag Weltarchiv, 1974.

International Trade Unions

Elsner, Wolfram: Die EWG. Herausforderung und Antwort der Gewerkschaften. Cologne, Pahl-Rugenstein, 1974.

Piehl, Ernst: Multinationale Konzerne und internationale Gewerkschaftsbewegung. Ein Beitrag zur Analyse und zur Strategie der Arbeiterbewegung im organisierten Kapitalismus insbesondere in Westeuropa, Frankfurt, EVA, 1974.

Tudyka, Kurt P. (ed): Multinationale Konzerne und Gewerkschaftsstrategie, Hamburg, Hoffmann und Campe, 1974.

Other

Dejung, Karl-Heinz: Die ökumenische Bewegung im Entwicklungskonflikt 1910-1968, Stuttgart, Klett; Munich, Kösel, 1973.

Lohmann, Reinhard/Manfrass, Klaus (eds): Ausländerbeschäftigung und internationale Politik, Zur Analyse transnationaler Sozialprozesse, Munich, Vienna, Oldenbourg, 1974.

Timmermann, Heinz: Die europapolitische Konferenz westeuropäischer kommunistischer Parteien in Brüssel. OE, 1974, 442-453.

International Organization and Integration

General Studies

Horstmann, Hans-Henning: Der Drang zum Rohstoff-Kartell. Die OPEC als Vorbild internationaler Produzentenorganisationen? EA, 1974, 738-744.

Meister, Roland: Ideen von Weltstaat und der Weltgemeinschaft im Wandel imperialistischer Herrschaftsstrategien, Frankfurt, Verlag Marxistische Blätter, 1973.

The United Nations System

Heiduk, Günter: Die weltwirtschaftlichen Ordnungsprinzipien von GATT und UNCTAD. Instrumente der Entwicklungspolitik, Baden-Baden, Nomos, 1973.

Hüfner, Klaus/Naumann, Jens: Das System der Vereinten Nationen, Eine Einführung, Düsseldorf, Bertelsmann Universitätsverlag, 1974.

Pawelka, Peter: Vereinte Nationen und strukturelle Gewalt, Munich, Piper, 1974.

Pawelka, Peter: Internationales System und Internationale Organisation. Die Autonomie politischer Einfluß-Strukturen in den Vereinigten Nationen. Hannover, Niedersächsische Landeszentrale für Pülitische Bildung, 1974.

Scheuner, Ulrich/Lindemann, Beate (eds): Die Vereinigten Nationen und die Mitarbeit der Bundesrepublik Deutschland, Munich, Vienna, Oldenbourg, 1973.

Tetzlaff, Rainer: 'Die Entwicklungspolitik der Weltbank', Lev. 1973, No. 4, 489-532.

Zemanek, Karl: Die Finanzkrise der Vereinten Nationen. EA 1974, pp. 555-563.

West European Organizations

Dahrendorf, Ralf: Plädoyer für die Europäische Union. Munich, Piper, 1973.

Ehrhardt, Carl A.: Die EG-Assoziierung der AKP-Länder. AP, 1974, 384-399.

Das Europa der Siebzehn. Bilanz und Perspektiven von 25 Jahren Europarat, Bonn, Europa Union Verlag, 1974.

Groeben, Hans von der/Mestmäcker, Ernst-Joachim: Verfassung oder Technokratie für Europa? Ziele und Methoden der europäischen Integration, Frankfurt, Fischer Athenäum, 1974.

Köhler, K./Scharrer, H. -E. (eds): Die Europäische Gemeinschaft in der Krise. Ursachen und Lösungsansätze, Hamburg, Verlag Weltarchiv, 1974.

Kohnstamm, Max/Hager, Wolfgang (eds): Zivilmacht Europa — Supermacht oder Partner? Frankfurt, Suhrkamp, 1973.

Krämer, Hans R.: Die Europäische Gemeinschaft, Stuttgart, Kohlhammer, 1974.

Läufer, Dirk: Krisen in der Europäischen und Atlantischen Organisation, Berlin, Duncker und Humblot, 1974.

Loch, Theo M./Hasenpflug, Hajo: Die Assoziierungs- und Präferenzpolitik der EG. Ein Beitrag zur Entwicklungshilfe, Bonn, Europa Union Verlag, 1974.

Mickel, Wolfgang W.: Europäische Einigungspolitik. Vol. 1. Didaktischer Aufriß. Vol. 2 Quellentexte. Neuwied, Luchterhand, 1974.

Regionale Verflechtung der Bundesrepublik Deutschland. Empirische Analysen und theoretische Probleme, Munich/Vienna, Oldenbourg, 1973.

Sasse, Christoph: Kooperationsabkommen und EG-Handelspolitik. EA, 1974, 695-706.

Scharrer, Hans-Eckart (ed): Europäische Wirtschaftspolitik. Programm und Realität, Bonn, Europa Union Verlag, 1973.

Weinstock, Ulrich (ed): Neun für Europa. Die EWG als Motor der europäischen Integration, Düsseldorf, Cologne, Diederichs, 1973.

Well, Günter von: Strukturelemente eines neuen europäischen Staatensystems in der Diskussion. EA, 1974, 643-649.

Thiel, Elke: Chancen und Risiken einer Währungspolitik der Europäischen Gemeinschaft. EA, 1974, 825-832.

Other

Gumpel, Werner: 25 Jahre 'sozialistische' ökonomische Integration im RGW. OE, 1974, 13-26.

Steffens, Rolf: Integrationsprobleme im Rat für Gegenseitige Wirtschaftshilfe (RGW). Lösungsansätze bis zum Komplexprogramm des RGW, Hamburg, Verlag Weltarchiv, 1974.

Notes on Contributors

Ulrich Albrecht is Professor of Political Science at the Free University of Berlin. He specializes in Peace Research and studies on the military-industrial complex. Publications: *Der Handel mit Waffen* (1971); *Deutsche Waffen für die dritte Welt* (1972); *Rüstungsexporte in der BRD* (1972).

Clemens Burrichter and **Eckart Förtsch** work at the University of Erlangen. Förtsch has published a book on the GDR's leading party: *Die SED* (1969) and both of them in cooperation with M. Zuber edited: *Produktivkraft Wissenschaft* (1970).

Christel Eckart and her collaborators work at the Institut für Sozialforschung at the University of Frankfurt. They have published numerous articles on trade unions, and social policy problems. Ursula Jaerisch has published a survey study: *Arbeiter authoritär?* (1975).

Gerd Junne teaches political science at the University of Constance. His field is Theory of International Relations. Publications: *Spieltheorie in der internationalen Politik* (1972); and with Salua Nour) *Analyse internationaler Abhängigkeiten* (1974).

Heide Gerstenberger is Professor of Political Science and Political Economy at the University of Bremen. Her field of interest is political theory, especially theory of the capitalist state and history of the bourgeois society. Publications: *Die konservative Revolution* (1969); *Zur politischen Ökonomie der bürgerlichen Gesellschaft. Die historischen Bedingungen ihrer Konstitution in den USA* (1973).

Max Kaase is director of an institute for Survey Studies at the University of Mannheim. His main fields include: political socialization, voting behavior, radical political movements. Publications: *Wechsel von Parteipräferenzen* (1967).

Heribert Schatz was for several years a member of the planning staff in the Federal Chancellor's office. He is now Professor of Political Science at the University of Bochum. He has published *Der Parlamentarische Entscheidungsprozeß* (1970).

Gerda Zellentin is Professor of Political Science at the recently established University of Wuppertal. She has written several books in the fields of the European Community, East-West Relations and Peace Research. Publications: *Der Wirtschafts- und Sozialausschuß der EWG und Euratom.* (1962); *Die Kommunisten und die Einigung Europas* (1964); *Budgetpolitik und Integration* (1964); *Intersystemare Beziehungen in Europa* (1970); *Europa 1985* (1971); and *Les Représentants permanents auprès des Organisations Internationales* (1972).